LAWRENCE MALKIN

THE NATIONAL DEBT

**How America Crashed Into a
Black Hole and How
We Can Crawl Out**

Revised and Updated Edition

A MENTOR BOOK

NEW AMERICAN LIBRARY

NEW YORK AND SCARBOROUGH, ONTARIO

MENTOR TRADEMARK REG. U.S. PAT. OFF. AND FOREIGN COUNTRIES
REGISTERED TRADEMARK—MARCA REGISTRADA
HECHO EN CHICAGO, U.S.A.

SIGNET, SIGNET CLASSIC, MENTOR, ONYX, PLUME, MERIDIAN
and NAL BOOKS are published *in the United States* by NAL PENGUIN INC.,
1633 Broadway, New York, New York 10019,
in Canada by The New American Library of Canada Limited,
81 Mack Avenue, Scarborough, Ontario M1L 1M8

Library of Congress Catalog Card Number: 88-60737

First Mentor Printing, July, 1988

1 2 3 4 5 6 7 8 9

PRINTED IN THE UNITED STATES OF AMERICA

In Memory of My Mother and Father

For whom America was a land of hope and a Golden
Door, and by whose patient work it became a land
of miracles for me, and whose virtues its illusions now
dishonor.

Contents

Introduction to the Paperback Edition

On the afternoon of August 13, 1987, about a fortnight before the New York stock market reached what we now know was its peak, I was chatting with James Grant, the wry and respected editor of a Wall Street newsletter. We were musing about things like speculative bubbles and how long they could defy the laws of hydrodynamics. He reached for a historical analogy: "All I know is that this market can't go on forever, and everyone on Wall Street knows it. Down here it's like the eve of the First World War. Everyone knew it would start, but no one knew how or when it would start until Archduke Ferdinand was shot." Finally they heard the guns of August, and they knew. And now we know. Or do we? If anyone in the streets of Sarajevo could have foreseen the imminent slaughter on the Somme, would they have cried out to stop it?

The warning shock of Wall Street's Black Monday dispatched one of the few unambiguous messages ever sent from the hurly-burly of that market: the United States faced a reckoning in its national accounts—financial, political, and even moral. Everything that came to a head in the autumn of 1987 had been building up with the giddiness of a high-flying balloonist. Alone and rising, he feels he can touch the sun. This is the myth of American exceptionalism, and the air began coming out of it. As our predecessors in the business of global hegemony discovered to their cost, God is not an Englishman. We now know (pace the televangelists) that he is not an American, either. This human story is as old as Ilium and Imperium, except that it can no longer be told through upended cuirassiers or soldiers in blood and mud. To borrow an appeal from *Death of a Salesman*, one of the classic American stories of tragic optimism, "attention must be paid"—to debts and deficits, to how they drag us down in our livelihood, how our private as well as our public debts leave us collectively vulnerable, and to how we owe the world a living because of the national illusions that predate and also helped cause the foolish spending spree of the Reagan years.

In this book I have tried to write a history of how the United States slid into an economic and financial black hole and to offer some ideas about how it might crawl out. What deepens the pit is that foreigners have kept us afloat, as never before in American history. With childish arrogance we believed they were doing it simply because they liked our beautiful faces. What makes it frightening is that unless the United States adopts a coherent policy that allows its accounts to add up over time, it can tip the world into a real crash. That would truly destroy the Old Order, as an earlier one foundered in the blood of the Somme.

One place to look for cataclysm is Tokyo. Historians have seen such things before. Whenever the world's financial system has shifted its center of gravity, the movement has spawned speculative bubbles. Each shift produces a new group of speculators who are excited by new opportunities but lack the experience to understand them. The shift from the Lombard bankers to Amsterdam led to Holland's tulipmania. Early in the eighteenth century the world's financial capital moved from Amsterdam to London, inflating the South Sea Bubble that popped when capitalism was still young. In the 1920s the headquarters of capitalism moved from London to New York, accompanied by the historic collapse of 1929.

In Tokyo, a whole new class of investors has learned to play the market by trial and error. Some of the biggest manufacturing companies speculated with company money; they call it *zaitech*, a neologism composed of the Japanese word for finance and the English word, technique. Ordinary Japanese switched from reading comic books on the subway to the stock tables, just as Americans switched from baseball box scores to the stock market tables in 1928. Japan's markets rode up on a bubble of their own: stratospheric Tokyo real estate prices and the profits of Japanese export companies. Neither could hold up in an economic downturn, and nervous investors in Tokyo watched the dollar values of their Wall Street holdings slide. A Tokyo collapse always threatens to suck money home to fill a financial void in Japan, and that could tip Wall Street into a downward spiral. A different slow-burn scenario is less frightening but not very different: Japanese bond buyers decide to keep their money at home and stop filling America's financial black hole. Americans would have to start filling it themselves, quickly, with money coaxed into government securities by stratospheric interest rates. Readers will find this elaborated in Chapter 15, an increasingly plausible fable entitled "How to Go Bankrupt."

Why did Black Monday take place on that Monday and no other? In the week following the Crash, the analysts were all over television and the newspapers explaining how paper values had outraced real values. Obvious—and late. Before that, there were differences of opinion on whether such a divorce between financial illusion and economic reality was really justified. But differences of opinion are what make a market. When most opinions suddenly line up on one side, markets usually shift. When illusions collide with reality, there generally is some kind of bump in the night. But why should it matter to the most powerful government on earth when a speculative bubble goes up on Wall Street? At the risk of stating the obvious, it matters because that government is borrowing through Wall Street to avoid making hard choices about the nation's priorities. When bankers stop lending, the hard choices will be even harder.

It was not widely realized that by the start of 1987

the air that had been pumping up the American economy had quietly begun to leak out. Private foreign investors stopped lending the United States money to fill the huge financial hole created by our twin budget and trade deficits. Some of them, especially the Japanese, switched to American stocks, which largely explains Wall Street's self-levitating rise in the first half of 1987. When foreign investors walked away from the government bond market, the job of filling the black hole was left to their governments. Japanese and Europeans may have been buying office buildings and factories and stocks for most of the year, but for the first time since Ronald Reagan assumed office they also began voting against him with their checkbooks. They stopped buying government bonds and began to withdraw the short-term deposits that bankers call "hot money" because it chases higher interest rates. Once American rates started going down, the net private capital inflow to the United States dropped to zero.

Some kind of crunch then was inevitable. First, foreign governments stepped in to help prevent a nosedive for the world's most important currency. (Imagine the blow to confidence if the dollar itself, whose exchange rate is the most important single price in the world, had also done a Black Monday dive on the currency exchanges.) It is estimated that the central banks of foreign governments bought up 70 billion dollars through the first nine months of 1987. By early summer they were already bloated with these IOU's of the United States government and started grumbling about swallowing more. Rightly or wrongly, they feared a dose of imported inflation through too many unwanted dollars. They raised their interest rates. In September the U.S. Federal Reserve followed and raised American interest rates a notch. Wall Street nervously began to understand. In October the American Secretary of the Treasury declared war on the Germans for raising rates and threatened like Samson to pull down the dollar on everyone's head. With that clear warning that the price of the dollar might go down even more, the smart money on the street got the message. Propelled by fear and computers, everyone piled toward the exit in a classic panic.

After the fall, the world was left dangling. The U.S. government obtained a rare chance to retrace its steps. The Crash thus presented an opportunity. But in attempting to climb up again, the government was left Sisyphus-like with a narrower margin for error and a heavier burden of debt than if it had changed course the year before. The people who decide such things in Washington must tread a fine line indeed between bailing the country out of debt by printing too much money (which can destroy society by inflation), or moving too decisively by squeezing money out of ordinary people (and destroying society by depression). On balance, the risk is the former, because folk myth of disaster prompts governments to guard against depression.

Assuming that governments will act as they have in the past is the principal error made by Professor Ravi Batra, the author of *The Great Depression of 1990*, who has waxed fat as a plague-years fakir. A heretofore obscure theorist whose personal Indian guru was once convicted of murdering six defectors from his Path of Bliss (the conviction was reversed on appeal), Batra (like most Hindus) believes that life and history recycle themselves. This leads him to the conclusion that 1929 will come round again, followed in the same way by the 1930s. Indeed, the academic title of his book was *Regular Cycles of Money, Inflation, Regulation, and Depressions*. It was published by a personal press with an introduction by Dean Lester Thurow of the Sloan School of Management at MIT. Thurow now says he wishes he hadn't written it, because one of the New York publisher's demands was the addition of a chapter advising ordinary folk on how to escape imminent catastrophe. In it Batra advises his readers to sell their houses and sit on the profits, because he believes that the hard-money 1930s are certain to come round again. Neither Thurow nor most economists, including the present and previous chairmen of the Federal Reserve Board, believes any such thing. The unfortunate Thurow turned to his lawyers, but they were unable to sever his introduction for the new edition, and he frets that one day he will meet someone who actually followed the book's investment advice and sold out. In Thurow's nightmare, that sucker will be lying broke in a New York gutter and will look up and blame him and Batra.

Batra's tacked-on advice to readers to flee into cash might be fine if history ever did repeat itself. In 1929 the Federal Reserve Board helped turn a financial panic into an economic catastrophe by tightening the supply of money, forcing banks to close and bringing down their business clients with them. This time the risk is otherwise. Alan Greenspan, the new Chairman of the Federal Reserve Board, signaled during the week of the October panic that America's central bank would not repeat the mistakes of the last crash. Even his predecessor, Paul Volcker, the man who stopped The Great Inflation, fears that in order to unshoulder the burden of their own debt both public and private, businessmen and politicians will create irresistible pressures for another dose of inflation. After all, these insistent inflationists argue, it would only be a little dose. If that happens, cash will shrivel and house values will inflate—*after* Dr. Batra's faithful followers have sold the roofs over their heads.

What most people do not realize—and what this book tries to explain—is that a decision to juice or squeeze the economy in response to financial upheaval would be a political decision and not an economic one. The way the authorities turn the dials between deflation and inflation also decides who gets hurt: The savers or the speculators. Anyone who gambles his house on a decision of this kind, usually made in secret and in haste under intense political pressures, deserves to lose it. That is why *The National Debt* is not a book of financial but one of political advice; its fundamental message to Americans is to face reality and demand the same clear-eyed honesty from their leaders. On his travels abroad, foreigners urged Ronald Reagan for several years to recognize that his policies did not add up and could only bring America to grief and the world with it. A vignette of how he blithely ignored them will be found in Chapter 30. In Chapter 31 are assembled the signals that long had pointed toward crash.

The year 1988 is crucial in deciding whether the United States reads the handwriting in Wall Street. As an election year, it is a year of dangerous living, and the dangers extend from continued dumb incomprehension in the White House to demagoguery in the campaign. The first could foolishly raise the hopes of a nation facing judgment. The second could dangerously play on its fears. Peace and prosperity are the classic rhetorical twins of American political campaigns because they are the ideas that really matter to the voters. Ronald Reagan may have begun stumbling toward peace with the Soviet Union in the same undirected manner that the incoherence of his policies pulled us back from prosperity. But the passage into the next phase of the American economy is much easier to understand than the arcana of arms control. Historically, great inflations are followed by slumps. Most obvious is the slump in economic activity: businesses fall, people lose their jobs. But assets also are written down. That sounds like a boring euphemism of accounting, but it is not. The process can have profound political and social consequences; bonds, stocks, houses, farms, and, most painfully, the savings invested in them lose their value, sometimes catastrophically as they did worldwide after 1929.

During any boom, small savers and entrepreneurs usually align themselves politically with conservative big business interests. But as the value of their property plummets on the way down, they discover that economic virtue is not its own reward. Then they cry foul and change parties. Professor Charles S. Maier of Harvard, an expert on the political history of boom and bust, has remarked on the pain of this discovery during the 1930s by small merchants and farmers in the United States, Germany, and most other industrial countries. They followed the classic pattern and switched sides in anger and frustration. In Europe half a century ago, most countries were unlucky because the disaffected could only turn to right-wing radicals, the worst of whom was Hitler. In Japan, it was the country's fate to fall under the control of military adventurers. The United States was lucky: it got Franklin Roosevelt. That same coalition of small savers and diligent businessmen still exists in the United States: it is called Middle America. Over the years it has given its undying loyalty to Roosevelt, its respect to Eisenhower, its heart to Kennedy, and its head to Nixon, at least until until he broke the rules by which they live. Finally they fell, exhausted by inflation and national humiliation, into the comforting embrace of one of their very own, Ronald Reagan.

President Reagan, the summer lifeguard from Middle America, presided over the end of inflation and took out a loan on the future. But it was based on shaky collateral because the national assets had never been written down. They were only shuffled and creamed off by Wall Street's asset strippers. The market then followed by belatedly writing down the assets of the biggest U.S. corporations after their managements had demonstrated their inability to pay the nation's collective way in the world. (That's what a trade deficit means.) That also wrote down the value of most working Americans' savings, whether they were directly invested in the stock market or indirectly through pension funds. The next assets at risk are in the real estate market: housing, the foundation of most American families' personal wealth. That presents the final bill for inflation. Write-downs like this usually are done in the classic way: a massive devaluation of the currency that cuts everyone's standard of living. This is already underway. A mass of aggrieved Middle Americans may find their assets forcibly written down while they are already strung out by mortgage and consumer debt. If they do not understand what is happening to them, they can become bait for unscrupulous politicians. They form a potential swing coalition of angry, frustrated small debtors. Will politicians bid for them? Only if they are confused and unaware.

When I write about this, people ask: do you have to be so gloomy? The answer of course is no. Nothing is preordained in life; we in the Western democracies don't believe that finance is karma. Just because the world turns, 1929 and its aftermath do not have to happen again in 1988, 1989, or 1990. We have it in our hands to do something about it.

Ordinary people in America know what is at stake, that the world is different, that their lives have not improved much in a generation. Before the campaign began, the Washington political class was talking about the 1988 election as a battle of ideas. Then we switch to a campaign about "character"—a word defined as only the Washington wiseacres can. But the national debate really should be about competence, common sense, and national self-awareness. Above all, about honest leadership. The grand political intelligences in Washington have not really been thinking carefully about some of the most startling political facts of Ronald Reagan's two terms: America's dependence on foreign money and cooperation to maintain our solvency; the decline in our relative standing with the rest of the world; the lack of a real leader of the Western world's political economy, or, the more realistic possibility, a partnership among nations of the world to match a social consensus at home.

The task of the president who follows Ronald Reagan will not be to find new ideological directions for our country; two presidential terms of experimenting with ideology have scared people off. Reagan's successor will have to show us how to clean up after the party. The events outlined in this book prove that the most important qualifications for the next president lie beyond mere inspiration. He ought to be a proven specialist in management and he must be a leader. Leadership in America now consists of telling people hard truths and managing the Republic in hard times.

PART I

DEFICITS and DEBTS

THE GOVERNMENT'S DEBT— AND OURS

1

"What Is the National Debt, Really?"

When I told a Harvard professor—not an economist but a psychiatrist—about my plans for this book, he brightened visibly and said, "What *is* the National Debt, really? You'll have to explain that." My purpose, then, is to try to explain such ideas as debt, deficits, and economic adjustment in terms that even a Harvard professor can understand. This is a formidable task, not undertaken lightly, but nevertheless with a sense of public duty as well as a sense of fun. I am not trying to prove anything; but I am trying simply to warn against what could turn into a financial and public catastrophe if we cannot learn to live within our means, provide for our future, and cooperate with our trading partners. This book might not have existed at all if fewer members of the economics priesthood had not secretly shared the attitude of Professor Seymour Harris. In presenting a new style of economics to the American public forty years ago, he wrote, "Many a citizen will never be able to understand fully the problem of the public debt, for it is too complicated for the average layman. On these technical matters he will have to accept the word of the experts."

Economists have been getting off lightly by posing as technicians in white coats, when in reality their useful discipline, stripped of its pretensions, is far from being as forbidding as it seems. It is not a science, and it is no more dismal (Carlyle notwithstanding) and no less ludicrous than most human behavior. It tries to bring order to one aspect of behavior by postulating an ideal type of rational man as if "Everyman were indeed Economic Man," in the neat oxymoron of another Harvard professor, Charles S. Maier, who is a political scientist. Arbitrating the demands of Everyman, especially when the world around him changes, is the task of politics, which is the study of how we want to live. The economic concept of adjustment to technical innovation or changes in the balance of financial power is really a term of art drawn from psychology. Any therapist will tell you that the longer individuals postpone their adjustment to change or misfortune, the more difficult and painful the process will be. This is a technical insight with a moral foundation: when the discipline of economics was invented during the Enlightenment, it was a branch of moral philosophy. In the nineteenth century, it began to be thought of as political economy for thinkers as disparate as Mill and Marx. There is an old saying: politics proposes, economics disposes. Economics defines limits. It is no accident that Paul Volcker, when he was the most powerful economist in the United States, if not the world, as the chairman of the Federal Reserve Board, said that the Fed was "caught in the position of sometimes reminding people of the limits." After a quarter-century of writing about political economy, I have become convinced that the discipline of economics is essentially politics with a few numbers to illuminate its ideas. But not too many. Beware of the man who, like the drunk with a lamppost, uses numbers for support rather than for illumination.

The best economists instinctively know all this and become statesmen. John Maynard Keynes, the brilliant economist who marked this century, changed the way we thought about our national and international economy and laid the intellectual foundations for the greatest period of prosperity the world has ever known. The British government raised him to the peerage for his contributions to wartime finance, but Lord Keynes nevertheless had modest, even humble aspirations for his discipline. In an essay entitled "Economics for Our Grandchildren," he looked forward to the day when most economic problems would be solved, and when economics would be a minor, technical discipline that would help us make painful choices, like dentistry. He wrote: "If economists could manage to get themselves thought of as humble, competent people, on a level with dentists, that would be splendid."

One way to think about the phenomenal growth of the National Debt is to consider it as one price we pay for putting off a visit to the dentist. The flow of deficits we have been running throughout the decade as a nation and as individuals in what Volcker calls "a national binge of borrowing," has run off and collected into a huge swamp of debt. Mark that distinction between deficit and debt: one is what economists call a flow, the other, a stock. Think of deficits as a stream of borrowed money flowing steadily into a huge, stagnant pool of debt. When you run a surplus (which is increasingly rare), the stream flows out of the pool and lowers the level of debt. Some of the gross debt figures are so staggering as to be incomprehensible: 2.3 trillion dollars owed by the federal government, and rising; 1.5 trillion owed by American corporations; 1.8 trillion owed in home mortgages; 600 billion in installment credit; 300 billion owed in uncollectible debts by third world governments to American banks; and, for the first time since World War I, more owed to foreigners by everyone in America than they owe us. All of which makes that traditional debtor, the American farmer, a relative piker with only about 200 billion outstanding, except that about one-quarter of his debt has gone sour. Salomon Brothers, the huge Wall Street trading house, calculates that by the end of 1986 the pool of debt in the United States had reached $7,871,700,000,000.00—just short of a nice round eight trillion dollars or almost twice the gross national product. That represented an increase in everyone's total debt to everyone else by about 11 percent during only one year. It also meant that the level of this debt swamp was rising at about twice the rate of the dollar value of everything produced by the country the year of 1986.

If our debts were to hold steady, even around those awesome levels, the rest of us could catch up with them by the process of economic growth that has come to be considered normal in the modern world. But our debts refuse to stand still. Debt of all kinds has almost doubled in five years, growing twice as fast as our annual income. Such shifts in economic behavior traditionally signal wars, depressions, inflations, or other upheavals. What is underway now, in peacetime and relative prosperity, is unprecedented: perhaps some sort of national delusion, like the South Sea Bubble. For many years, we owed about 40 percent more than we earned. That ratio now has grown to almost 70 percent, largely but not entirely because of the increase in the federal debt. This burden of debt can never really be laid down, because debts of such magnitude can only be paid off by massive transfers of wealth from spenders to savers, and that would stop the economy dead in its tracks. Instead, we will have to carry interest on it. And so will our grandchildren.

In coming generations, debt may simply turn into an ugly four-letter word: resentment over it may distort the way we think about, finance, and organize our society. *Credit,* which derives from the Latin verb *credere,* "to believe," is not a term of purely financial application. The word is allied to the quality of *credibility,* which lately has extended its use into the world of politics, not always in a positive sense. For, make no mistake, debt is not just a simple sinew of commerce but a fundamental relationship of civilization. It must be founded on trust between creditors and borrowers, even when they span generations. Debt is the foundation of capitalism: it is a social contract linking savers, spenders, and investors—the old and the young who together compose the flour and the yeast of society. Debt is the lubrication of society's dreams; it transfers wealth from secure savers to adventurous investors and offers the possibility of enriching them both. It gives a prudent government room for maneuver to help its citizens in need, and a bold one the leverage to chance its ambitions.

One imaginative economic historian reckons that the foundations for England's foreign treasure were laid by Queen Elizabeth I wisely investing the profits from the expedition of Sir Francis Drake's *Golden Hind* in 1580. She paid off England's foreign debt, balanced the budget, and invested 40,000 pounds in the new East India Company. Compound interest on that sum would have increased it one-hundred-thousand-fold by 1930, when Great Britain's foreign investments stood at about four billion pounds. Yet within a generation they were gone, and Britain was a debtor, its investments burned up in a war for survival.

However sad this tale may be, it bears considerably more nobility than the one we have to tell of America financing its consumer culture by borrowing from its friends abroad and its unborn children. This is a stock of debt with socially destructive potential. Normally, nations, just like companies or families, reduce their debt according to the same principle: by growing out of it. As any businessman knows, if his gross receipts grow faster than his interest costs, he is keeping his head above water. Borrowing to build something bigger or better creates jobs and improves people's lives, and it is the basic rationale for going into debt. That is what happened as we came out of the Golden Age of the postwar world: from 1955 to 1975 the National Debt was steadily reduced as a share of what the nation earned—not by paying off the money, but by amassing more wealth so the burden of debt became relatively lighter.

But then the world turned upside down. Inflation and its aftermath changed the rules. Lyndon Johnson financed the war in Vietnam with the printing press. Richard Nixon helped guarantee his reelection with the same blunt instrument, more subtly used. Poor Gerald Ford and Jimmy Carter, still trying to fine-tune a tradeoff between inflation and unemployment according to their divergent political predilections, were simply overwhelmed. When Ronald Reagan came to office, he brought with him a simplistic, old-fashioned plan to cut everyone's taxes, free up the country's energies, restore its military strength, and then let nature take its course. The President is a romantic; that is part of his attraction and accounts for a great deal of his charm. He was thinking of the old-fashioned values bred in the limitless opportunities of another age, and he wanted to restore them. Like the frontiersman, he thought we could borrow ourselves rich. We now know, in some inchoate way, that we cannot. The purpose of this book is to explain why that is so and to introduce a sober measure of realism to the ordinary and puzzled reader.

The last generation in America has ridden on an economic roller coaster. First it went upward into inflation in the 1970s, and then down into debt. This left the country vulnerable to forces it can no longer be sure of controlling. Options are limited. Higher taxes are necessary, but they pose a dilemma. If they are imposed to slow the growth of debt, they produce an economy that is more financially stable but simultaneously has less spending power. That would make the economy more sluggish, but also make life in America less promising. Ideally, the air should come out of the debt balloon slowly, so that it does not land on solid ground with a thump. But that means the descent may take a generation. It may well stretch into our children's early adulthood and constrain their opportunities, their hopes, and therefore the tone of our society. Borrowing from foreigners has also constrained our political maneuver. In an extreme case of misrule and stubbornly persistent public illusion, it is not total fantasy to envision our country shredding at the edges like a third world nation, where things are not under our own command. So it is not impossible to discard the possibility that debtors and creditors will lose patience with each other, and that the air in the balloon will all come out with a big whoosh.

There is a fundamental difference between observers who transmit the information and analysis about the world and the people who make things happen without necessarily understanding why they worked that way. If they did ask themselves why, they might realize the risks and probably would never dare to take them. Inevitably, some of them fall off the high wire in real estate, finance, or other risky occupations. One position is that of the skeptic, the other of the believer. They go for the bigger reward, and they rise higher or fall farther; that is the way of the world. To those who see themselves exploring new territory, whether physical, intellectual, or ideological, the skeptic's caveats are a bore. To Mr. Walter Wriston, late of Citicorp, for example, the reservations expressed about his banking practices by Ms. Karin Lissakers, late of the U.S. government, had the annoying ring of a Cassandra. Had Mr. Wriston retained the classical teachings and wisdom of his father, who was president of Brown University, he would not have needed her rejoinder: "He forgot that Cassandra was right." Once in a generation or so, when memory fades of the last time the high wire itself collapsed, the Cassandras do, in fact, turn out to be right.

2

Whose Debt Is It?

Almost every week of the year, usually on Monday, the United States government has to go out and buy money. *Buy* money? When they can print all they want? Well, no. Not if dollar bills are to retain at least some correlation with the value of the goods they can purchase. So the government actually borrows billions of dollars in the money markets to buy things that we want, but for which we cannot always pay with this year's taxes. One example would be something that costs a great deal but must be undertaken with great urgency, such as a war. Another would be something that repays its cost slowly, such as a hydroelectric dam or a cancer research laboratory. When the government buys money, it pays with nothing more than its own promise to pay back later. That is why its promise is called a government security; it is secured only by the full faith and credit of the United States. If the promise lasts for a decade or more, the security is called a bond; if for two to ten years, it is called a note; and if for one year or less, it is called a Treasury bill. Since Treasury bills are the promises that fall due most often, groups of them have to be renewed, or "rolled over," in the quaint terminology of finance, every week. All these promises yield interest, which is how the government pays rent for the use of the money. The rent, of course, is paid by the taxpayers. Like any prudent steward, the government seeks to pay the lowest possible rent.

Several weeks before the government knows it will need large chunks of new money, its operatives start sounding out the big Wall Street houses to determine what kind of rent would make it worth their while. One week in advance, the Treasury announces its terms; it is planning to sell, let's say, $15 billion in bonds and notes to accommodate people who want to park their money with the world's safest borrower for a few years, or perhaps for as long as thirty years to build up a nest egg for retirement. They usually do not buy directly from the government, although they can do so. Instead, they go to a bank or a broker who has bought the bond wholesale at the government's auction. Major bond auctions are important events in the world of finance, because they test the credit of no less than the United States government. They are conducted at least four times a year and usually are spread over several days, starting on a Tuesday. All of the auctions are conducted by the government's own banker, the Federal Reserve System, which has its headquarters in Washington and regional banks in the major commercial cities, such as New York, Chicago, San Francisco, Atlanta. But it is in New York where most of the money is sold, at the forbidding Federal Reserve Bank on Liberty Street in the center of the Wall Street district, which is the financial capital of the world.

Since the government's aim is to obtain use of the money at the lowest possible cost, it conducts a curious kind of auction. Those who promise to pay the most money for their bonds are in effect offering to accept the lowest rate of interest; they win the auction. Follow closely: if you buy a $10,000 bond for $10,050, and that bond pays 10 percent interest a year, you receive $1,000 a year. But the government in fact is paying a rent of only 9.95 percent a year because of the extra money it has received. So why would anyone pay a $50 surcharge for a $10,000 bond? Because if he believes that at the next auction the government will only have to pay 9 percent interest—or $900 a year—a return of $1,000 a year will then look very nice indeed. By contrast, if you think that interest rates are going to go *up*, and next time the government will have to offer a rent of $1,100 a year for $10,000, you will not offer a surcharge but bid for your bonds at a discount. When the government's accounts are in order, its credit rating tends to be better, and the rent for its money lower. Interest rates on government bonds set the baseline for the cost of credit in the country, so these regular auction sales of the government's debt are one of the most important links between the government and the everyday economy, which also runs on credit.

When billions of dollars in bonds are sold like this in one day, huge amounts of money can be won or lost by guessing what the wholesale price of the bond ought to be, so that it can be resold later at a profit. Guess too low and try to make too big a profit, and you lose the auction because you will receive no bonds. Guess too high, and you have to resell the bonds at a loss to your customers, which means you lose the auction in a different way. This is not just some game for traders: the full faith and credit of the United States is not just an idle cliché. If everybody decides the government is either not to be trusted or trying to get away with too low a rent for its money, nobody buys bonds, and the government either goes out of business, borrows money elsewhere, or prints it up anyway. All of these things have been happening in Latin America for years.

So, it is just before 1 P.M. on a Tuesday. Runners dash into the New York Fed with sealed bids for a share of the bonds. Bids for billions in government securities during the year come from one group of about three dozen big buyers, and some of their names are as familiar to readers of the financial pages as Billy Martin and John McEnroe are to readers of the sports pages: Salomon Brothers; Goldman Sachs; Shearson Lehman. They are known as "primary dealers" because of their size and the amount of regular business they handle to keep the bond market turning over. As such, they rate special telephones at the Fed with direct lines to their offices. That allows each firm to phone in its bid at the last possible moment to its man stationed at the special phone inside the Fed. In this way, they can avoid being trapped by any sudden change in the bond market. The Japanese, recent buyers in quantity of thirty-year bonds, are trying to join this select group of primary dealers. For the present, however, they must resort to such expedients as that employed on one recent auction day by Nikko Securities. Traders at its New York office parked the chairman's stretch limousine outside the Fed's huge iron front gates, opened up a line by the car's radiotelephone to their thirty-seventh-floor office a few blocks away, and sent in a runner with their bid in a sealed envelope at 12:56 P.M., just before the 1 P.M. deadline.

With the bids assembled, clerks slit open the sealed envelopes, and the Fed quickly starts allocating the bills, notes, and bonds to the winning buyers. Their accounts are later debited by computer, and the government's own bank account at the Fed is credited in the same way. The primary dealers have huge trading rooms, some of them a block long, to retail the bonds they have just bought. The prices appear on flickering monitor screens so mesmerizing to the bond traders that they rarely pause to look out at the stunning panorama of New York Harbor. The bonds are sold in huge batches to banks and pension funds, and a few may even find their way into the classic widows-and-orphans' portfolios. The big-name traders buy and sell among themselves in a perpetual auction: an insignificant piece of news such as the previous month's level of factory orders can affect their view of the economy, which in turn will affect their view of interest rates, which can add or wipe away millions in the value of the bonds within minutes. As the National Debt has increased, and as interest rates have become more volatile, so has the trading in government bonds. Ten years ago, the bonds changed hands twice a year; now they are traded on average once a month. They are hardly recognizable as bonds. No more gilt-edged engraving, even if the buyer insists. For that, he has to go into the retail market and buy an old bond. Except

for short-term bills, new government securities now
are just entries on a computerized master list.

Inside the Treasury in Washington, the bonds, notes,
and bills are entered in the government's accounts.
These, too, are stored on computer tapes. While the
winning bids were being parceled out, each sale was
reported on the Federal Reserve System's communications network, which is hooked into a floor full of
computers in an unexciting federal building at 13th and
C Streets SW, Washington, D.C. It stands in a wind-
swept urban desert across from the Central Heating
and Refrigeration Plant and is appropriately located in
an annex to the Treasury's Bureau of Engraving and
Printing, where they actually produce dollars. The computers belong to the Treasury's Bureau of Public Debt,
and they are detailed to the Division of Public Debt
Accounting, where they form the heart of its Financial
Accounting Branch. It is these machines that mark the
prices of the bonds received by the government as the
Fed sells them, note the interest payable, and keep
track of the National Debt. About forty people work
in the Financial Accounting Branch, but the work of
adding up the National Debt is detailed to three or
four senior clerks in the Financial Reports Section.
The task rotates among them because it is a taxing
one, especially as the National Debt continues to grow
almost beyond human comprehension. At any moment of the day, however, the section can capture the
precise figure. For example, Mrs. Marsha Adams, a
handsome black civil servant whose photograph has
graced the national magazines, is able to walk down a
corridor over some brown government-issue carpeting,
open a door with a hand-lettered sign (PLEASE KEEP
DOOR CLOSED), and tap a small computer terminal
about the same size as those used by the millionaire
Wall Street traders to shovel masses of that same debt
back and forth among themselves. Out comes the latest figure. On January 5, 1987, the day Congress received history's first trillion-dollar federal budget, the
National Debt was $2,218,428,901,299.50, or eight times
larger than in 1956, the year that Mrs. Adams was
born. When she finishes her work, she goes home to

the suburbs in Hyattsville, Maryland, where she helps her schoolboy son with his arithmetic.

So the bottom line of the National Debt is, after all, only a matrix of electronic pulses in a computer, binary charges nestled in the atomic interstices of a silicon chip. They record what the government owes in the most ephemeral manner, as if written in sand. But financial obligations are by definition fragile things. Promissory notes, banker's bills of acceptance, and Treasury bills and bonds have always been called paper. Just paper, because that is what they used to be written on. That gives some indication of how they are simultaneously weak and strong. The computer across from the heating plant could blow a fuse and wipe out the records of the National Debt. The paper could simply be torn up. But the obligation, the debt, would remain. Debt is not a thing; it is a moral concept. By no coincidence is it called a *bond,* as fragile and as strong as the word implies, part of the skein of human relationships that make society. You cannot touch it or feel it, but you know it is real.

Such paradoxes make the National Debt one of those perennial mysteries, like the Holy Trinity or the Fourteenth Amendment to the Constitution, that are excessively vulnerable to the rhetoric of religious charlatans, political demagogues, presidential candidates, or a combination of all of them. Every presidential candidate from Franklin Roosevelt onward has campaigned on a promise to balance the budget and control the size of the debt. Roosevelt both set and broke the mold when he realized he could not keep his promise, which he made in a stump speech in Pittsburgh in 1932. The best way out, suggested his speechwriter and confidant, Judge Sam Rosenman, might be to deny that he had ever been in Pittsburgh. For as long as I can remember, deficits and the debt they left behind have been subjects best left to politicians and other cranks, while the rest of us have gone about our business of making, and sometimes losing, real money. The National Debt was something so forbidding in concept that it was paradoxically regarded as a trifle, despite its huge size. It has provided occasional employment for cartoonists who enjoy sketching taxpayers clad only in barrels en route to the poorhouse, or piles of pennies reaching as high as some celestial body.

But the size of the debt also has doubled in only about five years. During that period, the government's debt increased by the same amount that it had earlier grown in only fits and starts during the entire history of the Republic. By any measure, it now is the largest in peacetime history—anyone's history. When Ronald Reagan assumed the presidency in 1981, the National Debt, then about one trillion dollars, would have stretched into a stack of thousand-dollar bills sixty-seven miles high, assuming someone wanted to print up all that money. In his first televised speech from the White House, he sought to horrify the ordinary citizen with the fiscal excesses of his predecessors by invoking that measure, which his staff actually went to the trouble of verifying with the Bureau of Engraving and Printing. "A monument to the policies of the past, which as of today are reversed," said the President. The President did not advertise that during his presidency this monument grew to a height of at least 155 miles, or that its sudden growth took place under the stewardship of the most conservative president of this century, the man who had built a brilliant political career late in life partly by denouncing deficit spending and attacking the National Debt with the zeal of a parson secretly maintaining an intimate emotional relationship with sin. Anything that grows so inexplicably and exponentially, whether it be supposedly benign phenomena like waterlilies and human births, or more threatening explosions like kudzu and cancer, deserves our full attention.

3

Vigorish

Borrowing and saving are two sides of the same coin. You can only borrow money that someone else has put in a bank to save. In modern times, governments used to borrow money in peacetime in order to run deficits during recessions. They could scoop into the national pool of savings and borrow because a stagnant industry did not want the money. That pool of money had been put aside by individuals for retirement and by businesses fer investment when times turned better. It provided a natural limit to the appetites of borrowers and was curbed by interest rates, which are the price we pay fer borrowing money. But why save when you can borrow? With our natural optimism reinforced by a tax system that still rewards borrowing more handsomely than any other, even after the most thoroughgoing reform in a generation, our savings rate is the lowest in the industrialized world. A generation ago, the country as a whole— individuals, businesses, and the government—saved about 18 or 19 percent of its earnings. The major European nations still do. Japan puts aside a positively masochistic 30 percent. But Americans save only half that, about 14 percent.

But now we have started moving into uncharted territory, at home and abroad. As individuals, we have been saving at about half our habitual rate, while the government borrows the difference on our behalf from foreigners. The Reagan administration's vaunted supply-side savings incentives have had little effect. We now save only about 3.5 percent of our personal earnings, leaving a smaller pool of savings for the government to tap. When the administration started to run up record deficits, no one of importance believed it could actually find all the money it would have to borrow. There just were not enough savings. The chairman of the Council of Economic Advisers, the chairman of the Federal Reserve Board, the blue-chip forecasters who point the way for Wall Street, the number-crunchers with their computers—all warned that the government, like a thirsty elephant, would crowd all the other borrowers out of the national savings pool. Not one of these gurus of capitalism foresaw that the more parsimonious Japanese and Europeans would willingly lend us a sizable share of their savings, as long as we paid them enough to make it worth their while. They were attracted by our high interest rates; America had become one vast money-market fund for the rest of the world. But no one imagined that the country would also be able to live with the high interest rates. The persistent economic and political imbalances that this situation created are an important part of the story of the National Debt. Now, for the first time since America succeeded England as the preeminent country of the capitalist world after World War I, we owe our foreign creditors more than they owe us.

Economists used to pooh-pooh the National Debt. They argued that spenders in one part of society merely owed it to savers in another, and we simply "owed it to ourselves." But now that we owe so much of the debt to each other, as well as a rising proportion to foreigners, paying the interest on it has become a major consideration in the government's national finances. The annual interest bill exceeds $150 billion. In the space of five years, interest payments as a share of the budget doubled, to 15 percent of total spending. That may not sound like much until you realize that the amount the government pays in debt interest has risen from one-third to one-half of what it pays for our military establishment. Since we have financed the greatest peacetime defense buildup in history on the never-never, those figures are not entirely unrelated. The government's relentless demands for credit have also driven up its long-term price; it is no news that interest rates have tended to go up rather than down in the postwar period, especially during the first half of the 1980s. Interest paid by short-term Treasury bills averaged 2 percent in the 1950s. In the early 1980s, they yielded an astounding six times that, then gradually slid back to about 6 percent. High rates add to the cost of financing the debt. As rates rose, interest on the debt grew four times faster than the debt itself. Thirty years ago, interest paid to the public on the debt accounted for only a sliver of the gross national product. It now has almost trebled, to 3.8 percent of the GNP, twice as high a proportion as in 1978. The federal government now spends more on debt interest than on income security for the poor.

Who pays the interest, anyway? Not just big companies; all the corporate income tax collected in 1986 would not pay two-thirds of the interest bill. So it is not some sort of irrelevant shell game of shuffling money back and forth from rich companies to rich bondholders. The interest is paid by everyone. At the start of the decade, one dollar out of every five paid in personal income taxes was spent on interest payments on the National Debt. In five years, that proportion has increased to two dollars out of every five. Interest payments already eat up the rough equivalent of all the individual income taxes collected from everyone living west of the Mississippi River. As for the future, it is always problematical, hence the first rule of financial forecasting is: give a number or a date but never both. Physicists can forecast both because there are far more constants in the physical universe than in human behavior. Einstein could predict precisely how the sun's light would bend when it passed near a planet, but financiers cannot even predict the prices at next week's government bond auction. But let's be bold. After all, like Einstein, we're moving into such uncharted territory that we need to get our bearings.

Each year that the government ran a deficit of $200 billion, the taxpayers paid for about four-fifths of the budget, and lenders made up the difference. Averages can be deceiving, yet they help in understanding financial flows of such magnitude that no one person can ever pick them up and handle them. If you average out each deficit of $200 billion among the country's approximately 100 million taxpaying workers, each one ends up being responsible for $2,000 worth of the deficit. Or turn it around and put it another way: each one of them (you, us!) managed to postpone paying $2,000 in taxes and borrowed the money instead. Pretty clever, especially since it will never have to be paid back. As long as the credit of the United States holds good, it can be borrowed, rolled over, and reborrowed. With interest, of course.

At what cost? At 10 percent, the interest on one year's deficit works out at only $200 per person. Not bad. Less than the annual charges on the MasterCard. Beats paying $2,000 extra to the IRS, until it starts to add up. Even then, five deficits at give-or-take $200 billion each (there's Ronald Reagan's extra trillion, all sixty-seven miles of it) add up to an additional $1,000 in interest per person. Relax, all that extra money isn't going to come directly out of your pocket, since the federal government receives only about half the revenues for its budget from individual income taxes. So the IRS will need to add only half of that additional interest to your tax bill. Go ahead, make a deal with the revenue agent before he decides he has a court case. You owe an additional $500 in income taxes for that five-year spending spree—*except that you owe it for every taxpaying year for the rest of your life.*

If you're a 27-year-old yuppie who voted for Ronald Reagan, you deserve each other. From now until retirement (not at age 65 anymore, but at 67 under the latest Social Security reform), you will have to pay extra income taxes totaling $20,000 as the morning-after bill for that glorious spending spree. Of course, that leaves aside the $20,000 for the other trillion dollars of debt you're already paying, along with the matter of how the rest of the interest costs will be spread out among cigarette and liquor taxes and among corporations, and finally how some of the rising payroll taxes for Social Security will go into Treasury bonds to help roll over the debt. Twenty thousand dollars bought a very commodious house at the end of World War II, or, if you were so inclined, a Rolls-Royce. With inflation, both cost much more, but debt incurred at that time is worth far less. Lifetime levies of such magnitude means that the people who have to pay them may prefer an inflation that makes it cheaper for them by devaluing the currency in which they have to pay it back. They may prefer that forty years from now $20,000 will buy only a cup of coffee, and two government bonds of that amount are only good for wallpaper. That's one way to escape from a financial hangover.

Now that we have an idea of who pays the interest, who gets it? The interest on the National Debt is transferred from ordinary taxpayers to the rich, who hold a disproportionate amount of the Treasury's notes and bonds (the government's IOUs), or the old, for whom the bonds are held in Social Security trust accounts. Because of political promises made to this largest and most conscientious of voting blocs, Social Security benefits have risen twice as fast as real wages in the past thirty years. The per capita income of retired families has about pulled even with that of working families. The old in America no longer live in a pocket of poverty; many seemed to be living off their money market funds. In 1982, half the interest income counted by the Internal Revenue Service was reported by people over the age of sixty-five; a decade earlier, the elderly had accounted for only one-fifth of the interest. In the charts on how people earn their share of the national income, a sharp change has taken place in the share for earnings from interest. From 1970 to 1984, employees' compensation declined slightly but hovered around 75 percent of the total. Corporate profits after taxes improved less than one percentage point, despite all the hoopla about revenue favors to business in the 1981 tax bill. But the share of income from interest almost doubled from a range of 5 to 6 percent in 1970–75, to a range of 9 to 10 percent from 1980–85.

As these trends continue, we risk the creation of a rentier class partly dependent upon high interest rates for its continued comfort. In France in the 1880s, about four million people, or 10 percent of the population, held bonds—*rentes* in French. When the government decided to exchange new bonds for old at lower rates, these *rentiers* formed themselves into a political bloc and forced the government to maintain the high rates for a number of years. It was then, and would be now, an intergenerational and interclass tug of war, with the federal government's balance sheet as a political battleground.

Federal Reserve Board economists surveying the personal wealth of all American families found that in 1983 they owned $93 billion in Treasury securities. But the top 1 percent—all the families earning over $150,000 a year—owned $40 billion worth, or almost half of them. The top *one-half* percent, those earning $280,000 or more, owned a startling one-third of the total, an even sharper concentration of the government's wealth among individuals. That meant about 320,000 families owned $30.8 billion of the National Debt, an average of about $100,000 per family, yielding about $10,000 a year in interest, all paid by the taxpayers. This stock of Treasury securities held by the rich and the super-rich is larger than the $34 billion held by U.S. pension funds, which are set up for the middle class. This concentration is unlikely to change over generations, since 80 percent of household wealth in America is inherited.

The largest single holders of the debt, however, are the government's own Social Security and other retirement, unemployment, and Medicare trust funds. These funds, which now hold about $300 billion, are really an elaborate accounting device designed to ensure that when the sick, the old, and the unemployed claim their portion, it is there. It almost wasn't there in the recession year of 1982, because the contributions from the payroll taxes of wage earners could not match what the politicians had promised their parents. The system was overhauled and payroll taxes were raised. While income taxes decreased under the Reagan tax cuts, payroll taxes had to be increased sharply. Their contribution to federal revenues has quickly tripled to one-third, producing a surplus in the trust funds, which are invested by law in Treasury bonds.

The government forecasts that the trust-fund surplus will double in the next five years. If the deficit is erased by then, it will have been accomplished largely on the backs of workers and their employers dutifully depositing payroll taxes in the government's trust funds. But meanwhile, the Medicare fund is likely to run out of money early in the 1990s. The same choice will face the country as existed with Social Security earlier in this decade: severe economies in treating the elderly or further increases in payroll taxes. When the young awaken to the implications of this, a public policy debate could turn into ugly intergenerational warfare. The most obvious target for Medicare economies is in the care of the terminally ill. Medicare spends one dollar in every five on patients during the last six months of their lives. That proportion can be reduced by pulling the plug earlier, or it can be financed by raising payroll taxes. Which? How many people have watched an aged parent in a lingering death, longing for relief? From pain? Or from expense?

Although few fiscal dilemmas pose quite such stark alternatives, none of these financial and political storm signals is going to turn toward calm anytime soon. Even if the federal deficits start shrinking, government interest payments will continue rising, and, by the end of the decade, they will level off at somewhere between $160 and $180 billion (depending on whose entrails the forecasters examine). Congress can vote to cut defense and has improved the fiscal situation considerably by doing so. But it cannot legislate a cut in the National Debt or the interest on it, short of defaulting on it. Lower interest rates cannot offer very much help either. About half of the federal debt is locked into bonds with a lifetime of five years or longer, yielding their lucky, or prudent, holders 10 percent interest or better. And if (but more likely *when*) interest rates move up, the Treasury gets hit quickly with the rising cost of short-term borrowing.

The most awesome quality about these numbers is that they can take on a life of their own, whether on the most imperial or intimate scale. The miracle of compound interest works in favor of savers but with equal force against debtors. In 1560, Philip II of Spain, who was then singlehandedly directing the largest empire theretofore assembled, reported that his royal indebtedness was seven times his total revenue. By 1574, he was paying more interest to his bankers in Italy and Germany than he was collecting in taxes; his Italian creditors continued carrying this potential rival because they knew he would waste his treasure on military rather than industrial adventures. Right they were. In 1588, the dour and obsessive Philip, misjudging the world from his refuge in the Escorial, made one final thrust to save Spain's fortunes by launching the Spanish Armada against England. We know how that came out. Spain, still nominally the richest and most powerful country in Europe, fell into a rapid decline from which it never recovered. On a personal level, the phenomenon has been described by Senator Daniel Patrick Moynihan, recalling his boyhood on the West Side piers of New York. He compares it to the usurious "vigorish" (actually a Mafia term lately shortened to "the vig") and describes its operations as follows:

> If you were broke on Monday morning, no problem. You could borrow $20, with $30 to be paid back on payday, which was Friday. If you didn't have $30 on Friday, that was no problem. You could pay $40 on Wednesday. The extra $10, then $20, was called "vigorish." It kept mounting. Sooner or later your family bailed you out in a big scene, or you ended up in St. Clare's Hospital. That is what the U.S. federal deficit is all about. Not spending; interest.

Such homely comparisons between personal and federal finance have been frowned upon by the grand panjandrums of national accounting since they began playing around seriously with public deficits in the 1960s. But now the incongruities of federal finance refuse to be ironed out. The Congressional Budget Office began warning in its February 1985 *Economic and Budget Outlook* that "the inost insidious danger of persistent large deficits is that they may result in a runaway accumulation of federal debt." The CBO was cautious not to predict that it would actually start running away, but the agency has demonstrated how a combination of slow growth, low taxes, and high spending could make it happen. Put simply, if the National Debt grows faster than our national economy, we reach a point where the mounting vigorish becomes unbearable. It becomes politically impossible to cut spending further or to raise new taxes. The continuing drain to pay ever-higher interest leaves fewer savings to invest in new factories to increase our wealth, and, consequently, the government's tax receipts also grow more slowly than its spiraling debt. Unease or worse sets in, and government bondholders start dumping them and turning their bonds into cash at whatever price they can get. Floating new bonds then demands a prohibitively high rate of interest. The government begins to resemble a business that borrows simply to finance last year's debt and this year's interest. The bankers start thinking about reorganizing their clients' debts under Chapter 11 of the bankruptcy laws (and their clients start thinking about bankruptcy), but governments aren't supposed to do that.

They don't. In the days of Philip II, the Spanish Hapsburgs clipped the coinage as an expedient, and the Armada was Philip's last throw of the dice. Now governments print money to inflate their way out of debt. The money raises the national wealth, at least on paper, but the debt, also on paper, is smaller. Such paper expedients work for only a time, as the nations of Latin America have recently had occasion to learn. When a cup of coffee costs 20,000 pesos, the Argentine government finally has to wipe the slate clean, devalue the peso right out of existence, and find some other name for its discredited currency. Homely metaphors still hold good even in international finance. In earlier generations, the United States sent in enforcers known as Marines, and a spell under guard in the tropical equivalent of St. Clare's Hospital was not unknown for debtors. The world now is a more civilized place, and the family of nations has helped bail out the errant debtors. Their bankruptcy has not yet been financial, but it has been moral. If we teetered on the same precipice by refusing to face the reality of our commitments, which is to say our debts, our bankruptcy also would be moral.

4

How It Got There

The nation was born in debt. The first deficit, totaling $1.4 million, occurred at the dawn of the Re-
public in 1792. Superficially, our view of the National
Debt seems quite different from today's. It was only in
the 1930s that the government took a major role in
stabilizing the economy and began to spend money in
order to pull us out of slumps by our own bootstraps.
That was when the budget became the fulcrum of the
national economy. But the argument over the function
and therefore the fiscal role of government is as old as
the nation. Follow the story carefully; let the past
instruct the present.

From 1789 to 1930, there were only forty-five deficits, an average of one every three years. Almost all of
them were associated with the country's major wars,
when governments traditionally borrow to finance a
national emergency. The first deficit crystallized the
great debate of the era between Thomas Jefferson, the
author of the Declaration of Independence and the
defender of the then-revolutionary concept of the rights
of man, and Alexander Hamilton, the illegitimate West
Indian who was the country's first financial genius.
Would the new nation remain a homeland for Jefferson's incorruptible yeomanry, or would it industrialize
and fall under the sway of "the mobs of great cities"?
Hamilton championed industrialization by using the
government's taxing power and its right to run up debt

as a "useful illusion" of its political credibility. He
wanted to advance the economy in ways that Keynesian
economists of today would hardly find strange. Long
before, he had written Robert Morris, the wartime
superintendent of finance: "A national debt, if not
excessive, will be to us a national blessing." Hamilton
knew there was no way the new nation could raise
money for industrial development until it established
its public credit and financed the war debt of $79,124,465
that he inherited as the first Secretary of the Treasury.
In the process of doing so, the thirteen states would
also learn how to operate as a commercial and thus a
political union. As he told Congress, "Credit is an
entire thing; every part of it has the nicest sympathy
with every other part; wound one limb and the whole
tree shrinks and decays."

Jefferson disagreed. He wanted to pay it off, but for
moral rather than economic reasons. He argued that
"the laws of nature" made it unfair to impose the
debts of one generation upon another, and he therefore proposed that the debts be paid off in nineteen
years, or one generation less one year. Since the debt
was then equivalent to 40 percent of a year's income,
Jefferson's dictum would have condemned the post-
Revolutionary yeomanry to virtual servitude as it repaid the nation's creditors by annually skimming off 2
percent of the national income, plus interest, of course.
Jefferson's real target seemed to be Hamilton, whom
he accused of furthering his "monarchical" ambitions
by using the debt "to corrupt and manage the Legisla-
ture." The gravamen was that federal money would
purchase political loyalty. This was long before the
first reclamation project was even conceived for a congressional district, long before the new Capitol was
built, or before its first lobbyist had to register.

Congress, jealous of its power to tax and spend,
refused to grant Hamilton a public hearing to present
his plan for funding the debt. So he sent it up in
writing, then retaliated by sending his annual appro-
priations request in lump sums. With no opportunity
to examine the requests, Congress had little choice but
to rubber-stamp them. The elders fired back by setting

up the House Ways and Means Committee for permanent oversight of public money, a thorn in the side of administrations to this day. Hamilton nevertheless prevailed. He reorganized the country's chaotic finances by floating long-term bonds, selling off lands in the West, and issuing a charming but alas now extinct form of annuity known as a *tontine*. Named after Lorenzo Tonti, a wise Neapolitan who invented it, this form of annuity splits up the interest among the surviving holders, who gamble that they will be among the last few left to profit from this ghoulish lottery. The quarrel drained and embittered him. Upon leaving the Treasury, he wrote a friend in 1794: "Believe me, I am heartily tired of my situation and wait only the opportunity of the quitting of it with honor and without decisive prejudice to public affairs."

George Washington's role in this dispute is both obscure and familiar. He issued regular appeals for the government to redeem the National Debt, but he seems to have been as dilatory as Congress itself in agreeing to raise the tariffs on wine, spirits, tea, and coffee that were needed to pay the interest on Hamilton's bonds. In a passage in his Farewell Address worthy of Polonius, he urged his successors to borrow sparingly, but seek peace with a strong military, and nevertheless pay off war debts to avoid "not ungenerously throwing upon posterity the burdens which we ourselves ought to bear." This Reaganesque policy of trying to mix high defense spending with prudent debt management sounds like rousing good stuff from the soldier-president who founded the nation. But the bottom line was that after twelve years of Federalist government under Washington and John Adams, their expenditures to fight off Indians, pay tribute to Barbary pirates, build forty ships for the navy, and start work on the new capital city, left Jefferson a National Debt of $76 million when he succeeded them as the third President. The sum was almost exactly what Hamilton had inherited from the Revolution.

From the moment he was inaugurated in 1801, Jefferson set the pattern for the nineteenth century by trying to liquidate the National Debt. Even though he had to borrow $11 million for the Louisiana Purchase, he had paid off $25 million of public debt within six years. The principal aim of government finance then was to retire the federal debt by earning surpluses, not always to the advantage of the economy. Assisted by westward expansion, the United States ran a surplus from 1816 to 1836. Andrew Jackson's Treasury Secretary, Roger Taney, proudly announced that as of January 1, 1835, the United States "will present that happy, and probably in modern times unprecedented, spectacle of a people substantially free from the smallest portion of debt."

This fiscal utopia was unnatural, unjustified, and consequently short-lived. Customs duties, which were the main form of taxation, had already been reduced. Instead, Jackson's government depended on the continued sale of virgin public lands for new revenues. Until the bubble burst, that satisfied planters and speculators alike. Cheap credit boosted prices by fueling speculation. To limit the powers of the federal government by starving the Treasury, Jackson's populist administration decided in the election year of 1836 to divide a surplus of $37 million among the states. The first two installments were paid in gold, the third in devalued bank notes, and the fourth not at all. A recession had cut imports, and tariff revenues accordingly plummeted. The surplus vanished, and the land speculation boiled over into the Panic of 1837.

The surplus did not become a problem again until the 1880s, when hard-money Republicans of the Gilded Age squeezed the economy, reducing the Civil War debt and living standards with it. Once again, the surplus era ended in crackpot financial theories, this time the free coinage of silver, and the financial panics of the early 1890s. The surplus came back again during the happier but more ominous 1920s. General H. M. Lord, the director of the Bureau of the Budget, reported in 1927: "Despite persistent efforts to reduce revenue by cutting [income] taxes to a point barely sufficient to meet our annual demands, we seem helpless in the face of the country's continuing prosperity. Reduction in taxes has come to be almost synonymous with increases in public revenue. At the end of each year we are called upon to determine what to do with the surplus millions." Lord served Calvin Coolidge, whose partiality to commerce is memorialized by his classic assertion that "the business of America is business." No wonder that Silent Cal is Ronald Reagan's favorite president. Reagan keeps Coolidge's portrait on the wall of the Cabinet Room and argues against raising taxes by asserting that tax cuts always raise revenue, just as they did in Coolidge's day when Dutch Reagan was a teenager.

Is history trying to tell us something? That surpluses are bad and deficits are good? That Keynes and Roosevelt were right and Hoover was wrong in trying to balance the budget in the middle of a worldwide depression? Neither. It tells us that politicians usually fight in the trenches of the last ideological war even while the battlefront of the present one shifts around them. But the issues hardly change. Hamilton and Jefferson defined the two opposing ideological strands in American life. Hamilton borrowed unashamedly to create the industrial and military underpinnings that would defend the country against its enemies. Jefferson scorned his Big Government policy. For him, "that government which governs best, governs least." His ideological successor was Jackson, the frontier general, who ran the central bank out of Washington because he favored cheap and unfettered creation of credit by country banks for little people. The result was a financial crash. The ironies of history are exquisite. The Democrats, today's party of Big Government, venerate Jefferson and Jackson. The Republicans, who lean toward Jeffersonian rhetoric when it suits them, owe their birth to Abraham Lincoln, who put the nation through a Civil War to preserve a strong central government that oversaw America's economic emergence into a world power. Franklin Roosevelt, a Democrat, conserved and expanded that role of government. And what about Ronald Reagan? He seems like a Jeffersonian in thought but a Hamiltonian in action. But that is getting ahead of the story, into an area that Marx might call The Contradictions of Capitalism.

Even after the Crash of 1929 or the Great Inflation of the 1970s, Herbert Hoover (while in office) and Ronald Reagan (like Roosevelt, while campaigning) insisted on a balanced budget. They argued that it was essential for reviving business confidence and restraining inflation. Hoover and a Republican Congress followed this idea right out the window in 1932, when the GNP contracted by 15 percent. Victims of past obsessions, they quadrupled income tax rates and made them retroactive. Taxpayers had to dip into savings to pay, and the drain on the banks helped pull the plug on the banking system. One of Roosevelt's first acts as president in 1933 was to close the banks for a week to reorganize them.

Roosevelt cautiously introduced the concept of "compensatory finance," which meant compensating for a slack economy by government spending. Keynes gave it a theoretical justification and helped save capitalism. He fully accepted the capitalist laws of supply and demand, but he discovered that they could end up balancing in such a way as to leave the economy operating only at half-speed. His remedy was the simple application of money to fill the gap, either government bonds to make the rich feel wealthy enough to spend, or highway projects to give the poor jobs and money to spend, too. And if the bureaucratic imagination was bereft of ideas for new projects, the government could simply bury banknotes in old coalmines, fill them up with garbage, and let people find them. Mind you, this was to be neither charity nor socialism. Keynes's idea was to start recirculating idle wealth on the basis of prudent public finance: "Leave it to private enterprise on sound principles of laissez-faire to dig up the notes again, the right to do so being obtained, of course, by tendering for leases of the note-bearing territory." As long as money was idle, which surely it was in the Depression, the idea worked. Although it took a war to pull both the nation and the world out of the Great Depression, when Roosevelt tried to balance the budget, the economy slumped.

Once businessmen saw how well this policy worked, they dropped their scruples. In the 1950s, Republican businessmen quickly embraced the idea of economic stimulus. Herbert Stein, the country's leading conservative economic historian and one of the Republicans' best economists, wryly notes that then, as now, it offered a ready-made rationale for what businessmen always want to do, which is to reduce taxes. Their real opponents entering the 1960s were not the few remaining hands-off Hooverites but the minority of hands-on public spenders in the Democratic Party. These Democrats saw deficits as a means to increase the task of government and hence the quality of public welfare over the claims of private affluence. The social reformers were led by the Harvard professor John Kenneth Galbraith, who was reviled by conservatives like Stein as an intellectual dandy. Galbraith caught John F. Kennedy's ear with his style and sardonic charm, but he lost the argument to the President's pragmatic New Economists and was happily consoled by appointment as Ambassador to India. There he kept a diary, collected Indian miniatures and felt at home because, as he recognized even before departing, "I enjoy stating moderate positions in abrasive form."

These Keynesians finally made deficit spending more fashionable than Galbraith had ever intended to do in his best-selling books. To distinguish themselves from classical theorists who worried mainly about how prices were set in the marketplace, they called their ideas the New Economics and worried mainly about how the government could stimulate enough action to keep the marketplace going. Kennedy's economic witch doctors were led by Walter Heller, an articulate professor from Minnesota, ever a state of rationally optimistic American expansionism. He quickly recognized that cutting taxes was the only politically plausible way to stimulate the economy. Heller argued that the economy was being dragged down by high taxes that created a gap between what it was doing and what it should do. Result: factories operating below capacity, people out of work, and the federal budget in deficit.

But cutting taxes when the budget was in the red seemed anathema to simple folk, and there are many such in Congress. Hadn't President Eisenhower's Treasury Secretary, George Humphrey, warned against the dangerous impossibility of trying to "spend yourself rich"? In his fear of inflation, Eisenhower had tipped the economy into three recessions, one of the principal reasons Kennedy had won the presidency. Kennedy did not want to lose it in 1964 because of a fourth slump, so he decided to peddle the medicine of a tax cut. The proposal was mired in a skeptical Congress when he was assassinated in 1963, but then it was passed quickly into law almost as a national expiation. Deficit finance was thus converted into public dogma as a monument to the martyred President.

A cut of $11 billion in personal and corporate taxes went into effect in 1964, when the budget was $6 billion in deficit. By the following year, unemployment was down to its target, inflation was quiescent, growth was up, and the resulting increase in federal revenues cut the deficit to a mere billion. This was the apotheosis of Keynes. *Time* magazine put him on its cover, the first dead person ever to achieve this secular canonization. Heller was invited to give the Godkin Lectures at Harvard in 1966 to explain his fiscal wizardry. Proclaiming that "economics has come of age," he said: "One finds it hard to imagine a future president spurning professional economic advice and playing a passive economic role." Yet that was precisely what was already happening. It was high noon for the New Economics.

While Lyndon Johnson was publicly committing the revenues produced by the New Economics to the social welfare programs of his Great Society, he was also secretly supplying the military to fight in Vietnam. The buildup for the Vietnam War was concealed from his economic advisers. They suspected it was underway, tried in vain to prove it, and nevertheless argued for a surtax to pay for it. Their advice was spurned. In bureaucratic slang, they were being cut out of the loop. The Pentagon sent regular spending estimates to the Council of Economic Advisers marked "for internal use only." Arthur Okun, the youngest and most irreverent of these advisers, scribbled underneath: "but not to be swallowed." When the public finally was forced to swallow the truth, it was too late. From the start of the Vietnam buildup in 1965 to its height in 1968, military expenditures rose 47 percent. Transfer payments, the best measure of government money transferred through Social Security and welfare programs, rose 51 percent during the same three years. In 1968, the deficit jumped to $25 billion. It was to be followed by a virtually relentless march of deficits straining the economy beyond its limits and igniting the Great Inflation of the next decade.

5

Sisyphus

The more rigorous aspects of the New Economics can be found even in the Bible. The idea of putting aside something in fat years for lean is primitive Keynesianism. In the modern world, it means raising taxes during periods of economic euphoria. Politicians living only within the horizon of the next election are usually not interested in hearing Biblical wisdom, even in modern dress. Like the plague, they have avoided raising taxes ever since Congress belatedly placed a special surcharge on income taxes in 1969 to help finance the Vietnam War. The result was a slump in 1970. Politicians do not easily forget such things and will seize any available rationale to avoid them. In 1971, Richard Nixon produced a budget to expand the economy before his reelection. He justified the stimulative deficit by declaring, "Now I am a Keynesian." Ronald Reagan did not even bother to seek theoretical justification for his deficits; he blamed it all on Congress.

Patriotic souls who prudently wish to send along a little something extra with their income tax to help reduce the National Debt have been gently reminded by the Commissioner of Internal Revenue on their Form 1040 that he will look upon it kindly, but only as a mere charitable contribution. Thus, the naive restraints of debt retirement no longer are taken seriously, and deficits not only have become a way of life but also a tactical handmaiden of policy. For Johnson, they sanctioned a guns-and-butter policy that permitted the proliferation of government programs. For Reagan, they turned out to be the cutting edge of a policy to reduce Johnson's Great Society programs by starving them of tax money, but the policy still ended up in guns, butter, and debt.

Historically, debts of the massive proportions now being carried by the United States usually are associated with headstrong princes bent on conquest or democratic societies determined to resist them. But at least half of our $2 trillion National Debt is the bill for a spending spree that has continued during half a decade of ideological skirmishing over the size and role of government. During the same period, the governments of the industrial nations of Western Europe went through the same debate over the relative merits of public versus private welfare. Their welfare spending having reached the limits of fiscal prudence and public tolerance, they changed direction through electoral debates and enlightened public discussion. Not even as ferocious an ideologue as Margaret Thatcher was willing to force the issue by cutting taxes independently of cutting spending, and she even warned a visiting American Congressional delegation against it shortly after Ronald Reagan came to power. In the nations of Western Europe, public spending as a share of national earnings reached its postwar zenith in 1983. In 1984, it quietly began a relative decline, moving down by one percentage point as prosperity took hold. European society as a whole had decided to spend more of its wealth as individuals rather than through the state.

By contrast, the federal income-tax cuts proposed by the Reagan administration deliberately emasculated the government's revenue powers in order to curtail this spendthrift's "allowance." This was one of Ronald Reagan's favorite metaphors, and it revealed where government stood in his scale of adult values. Measuring the ensuing gap between income and outgo does not demand a knowledge of the calculus of exponential numbers, only simple arithmetic. But, as Bertrand

Russell once said, "People would rather commit suicide than learn arithmetic."

In the United States, we now produce goods worth about four trillion dollars a year. The federal government spends or redistributes about one trillion, or one dollar out of every four. Some dollars go to buy bombers with expensive toilet seats, some to prevent the old from falling into poverty, some to cancer research. After climbing for four years, Washington's share of our money crested at about 24 percent in 1985. If you add in all the money spent by states and cities, the proportion is closer to one-third. On a world scale, that is relatively low; the Swedes spend almost two-thirds of their national income through their government, the British and the Germans about three-fifths, and even the Japanese almost one-third. But the point is that the proportion of our income the federal government spends is actually higher, by about two percentage points, than it was when Ronald Reagan arrived in Washington pledging to shrink it. It is four percentage points above the postwar historical norm. The change in priorities wrought under Reagan, by accident and design, explains why.

In the process of deliberately doubling the amount spent on defense, and then being forced to triple the amount spent on interest, most everything else had to stand still or, as with programs for the poor, contract. Nevertheless, because of the Reagan administration's great tax-cutting experiment in 1981, income tax and most other receipts have increased more slowly than spending. The one exception is the Social Security tax, which now extracts about half again as much as it did from workers' payrolls before the system was reformed to save it from bankruptcy. After five years of fiscal fanfare, the bottom line was a flow of federal revenues at or just slightly below its historical postwar norm of 18.5 percent of GNP. This adds up (or more precisely, subtracts out) to a federal deficit of between 5 and 6 percent of GNP. The result of this gap between revenue and expenditure was that one dollar out of every five spent by the government had to be borrowed.

There is no precedent for this. No U.S. government

has ever gone right on borrowing at such a rate during a period of peacetime expansion. Even at its height in 1968, the Vietnam War deficit reached only half the proportion of the national income as the deficit in Reagan's most spendthrift year. The Vietnam deficit also lasted a much shorter time; by 1969, the budget was heading into surplus. This time, to find the money to finance our consumer boom and our military buildup, we have been forced to borrow abroad, since Americans do not save enough money of their own to lend the government all it wants. Three cents of every dollar spent in the United States was borrowed from foreigners. That is three cents of every dollar *everyone* spends. Three cents of every dollar that passes through everyone's bank account, not just the government's bank account. The largest single lenders have been the Japanese, who are also the industrialized world's most assiduous savers and prefer our bonds because they will pay a high interest rate for their own retirement.

During World War II, at least one dollar of every two spent by the government was borrowed from its citizens for a great cause. We emerged from the war in 1946 with the federal government owing $241 billion to its various public creditors, or 113 percent more than the nation earned that year. No one worried, not only because of the characteristic optimism of the period, but because the debt went around in a closed society, like water boiling, condensing, and then raining down in one of those sealed glass chemistry flasks. Economists argued that "we owe it to ourselves," and, further, that the debt would be no burden on succeeding generations because our children would simply shuffle the interest payments around among each other. (From poor taxpayers to rich bondholders, apparently, as we do now, although no one ever puts it that way because the government started the vicious circle by borrowing on behalf of the poor taxpayers in the first place.) During the early postwar period, these arguments stood largely unquestioned by the economics profession because the motives of politicians were seen as benign. A rare exception was James M. Buchanan, a Virginia professor who argued that politicians were more like private entrepreneurs using public funds to promote their electoral interests. The grandson of a governor of Tennessee, he may have known more about real life than his professional colleagues. In the 1950s and 1960s, he was dismissed as a crank; in 1986, he was awarded the Nobel Prize for economics.

The principal reason for public complacency was that the National Debt stabilized under Truman and Eisenhower. The budget was balanced except during part of the Korean War and some of the Eisenhower recessions. But those deficits were small, and the country grew out of debt, which plateaued while the gross national product doubled. Like Alice when she ate her cakes to fit through the door to Wonderland, the debt kept growing smaller relative to the increase in the national wealth.

That relationship represents the ratio of debt to GNP. It charts the relationship between what we owe and what we earn. It is the standard measure of the appropriate weight of the debt, just as a family's annual income sets its mortgage limit (or used to, in a more prudent era). Because of postwar growth, the National Debt declined to the equivalent of 58 percent of GNP within the decade after the end of World War II. It continued declining steadily to 24 percent of GNP in 1975. Then it started climbing again as deficits rose, but it stood only two percentage points higher when Reagan took office. After that, it took off, and federal debt equaled about 41 percent of GNP by the middle of Reagan's second term. This debt ratio, like Latin America's in the previous decade, can hardly do anything but continue to climb until at least the end of this decade. By that time, the United States will have run budget deficits for twenty consecutive years unless adjustments are made on either the revenue or the expenditure side of the ledger. This political confrontation finally caught up with the Reagan administration after the 1987 Wall Street crash, when it grudgingly negotiated a first and feeble adjustment with a feckless Congress.

There has never been any sign that the pulse of the real economy would respond to the exuberant finance of the Reagan administration and provide new stimulus to grow out of debt, as it did in the immediate postwar era. This was the misconceived gamble of the supply-siders in the Reagan political entourage. But growth in the 1980s averaged only about 2 percent a year. During the 1970s, growth of the economy averaged around the traditional upward trend line, which is 3 percent. In the 1960s, it had reached an unprecedented 4 percent, which is unlikely to be repeated. This steady decline in the growth of the national income carries an ominous message outside the realm of government finance. It means that although we live closer to the borderline of recession, we have less insurance against it.

In the eight postwar recessions, smaller debt ratios gave the government room to borrow something to prime the pump. The increase in the overall debt was hardly noticeable, and the deficit insurance it bought quickly restarted the economy, which would then pull ahead and decrease the debt–GNP ratio again. But as a government and as individuals, the United States now is mortgaged to its eyeballs. A healthy economy with growing room to spare, just like an energetic individual with an idea, usually needs only a short, sharp injection of borrowed cash to get started. But now the unprecedented weight of debt is more likely to slow the economy. A deficit of $200 billion could easily increase half-again in the next recession. Any government prowling through the world's credit markets looking for that kind of money would send interest rates rising at the worst possible time. The size of the deficit already sets financial limits on borrowing. The psychological weight of debt inhibits our traditional sense of risk. Americans have always imagined themselves and their country as Promethean. But the classical figure America begins to resemble is not that mythical Titan who snatched fire from the gods, but Sisyphus, the damned soul in hell. His avarice earned him the eternal punishment of rolling a marble block up a hill, only to have its huge weight tumble down upon him as soon as he reached the top.

6

Keynesians, RATs, and Why We Really Borrow

Some ingenious economists still argue that government deficits hardly matter in the real world, thus helping to prove the old Washington adage that where you stand is determined by where you sit. When big budget deficits began just in time to create an election boom for Ronald Reagan in 1984, administration apologists produced studies purporting to show that deficits had no connection with interest rates. This was tantamount to saying that the largest borrower in the nation, indeed, in the world, had no effect on the price of credit, inflation, or other things that go bump in the night. In trying to give respectability to such huge deficits, these boosters were aided by the existence of a theoretical no man's land that no economist has been able to take and hold. For no theory has been able to trace the precise effect on the economy of selling government bonds to finance deficits, any more than doctors can fully explain how most medicines work, accurately predict what they will accomplish, or foresee all their side-effects. Human behavior is no less mysterious than human biology.

For what it is worth, Keynesians believe what seems to be obvious: that government bonds represent wealth to the people who buy them and happily clip their interest-bearing coupons. They feel richer, so they go out and buy new cars or new clothes. That creates jobs and raises output. Never mind about repaying the bonds when they fall due. This government will be out of office, and we all may be dead by then, anyway. The original guru of this theory of government deficits was Professor Abba P. Lerner, a Keynesian who argued in the 1940s that the National Debt was no burden because it produced a circular exchange of income within a closed society. That was the we-owe-it-to-ourselves argument. As long as we did, the only people who objected were labeled cranks or old fogies, like Professor James M. Buchanan, who attacked Lerner's theories as "the new orthodoxy," or President Eisenhower, who worried about our grandchildren inheriting the debt. Professor Buchanan's reputation has since been redeemed by his Nobel Prize, and President Eisenhower has been similarly rediscovered by historians. But meanwhile, Keynesian finance justified itself by prosperity unparalleled in history. Raising the money in the bond market was a cinch for the Treasury. So why worry?

This line of reasoning has recently been carried to what one hopes will be its ultimate conclusion by Professor Robert Eisner of Northwestern University, a lifelong Keynesian fiscal specialist. Mark another distinction here, that between fiscal policy and monetary policy. It even confused John F. Kennedy, who devised a mnemonic to help him remember the difference between fiscal and monetary. It was the letter M. It also stands for money, which helps control the economy through its availability for business and other loans. That leaves the other main arm of government policy, which is not monetary but fiscal; it works through the federal budget (the letter F) by spending on public works, helping the poor, and taxing ourselves to pay for it.

As a fiscal specialist, Professor Eisner characteristically worries less about raising money for the government than making sure the government spends enough of it to keep the action alive in the marketplace. In a recent study, he concentrated on the government's accounting methods, and rightly found them somewhat eccentric. Unlike a corporation, most municipalities, or indeed the industrial nations of Europe, the U. S.

federal budget makes no distinction between, on the one hand, operating expenses for salaries or paperclips, and, on the other, investment for projects such as roads, airports, or national parks that legitimately can be expected to profit society over the years. The reason for this is probably ideological: in America, the government is not supposed to own anything that smacks of profitable enterprise, which is reserved for the private sector. Only in America do we socialize the losses of Chrysler or Lockheed and encourage them to capitalize their profits.

This accounting critique has merit, but Professor Eisner carries it one step further. He argues that if the government did its accounts properly, it could call on a sizable stock of assets to offset against the debt, at least on paper. *Voilà!* The national accounts would be back in the black. If potential bond buyers could be convinced of this, the government would never have trouble raising money. This is an intriguing conceit until one asks whether these public assets could ever be cashed in to turn the red ink to black and draw down the National Debt. How about a sale-and-leaseback deal with Disney for the Grand Canyon? Or an outright sale of the Bonneville Power Administration? The Reagan administration has actually proposed selling off the Grand Coulee Dam in its 1987 budget, but there has been no rush of buyers. This idea is about as helpful as selling off the Crown Jewels to help Mrs. Thatcher balance the books. And a good thing, too, says the Professor, since getting rid of dams or national parks "would be as bizarre as suggesting that a family sell its $100,000 home to make its $50,000 mortgage disappear." But it certainly does provide a nice feeling to know that the books are not as unbalanced as they seem. Here is a huge stock of assets that offsets the stock of debt and even the annual deficit itself, if only the accounts could be arranged properly.

Such sensible bookkeeping then begins to lead Professor Eisner awry. By a series of calculations correcting for inflation and for a measure of the government's assets, he reckons that, far from stimulating the economy during most of the postwar period, the federal budget was actually holding back the nation's economic growth. Only with the arrival of good, solid 200-billion-dollar deficits that you could almost smell and feel under Ronald Reagan, he argues, has the federal budget deficit really stimulated the economy. There is no doubt a large element of truth in this, although these calculations hardly seem necessary to confirm the evidence of one's own eyes. They pose only one problem. Theories not only must provide sound guidance to the future, but validate the past as well. The Professor finds that during the tearaway inflation years of 1977 to 1980, a nominal budget deficit was supposedly holding back the economy. How's that again? Other members of his profession have caught him on this in testimony before the Joint Economic Committee of Congress. What would have happened to inflation, already in double digits, if the country had run even larger and more stimulative deficits under Jimmy Carter? Perhaps we ought to try a different theory.

Economists of a different persuasion known as "rational expectations" propound their theory from an opposing political nest. Known within their profession as RATs for short, and centered at the University of Minnesota with its freethinking traditions, this group has been trying to supersede the Keynesians. The RATs argue that government bonds do not really represent wealth. Instead of making their owners feel better, as the Keynesians believe, the RATs argue that government bonds make their owners feel worse because they know the government eventually will have to collect taxes to come up with the interest, either openly or by printing money. They suggest that everyone stays awake nights wondering how to protect himself and his descendants so they will be able to pay their share of the interest on the accumulated debt. Out of intergenerational altruism and foresight, these prudent souls then set aside the money to cover the debts of their children. *Voilà!* Their saving cancels out the effect of the deficit spending. "The key insight of rational expectations is that private agents change their decision rules when the government changes its policy," says RAT guru Thomas J. Sargent in the blood-less language that modern economists seem to prefer. The convenient corollary to the RATs' thesis is that since people supposedly plan ahead so rationally, they make government management of the economy not only unnecessary but harmful. The conclusion is that by their concerted actions in bidding bond prices up or down in the market, investors conspire to outwit the Treasury. This automatically irons out the ups and downs of the business cycle.

Professor Eisner and the RATs have developed intriguing if excessively narrow explanations for human behavior. This is a characteristic failing of economics when it tries to pose as a science (which is a point we will take up in the second part of the book). These serious social scientists, who forget that their assumptions about economic behavior grow in part from the history and society that shaped them, represent extremes in a serious mainstream argument over whether the deficit mechanism has been blunted by overuse. Eisner, a product of the 1930s, still credits a benign government, in all senses of that word, and argues that it is rich beyond its dreams. If it is short of cash to stimulate the economy, it only needs to borrow some more. The RATs, having watched politicians first cheat the country in Vietnam (Sargent was obviously marked by his military tour as a systems analyst at the Pentagon), and then cheat savers by inflation, claim that the tide has turned. The people who buy the government's bonds can force its hand by making credit prohibitively expensive when they fear it is going to devalue their savings by inflation. They watch Congress and the Fed playing a game of chicken over whether the Fed will print money to finance the deficit, and supposedly they know how to get out of the way by demanding a huge price in interest for their money. And if the government cannot sell bonds at a reasonable price, the RATs argue, it also can never afford to run a deficit large enough to boost the economy. So it should not even bother to try.

Despite their helpful insights, both cannot be completely right, and in fact neither is. If one of them were, the history of the past five years would have been very different. If the RATs are right, rational people should have nullified the Reagan tax cuts by socking away the money against the inevitable day. when the deficit will have to be repaid by higher taxes. Precisely the opposite happened; we spent as if there were no tomorrow. But events also prove that there is an element of truth in both strands. In the late 1970s, the then-unprecedented deficits of the Carter presidency flowed like water into the sand because bond buyers literally went on strike, as the RATs' theory said they would. Only the Federal Reserve's record interest rates lured them back. Result: recession in 1982. The deficits had backfired. Here Eisner's Keynesianism argues that the Reagan administration still should have no trouble selling bonds because the money always comes from somewhere. He would be right, or anyway half-right. Half of it came from foreigners. They bought bonds instead. But they insisted on being rewarded for the risk by receiving the highest interest rates since the United States had to bid on world markets for money to finance its economic development in the late nineteenth century.

Such extremes in academe signify mainly that the economy is moving into uncharted territory, and that there are more things in heaven and earth than are dreamed of in economic theory. In one sense, the RATs' thesis is eminently true for Latin America. But a new theory is hardly needed to explain why no rational citizen there will lend his money to governments with such notorious financial reputations. (Instead, they might try explaining why New York banks were irrational enough to lend them the money anyway, a hilarious episode in the historic accumulation of debt that will be examined shortly.) In the United States, mainstream economists are not ready to turn to theories more suitable for Latin America, at least not yet. But they do see the deficit as a huge black hole swallowing up tomorrow's savings for today's consumption. They cannot calculate how long the process can continue before it swallows the country's economy as well. The classical danger is called "crowding out":

voracious government demand for credit crowds out industry's demands for money to invest for expansion, and the economy falters.

So far, crowding out the demand for credit in the United States has been avoided by luring money from foreigners. But this is becoming increasingly difficult and expensive, and there is in any case a price to be paid for that later, as we have to earn the interest on their bonds. Martin Feldstein, who publicly quarreled with his own administration while serving as chairman of Reagan's Council of Economic Advisers, has suggested a blackhole scenario of *super*crowding out: deficit-caused inflation that runs ahead of the supply of money and sends interest rates so high that they squeeze the entire economy and not just industrial borrowers. But in fact this eminent Harvard economist has no clear theory of what will happen if the United States continues to take in the world's savings to finance its deficit. He can only say that the prognosis is definitely malign.

The question that all these academics really are addressing is whether it is better for a government to borrow or tax when its promises outrun its resources. It is as old as the invention of government debt. A simple way to address the real issue is to ask whether a taxpayer would prefer to hold a $10,000 government bond or a cancelled check for his tax payment to the U.S. Treasury. The answer may seem obvious, but that only demonstrates that neither deficits, nor borrowing to pay for them, have gone out of style. Two centuries ago, Adam Smith railed at governments that had "enfeebled" themselves by passing their debts on to their successors and cheating lenders who received no guarantee that the money would be spent wisely, since governments could always tax their hapless citizens in recourse. He wrote: "When national debts have once been accumulated to a certain degree, there is scarce, I believe, a single instance of their having been fairly and completely paid." David Ricardo, the wealthy London stockbroker who laid the foundations for logical analysis in economics in the early nineteenth century, reasoned that the burdens of taxation and debt were equivalent, at least in theory. In the long run, the cost to the citizen is the same whether he pays the costs at once in taxes, or in installments by paying off interest and principal. But common sense told him that in fact they were not equal. Taxpayers are hardly rational enough to save and cover their own or their children's tax payments. If government borrows on their behalf, they will spend more now. Taxes enforce public saving. Borrowed money is spent. We know from the consumer boom of the Reagan era that this is precisely what happens.

DEBTS: BUSINESS, OIL, FARM, PLASTIC, JUNK

7

The Culture of Debt

Cheap credit and easy money are the foundations of the American Way of Debt. Hometown banks were as important as social equalizers on the frontier, as the Colt .45 pistol. This helps to explain the durability of both the bank and the handgun in our national life, even if their technical improvements have not always been benign. A loan for tools, stock, or land gave the mobile but moneyless newcomer a chance to become the equal of the settled man with capital. The banks that rose, and alas sometimes fell, with the price of cotton or wheat in the nineteenth century served as pillars of the young Republic. They were every bit as important, if not perhaps as durable, as its Constitution. Of course, the line between investment and speculation, between *Giant* and J.R., is always a fine one, but it is there. The unfortunate banks now struggling under the weight of bad oil and farm loans in the great central basin of the United States, can at least take some pride in their great, stained, financial tradition as they call in the federal examiners to help bail them out and transfer millions of their debts into the National Debt. They have operated on the honorable principle of lending to rich and poor alike, regardless of ability to pay. "Beautiful credit! The foundation of modern society," exulted Mark Twain, our supreme literary ironist. "Who shall say that this is not the age of mutual trust, of unlimited reliance on human promises?"

This equivocal moral stance toward credit has not changed, only grown more complex as society has grown more cynical. Christopher Lasch, in *The Culture of Narcissism*, describes what surely was a mythical figure: "The self-made man, archetypical embodiment of the American Dream, owed his advancement to habits of industry, sobriety, moderation, self-discipline, and avoidance of debt." If such a man existed—after all, even Henry Ford needed credit—he surely does not exist anymore, as Lasch is quick to stress. Paying cash is infra dig to the average American with his six credit cards. But it is also close to impossible for many. Average real incomes have been stagnant for more than a decade, but expectations most decidedly have not.

Consumer debt for everything from cars to college tuition has tripled in ten years. Installment plan and credit-card interest charges and repayments take almost one dollar out of every eight from the average after-tax paycheck. Add home mortgage payments, and debt swallows one spendable dollar out of almost every five. Plastic money, which now represents about one-fifth of consumer debt, is being printed as never before: credit balances on 97 million American Master-Cards tripled in only three years, to $28 billion. Banks have shaken off public criticism for mass mailings of these tempting invitations to the never-never land of credit to millions of potential customers who had never even met a loan officer. Although some of their marketing methods may have been foolishly scattershot, their motives were in no way altruistic. By charging credit-card debtors up to twice what it cost the banks to borrow the money wholesale in 1985, the banks made profits on their plastic business at five times the rate of what they earned on all lending. With federal regulators looking over their shoulders, the bankers have used these profits to protect their institutions against the consequences of their past mistakes. They have been putting away these profits in their capital and reserves against defaults by third world borrowers, and writing off their losses to delinquent debtors, including the very same credit card holders who walked away from them during the recession early in the decade.

Total consumer indebtedness may in fact be larger than the unprecedented $600 billion or so outstanding. Another $150 billion in second mortgages—secured by the inflated value of the old homestead but repaid out of current income—is heavily deployed paying for today's purchases and not for building up tomorrow's investment. To avoid the sting of what used to be a slightly dubious loan, banks change the name to things like "Equity Access" with no hint that it comes from a second mortgage. The 1986 Tax Reform Act makes this even more attractive under the rubric of a "Home Equity Loan." Repayment is not based on the value of the house but the efforts of the householder. Describing this with appropriate skepticism, the banking correspondent of *The New York Times* could find only one banker who fully understood the equation. Not surprisingly, he was located in California, where they have suffered more and know better about such things. "Collateral," he said, "doesn't make payments. People do."

Some Wall Street analysts try to console the stockholders of the great financial institutions that rising household debt is comfortably matched by rising asset values. That, of course, is what the analysts are paid to do. Had not the rise in debt, after all, been matched by the greatest Wall Street boom in a generation? A man with a bulging stock portfolio should feel even morally entitled to take on additional debt. No doubt some stockholders have felt richer since the market rebounded in 1982, but credit-card debtors have not necessarily shared their joy. The reason would be painfully obvious to the latter if anyone had bothered to ask them: they are not necessarily the same people. As the Federal Reserve Bank of New York pronounced dryly in a recent annual report, "It is very unlikely that the same households are acquiring large amounts of both financial and debt obligations."

At their extremes, these households probably stand at opposite ends of both the age and financial spectrums: on the one hand, yuppies (or, worse, would-be yuppies for whom the middle letters in the acronym do not stand for "upwardly mobile" but, more accurately, for "underpaid") are running up debt as if there were no tomorrow; on the other, their parents are luxuriating in their financial gains as if tomorrow had already arrived. Credit cards are used most actively by these two kinds of people: those who have to, because they find it hard to obtain credit anywhere else, and those who want to, because they find it a convenience. The banks, not surprisingly, prefer the former as customers because of their high interest payments, while the latter usually settle at the end of the month. But those who need credit also seem to be convinced that they can and should nevertheless live like those who really don't, a circumstance that has never prevailed in quite this way before.

Traditionally, the ratio of people who fall a month behind in their credit-card payments rises during hard times, and that is precisely what happened early in the decade. The delinquency rate, as it is called, hit a high of 2.6 percent in the 1981–82 recession, and then began declining as the economy was pumped up for the 1984 election, hitting a low of about 2 percent around Election Day. But then, unaccountably, the rate started climbing abruptly. By the end of 1985, delinquencies on bank credit cards were at a record 3 percent. Since Sears reports a similar credit cycle from its nationwide chain of stores, most of these unfortunates are probably not those upwardly mobiles climbing the walls of New York's Upper East Side, but workers in the factory towns of the American heartland. There, well-paid blue-collar jobs are hard to find. Wives have to take what work they can get to supplement the family income and are laid off with alacrity. But credit-card balances rise relentlessly, along with dreams of comfort and security. We shall meet this young generation of post-industrial "new collar" workers again.

American companies have also been borrowing at unprecedented rates. Their purposes may be accounted either more sinister or more noble, depending on which foxhole any particular management found itself in during the Great Merger and Acquisition Wars of the mid-1980s. Like the wars of kings, these also are run on borrowed money: image-makers serving the corporate buccaneers would be wise to remind them that even Louis XIV had to be buried secretly at night because his campaigns of conquest had bankrupted France. The advantage, if any, of this enforced corporate restructuring to the U.S. economy is a matter of fierce debate. The justification of the corporate raiders is that they represent the nemesis of the marketplace; this should be taken as the self-serving statement it is. The definitive verdict on them may not be known for years. It took roughly a generation to discover the wastefulness of an earlier wave of takeovers in the 1960s, and some of those conglomerateurs' constructions were the very ones being dismantled in the 1980s boom in mergers.

What has happened is that raiders borrow to buy out and capitalize on usually sound if sleepy companies with ample cushions of cash and goodwill. Thus threatened, the managers in turn borrow to defend their good life by buying their own companies' stock, keeping it out of the raiders' hands. If the raiders win, they often strip away and sell the cushion that the target company had built up to search for oil, do long-term research, or start new ventures. If they lose, they usually leave behind a wounded company, bound up with debt. Admittedly, the cushion may have given its employees or managers an easy life, but who is best fitted to serve as arbiter of that—the financial markets with their narrow horizons, or the real market for the company's goods or services?

But the raiders also can end up gasping for air. Consider Ted Turner, champion yachtsman, organizer and proprietor of an innovative cable network, and world champion debtor. In 1985 he went after MGM, itself the pyramided result of past merger booms, and had to raise $1.4 billion to conquer the movie company. The Turner Broadcasting Company had not made a profit in the nine months prior to the bid, nor had MGM made a profit for the entire year; together their losses would have been about one-quarter of a billion dollars. Turner bet he could turn a profit by selling off MGM's library of 3,800 films. Buyers were slow to appear, so he decided to jazz up his investment by coloring such black-and-white masterpieces as *The Maltese Falcon*. Usually, corporate raiders justify despoilment of this order under the guise of the more efficient use of resources. If efficiency means pure profit, Turner has a point, but mainly he was trying to keep the wolf from the door. As he was swallowing MGM, Turner boasted that his companies' debt was $2 billion, or more than some of the smaller third world countries. "I'm pretty proud of that," he said. "Today, it's not how much you earn, but how much you owe."

The merger wave rolled ahead on credit. At first, obtaining funds for a raid in the newly deregulated, competitive banking world was no more difficult than using plastic. The prudent banker of yore had metastasized into the "profit center" of a great financial corporation, backing all comers. Citicorp, as always in the vanguard of any fashion in moneylending, was the largest financial backer of T. Boone Pickens when the oil raider made his unsuccessful run against Gulf. But the commercial banks had second thoughts after their big corporate customers loudly wondered whose side the banks would be on next. The lucrative business of backing corporate raids went to the investment bankers, who offer tactical advice at fees that run to the tens of millions and invest their own as well as their clients' money backing the raiders.

The most ingenious of these was the investment banking firm Drexel Burnham Lambert, which at the height of its influence in 1986 raised about $15 billion through a financial invention known politely as the high-yield bond. It is in effect a substitute for money which is issued by those willing to pay heavily for it: interest rates of 13, 14, or 17 percent, twice as much as the safest Treasury bonds. But organizations that offer to pay such interest premiums do so precisely because they are themselves sometimes shaky and unprofitable—which is why their bonds are called "junk bonds." They are raiders such as Turner; Carl Icahn, who took over TWA and bid for USX; Pickens, after the commercial banks found the oilman too hot to handle; Rupert Murdoch, who buys and sells newspapers like a recycler of trash; and Oscar Wyatt of Coastal States Oil, a Texas trader who shows up at OPEC meetings, maintains a house in Monte Carlo, and is often taken as the model for "Dallas'" J.R. All were clients of Drexel Burnham's junk bond guru, Michael Milken, who operated from an office in Beverly Hills to be near his family in California. For Milken, work began at 5 A.M. so he could keep in touch with his Wall Street contacts and his huge network of high-rolling investors as soon as they arrived at work. Potential clients came in for early breakfast, very early, but they came anyway, because Milken's yea-or-nay on whether to underwrite an issue of junk bonds could make or unmake a potential raider's day. He spent the rest of *his* day trading junk bonds to make sure they had an active and liquid market.

Was Ivan Boesky anything more than "a piece of sewage" (his own sister-in-law's description) floating atop this roiled financial sea? Boesky was an arbitrageur, a member of an arcane group that makes big money trading on small swings in the daily price of large blocks of stock. Normally these specialists fulfill a useful function by helping to iron out the swings in the stock market, but Boesky exaggerated them. Obtaining inside information from the investment bankers who backed the raiders, including one officer of Drexel Burnham who was prosecuted for leaking to him, Boesky bought huge blocks of stock before the raiders struck, held the stock while the price ran up, and then sold it at a huge profit, often swinging the deal for the raider as he did so by making the stock available to him. In the takeover casino, he fulfilled a role somewhat more exalted than a shill, who is the man hired to keep the game in play; indeed, Drexel Burnham helped Boesky raise $660 million early in 1986 for his investment partnership. The apprehension of Boesky and his confederates slowed down the take-over wave, which foundered in the Crash. Boesky had been widely pictured as a sort of spider at the center of a web. But as details emerged, the web turned out to be more important than the spider. More important than either was the junk bond, which was also devalued in the Crash.

What has indisputably been left by all this corporate carnage is more debt. Corporate debt increased at an annual rate of about $150 billion in the mid-1980s. Salomon Brothers estimates that for three years running, U.S. companies borrowed about as much for mergers, takeovers, and the repurchase of their own stock, as they did for buying new plant and equipment or financial assets. Minus inflation, corporate debt grew more than 8 percent during the 1984–85 boom, almost four times the annual rate from 1975 to 1983. Corporate managements, who may have been reckoning on a revival of inflation to bail them out, now have to devote half of their cash flow to paying interest on their debt, compared to slightly more than a quarter of it in the late 1970s. Unlike stock, this implacable debt must be fed with regular interest payments. There is less opportunity to skip a dividend and stroke the stockholders. The risk of hard times and bad judgments is thus carried by the company as an impersonal institution, by the management, and by the workers (who of course have had no say at all in these financial star wars raging over their heads). The stockholders, owners of record and presumed arbiters of the company's destiny, end up with less risk and the chance of a quick profit in a time horizon shorter than a Wall Street trading day. This isolates the paper chase of the financial economy from the decision-making of the real economy that produces goods and services—but not, as we shall soon see, from its consequences for the government or the taxpayers. This hardly can be said to streamline America's companies for the challenges of deregulation at home, competition abroad, and the unwinding of inflation which favored debt. On the contrary, it leaves them more vulnerable, especially when cash flow to service their debts dries up in the next recession, just as streams dry up in an August drought.

This chapter began with a remark by Mark Twain on the beauties of credit. Here is the rest of the remark: "That is a peculiar condition of modern society which enables a whole country to instantly recognize point and meaning to the familiar newspaper anecdote, which puts into the speculator in lands and mines this remark: 'I wasn't worth a cent two years ago, and now I owe two million dollars.' " The source is a book by Mark Twain and Charles Dudley Warner entitled *The Gilded Age: A Tale of Today*. It appeared in 1873, during an international financial panic linked to foreign speculation in American railroad bonds. The Panic of 1873 was followed by a five-year depression.

8

Creative Regulatory Accounting Principles

The commercial and cultural hubris of the American heartland may be a taste of what is to come in corporate boardrooms and those of their fiduciary allies. For the taxpayer, the problem will be to avoid getting stuck with the check by corporate America. For the past half decade, a depression—not a mere recession—has been underway on the land, exacerbated by accumulated debt. In the 1970s, America persuaded itself that it could, and therefore should, feed the unfortunates of the earth, a mixture of charity justifying profit that once was called the White Man's Burden. The policy also had a dash of realpolitik; Richard Nixon hoped America's abundant grain would tempt the Russians into political bargains in exchange for cheap food. A preemptive strike on America's grain harvest by Russian buyers operating in secret should have alerted him that the whole enterprise was built on sand.

Farmers nevertheless were exhorted to expand their cropland; credit was made freely available to help them do it. Within five years, farm debt doubled to $180 billion in 1980, and in the following year American farm exports reached a historic peak of 162 million tons. Then, to the amazement of the Midwestern farmers with their huge combines, the rest of the world caught up. Agricultural production worldwide increased by one-quarter, and in the developing countries, it rose by one-third. Kansas and Iowa were supposed to be feeding the indolent of Europe and the hungry in China, India, Indonesia, and especially that darling of an earlier generation of rock stars, Bangladesh. Now those nations are feeding themselves, there is a world glut of foodgrains, and Midwestern farmers and their creditors have been left holding the bushel basket with little hope of emptying it. Third world debtors have no money to buy and every motivation to undercut American exports, especially (cruelest cut) to the Soviet Union.

A farm property is worth what it can earn, and on that basis, the value of farmland has plummeted by as much as one-half in some Midwestern states. Land is the main security for farm mortgages, because it grows the money to pay the interest and, in normal times, leaves something extra for the farmer's profit. When it doesn't, the sound of the auctioneer's hammer splits the autumn air, Hollywood suddenly finds it profitable to make populist movies like *Country,* and farmers with their life's work in ruins walk into country banks and shoot the officers dead. One-quarter to one-half of the $210 billion in farm loans outstanding in 1986 are euphemistically described as "troubled." The Farmers Home Administration, the government's lender of last resort for thousands of farmers who no longer can obtain commercial credit, found that half of them are either technically bankrupt or heading there.

About 300 commercial banks failed during the first half of the 1980s, twice as many as during the entire postwar period. About half of them specialized in farm lending. In 1986, 138 banks failed, the largest number since the Depression. One-fourth were in Texas and Oklahoma. Another, larger, and more speculative industry was in trouble, without the benefit of the official government safety net legislated for agriculture: the oil business. When oil prices collapsed early in 1986, government regulators were ready with a list of 563 energy banks that had $61 billion tied up in loans to independents. These are more ominous although less emotional: farm means family, but oil means speculation and boom-and-bust. Farmers are tied to their land, but even oil roustabouts grown rich know how to walk away from dry holes. Donald Hughes, the biggest well-driller in Oklahoma, shrugged as his Mercedes Turbo Diesel 300SD was taken over by the bank; he would declare bankruptcy and wait until oil prices turn up again. Meanwhile, he has his memories. As Hughes told *The New York Times*, "During the boom everyone was screaming and hollerin' for rigs. There was not a week that at least three bankers from the major banks weren't here trying to loan me more money for more rigs. Chase Manhattan, Continental Illinois, Seafirst. They told me I was a shining star."

Seafirst, did he say? Merged under pressure. Continental Illinois? The first major American commercial bank to have been effectively nationalized. It had bought packages of uninspected loans from an Oklahoma bank called Penn Square that started in a shopping center, then collapsed along with its wildcatting customers in 1982. It took two years for the cracks in Continental's foundations to show, but it nevertheless had to be shored up in 1984. The Federal Deposit Insurance Corporation (FDIC), a government agency formed during the Depression to protect small depositors from bankers who had been unlucky or worse, committed $4.5 billion in new capital, even though it had insured only $3 billion in Continental's small deposits. The Federal Reserve System, which was formed in 1913 to guard the banking system and provide an "elastic" currency, promised billions more in loans. Continental's unprecedented rescue operation, which guaranteed the money of even the bank's high-rolling corporate depositors, was undertaken to prevent a single bank from pushing over a row of financial dominoes. The FDIC is trying to recoup some of its money by selling Continental's stock to the public, but the prognosis is poor, and the government's eventual loss has been estimated by the agency's chairman at a cool billion. Losses at that level are covered by the agency's insurance fund, which totals more than $18 billion. But if oil and third world losses infect enough of Continental's brethren, the FDIC will have to turn to the taxpayers for replenishment. The mortgage banks and the government's last-resort lending agencies for agriculture already have done so.

In the Farm Belt, government credit agencies now are engaged in a discreet game of pass-the-parcel, to determine which of them will have to beg Congress for more money to prevent more farm bankruptcies. Their debtors remain a charge on the government's credit as long as its agencies carry them, but if the government forecloses, their debts are subsumed under the National Debt. To help commercial banks relieve the government of at least some of its burden, federal banking regulators decided that less stringent accounting of capital might prevail for banks that permit farmers to stretch out their repayments. When oil prices plummeted, these exemptions, originally designed for the Farm Belt, were extended to banks specializing in oil and gas lending. They, too, will have to wait longer for repayment on their loans.

Places like Iowa, Oklahoma, and Texas thus begin to take on a certain financial similarity to Mexico, Brazil, and Argentina. When such models of official probity as the FDIC bend the traditional rules, they usually find it necessary to invent some public euphemism to cover their embarrassment. With an almost audible sigh, this one was called Capital Forbearance. The FDIC has a sister organization, the Federal Savings and Loan Insurance Corporation, FSLIC for short and pronounced "fizz-lick." It insures depositors in the nation's three thousand savings banks, which specialize in mortgages. The Home Loan Bank Board, which regulates the savings banks, asked Congress early in 1986 to lend it $15 billion because its insurance fund was almost exhausted, despite four years of winking at what are known as the Generally Accepted Accounting Principles, or GAAP for short. So many of these banks found themselves with dubious assets after high interest rates deflated the housing boom of the 1970s that in 1982, FSLIC allowed them to spread their losses over several years. These exceptions are called Regulatory Accounting Principles, or RAP. Among the fraternity of bank examiners, whose job it is to apply accounting standards rigorously in order to protect depositors from overimaginative bankers, this and similar professional perversions, which had been designed to prevent one exuberant or unfortunate bank, or a small group of them, from dragging down many, carry another description. It more accurately conveys the examiners' feelings. Bending the rules in this manner is called, informally, it must be stressed, Creative Regulatory Accounting Principles. Its acronym will instantly explain why use of this term is strictly informal.

All these developments cast doubt on the wisdom of the banks in their logistical support for the Merger Wars. The business world will not know the outcome of these struggles until the next downturn discloses how the companies will survive in a colder climate with their assets stripped bare. Against all the evidence piling up in the American heartland, the banks, or at least their managers, believe they have adopted an imaginative stratagem to transfer the risks of these battles to their corporate clients. This stratagem needs to be explained; it is called a floating interest rate. Big commercial banks—and many previously sleepy savings banks—do not depend on lending out the savings of their longtime customers. With financial deregulation, they no longer see themselves as the guardians of the public's savings. They picture themselves as entrepreneurs buying and selling money across state and even national borders.

Can money actually be bought and sold? Absolutely: money is a ruthlessly neutral commodity. Its price is its interest rate, and the banks go to market anywhere for the cheapest money they can find. It can be a deposit left idle for years in a country savings bank, spare cash that a Fortune 500 company treasurer may not need for a month or two, or the dollar profits that a Japanese auto manufacturer is waiting to invest in a new warehouse for his imports. It can even be yen or deutschmarks that have been turned into dollars to fetch a higher interest rate. No difference; it's all money, and the big banks scoop it up, bundle it, and sell it to the highest bidder just as if it were bushels of wheat, cartons of tomatoes, or a boatload of iced fish. But this financial auction proceeds almost instantaneously by impersonal phone and anonymous computer screen, and not at some colorful market where buyers and sellers have dealt with each other for years and know who, and who not, to trust. The banks, like the fish wholesalers, make their profits on the difference—called the "spread"—between what they pay for the money, say 8 percent per annum, and the rate at which they lend it out, say 9 percent if that happens to be the rate for corporate customers. If, six months later, the wholesale cost of money goes up by a percentage point, so does the retail cost. The interest rate floats, and, in theory at least, the financial middleman still profits from his corporate customers' debts.

As long as the customer can pay them. A company squeezed between falling sales and rising interest rates is not a good bet to deliver its interest payments at the end of the month. If it is big enough, it can squeeze its bank just as hard as third world countries did earlier in the decade. They also had been considered impeccable risks, until their export prices collapsed in the recession and their interest rates also floated up to the point where they no longer could pay. Continental Illinois was more vulnerable than most banks to this type of squeeze. It was the eighth largest U.S. bank, the largest lender to corporations, and the quintessential buyer of money. It had to shop as far away as Tokyo and Frankfurt; it had few loyal or understanding depositors in the prairie states. Large loans were out to a number of energy companies and airlines that went bankrupt. The men at the computer screens across the ocean began getting nervous. They did not need to wait for the publication of that hilarious book *Funny Money* to realize that the Penn Square disaster was a terrible joke on Continental's management. One fine weekend in May, despite a multibillion-dollar credit line arranged with sixteen major banks and the Fed, they picked up their telephones and asked for their money back. That's when Continental became a charge on the government's credit, like the farmers in Iowa.

Perhaps Continental's mistake was not to get a new

building. Its Chicago headquarters is modeled after an imposing Greek temple, pillars and all. Since banks are permitted to lend more money than they actually have, their architecture has traditionally stressed solidity to inspire confidence among the depositors, and thus both attract and hold them. But banks adopted the International Style in architeture to match the new international fashions in banking. From street level, the daring skyscrapers that cleave the air in lower Manhattan present a vertiginous contrast to the Federal Reserve's squat stone building, which is modeled after the grand palazzos of Renaissance Italy, where not only banking but double-entry bookkeeping were invented.

Some of the latest banking fashions would be unimaginable even to the subtle Florentine temperament. One is based on the idea of bundling up loans and selling them in packages like salami. It goes by the inelegant name of "securitization" and works like this: A bank has loaned money on a neighborhood of 100 houses and now is loaned up to its limit. It takes the 100 mortgages, each worth $50,000 and paying $5,000 a year in interest, and rolls them all together into an issue worth $5 million, paying a total of $500,000 a year in interest. Then it cuts them up into small slices, each worth $10,000, and sells them off to small investors. For the investors, this is a very good return on a security that literally is as safe as houses, or is supposed to be. The bank pockets a fee, and, with the money from the securitized mortgages, it can start lending out funds to roll another salami. About one-fourth of the $1.5 trillion in U.S. home mortgages have been sliced up and sold this way. Many homeowners hardly realize that their bank has sold their mortgage over their heads. The technique now is being applied to auto loans, computer leases, and who knows what next.

Some banks are reaching for the ultimate by reselling parts of loans as soon as they make them. For example, *The New York Times* reported that Manufacturers Hanover Trust loaned $180 million to a major oil company in October 1985, but within a few weeks it had sold half of it, interest included of course, to other banks in countries around the world. What's all this? First the banks buy the money, then they sell the loans to someone else, yet again? Exactly. They like to think of themselves as financial supermarkets. There is only one catch, and it sounds familiar. *How do the other banks know that the original borrower can keep up his payments?* The answer is that they don't—any more than Continental knew that Penn Square's oil loans really were based on a collection of dry holes. If the householder walks away from his mortgage, or the car owner stops his monthly payments, the owner of this new-style "security" can hardly seize the collateral, as banks have always done. He has no idea where it is. It may even be in another country. Such practices accentuate the divorce of the financial world from the real world. The paper chase seems to proceed under its own power. This is a dangerous illusion. But bankers are eager to share in it, as we shall see when we come to explore the jungle of third world debt. Their profession demands that they must on occasion lend credibility to the most outlandish projects while maintaining an outward respectability, a combination that Keynes once said made them "the most romantic of men."

Daniel Brill, a genial man whose hooded eyes witnessed much folly in a lifetime of finance, retired in 1969 as chief economist of the Federal Reserve Board in Washington and moved to Baltimore to head the Commercial Credit Corporation. It then was doing a thriving $3.5 billion annual business writing three-month promissory notes for the spare millions of blue-chip corporations. Commercial Credit would then lend the money to small borrowers at higher rates of interest. Banks also write these promissory notes, known as "commercial paper." Dealing in it is the kind of humdrum activity that has been going on in cities like Baltimore for generations, although the business in the late 1960s had begun to expand very rapidly and profitably. Then, one fine summer weekend in 1970, the Penn Central Railroad went broke. The Federal Reserve Board, in order to protect the banking system much as it would do almost fifteen years later to protect it from the collapse of Continental Illinois, quickly announced that it would relieve the banks of their millions of dollars of Penn Central paper. On Monday, the banks almost knocked themselves over to be first at the Fed's discount window to sell their worthless Penn Central paper to the government and get their money back. None moved faster than the First National City Bank, predecessor of today's Citicorp and then known in the trade as "Fat City." This fully belied the tireless homilies of its Chairman Wriston extolling the rigorous spiritual uplift offered by the risks in the Great Game of Capitalism. No such uplift was immediately on offer to such smaller players as Commercial Credit. Its market in buying and selling commercial paper immediately came to a halt, even though it did not have a single piece of Penn Central paper on its books. Bankers and companies alike had become so frightened that Penn Central would be just the first of the corporate dominoes that the market seized up, and no one would park money in any kind of commercial paper at all.

Mr. Brill recently reminisced in his office at the Brookings Institution, where he was organizing a scholarly study of the nation's newly deregulated financial industry.

> I don't know if you know what it's like when the treasurer of a major American corporation, with whom you have been dealing for a very long time, suddenly will not answer your phone call. Or if you know what it's like to try to get your banker, or *any* banker, when he is out sailing on Long Island Sound. We were stuck with hundreds of millions in blue-chip corporate paper and we couldn't sell a dollar of it. We had to go to the banks to raise cash, and the only way we could do it was to hint—on the highest authority, I assure you—that the Fed would back the loan. But the banks took their pound of flesh anyway. They bought the paper from us at eighty

cents on the dollar and redeemed it all at par [face value] because all those companies paid off. We never had anything to do with Penn Central. We were just caught in the middle.

Well, here I am studying the changes in the financial system over the last twenty years, and I feel like everything I wrote then was written in sand. Most of these new financial instruments you read about—options, futures, all the rest—have been invented by twenty-five-year-olds, and you should never trust a twenty-five-year-old, because he has never been through anything like this. All that's needed to shake their market, and God knows what else it will shake, is a limited number of failures. These young fellows who trade a hundred million Swissies [Swiss francs] on a phone call, I wonder when they last ran a credit check on the guys on the other end of the phone. And the transactions are also getting bigger as well as quicker; two or three Treasury bond deals in a day can equal the entire capital of a small bank. What happens if the guys on the other end of the phone go under? We've seen it happen already. What do you think sent people out to stand on those long lines in the rain outside the savings banks in Ohio? They wanted their money back, but some of it went up in smoke with some crooked dealers in government bonds. The government had to cover the loss. More debt.

Although these tangles of personal and business debt are unlikely to unravel at the same speed as that which produced the sudden estrangement between Continental's debtors and its creditors, their existence can have formidable yet subtle consequences for the economy. By rescuing Continental, the government has demonstrated that a safety net has been stretched under at least the largest banks. They now have the tacit assurance of no less than the Board of Governors of the

Federal Reserve System that the default of a major international debtor, say Mexico, or the bankruptcy of a handful of major corporations, would not break any bank. They have become, in Wall Street parlance, TBTF banks—Too Big To Fail. Their owners, of course, will be penalized and their managers disgraced. That assuages public morality, as it should. Nevertheless, the banks' economic activities, which are what really matters to their clients, would be curbed in more pervasive ways. Borrowers and lenders alike in many banks would heed such storm signals. The former group could be expected to exercise a preventive caution and slow their buying and investing in order to speed the reduction of their accumulated debt. The latter, however, would have to display prudence by law. Banks can lend only according to a multiple of the money invested by their owners. This capital base also stands as a guarantee against a rainy day, and a default by Mexico or some eminent members of the Fortune 500 would be a storm indeed.

After the flood, some of the bank's capital would have been washed away as the defaulted loans are given up for lost. That would leave less capital available as a guarantee for new loans to the public, which means, finally, fewer loans. The arithmetic was done for Congress by Donald Regan, then the Secretary of the Treasury, after he belatedly awoke to the international debt problem in 1982. Let us suppose that a medium-sized bank has $10 billion in loans outstanding. Under federal regulations, it must then have $600 million, or 6 percent of the loans, backed up by capital. It does not actually lend out the capital; it keeps that $600 million in reserve. But remember, that gives it the right to find up to $10 billion in deposits, which it then lends out. Then, suddenly, a handful of client companies declares bankruptcy. Not a mass bankruptcy, only a medium-sized one totaling $60 million. The bank must draw on that amount of its capital to make up for its losses on what now appears to have been a stupid loan. That leaves 10 percent less capital—and 10 percent fewer loans. One billion dollars less, as Regan explained, "in loans that can't be made in that community—20,000 home mortgages at $50,000 each that can't be financed, or 10,000 lines of credit to local businesses at $100,000 each that can't be extended."

Of course, if several major debt-laden corporations and a Mexico or two defaulted in a recession, the capital of more than just a few banks would be reduced. This would further choke off money available for business, personal, and mortgage loans. It is too late to ask why the banks were backing vulnerable corporations in the first place. We already know that, and we shall learn next what they were doing in places like Mexico in such a big way. But the arithmetic is by no means hypothetical. A similar infernal calculus helped convert a financial crash into the Great Depression because strict bank examiners refused to use Creative Regulatory Accounting Principles, even in sensible moderation. They ordered banks to reduce their capital because the value of the collateral for their loans had collapsed; farms and businesses were worth far less, and their losses had to be reflected on the balance sheets of their banks. That meant less capital on which to base new loans, and this helped turn a financial panic into a depression. Farms, businesses, and eventually the banks themselves lost value and fell like dominoes. What today's bank examiners have been doing is to tread a very fine line and so far avoid falling into an economic trap, winking here and borrowing there.

There is, of course, another escape, but it risks a fall into a financial whirlpool. The government can print money for the banks to lend without going to the trouble of borrowing it from someone else. That has a name of its own: inflation. As the postwar era demonstrates, it is a whirlpool that is also difficult to reverse. The other escape route puts government money directly into the treasuries of the banks themselves, increasing their capital in the same way Continental had to be bailed out. If that happened to enough banks, the price of that would be an increase in the National Debt.

THIRD WORLD DEBT AND OURS

9

"It Has Taught Us Nothing"

Borrowing by sovereign states creates almost farcical relationships between governments and banks. Sovereign debtors attempt to stay one step ahead of their bourgeois creditors. The creditors try to invent devices to prevent themselves from being plucked of their wealth. If an examination of the past helps clarify the future, here is the place to look. When King Edward I of England turned to Florentine bankers in the thirteenth century to finance his wars, he pledged an export tax on good English wool as collateral. The agents sent by the bankers from Italy were unable to station themselves in the English customs houses, unlike the U.S. Marines seven centuries later in Central America, to ensure that the duties were collected. King Edward III repudiated his predecessor's debt, and the Florentine banking houses of Bardi and Peruzzi failed. When Edward III tried to borrow more money from bankers in Brussels, they wisely insisted on taking his crown as collateral. To regain it, he was forced to turn to Parliament for money to repay the loan. In the seventeenth century, British kings amassed war debts fighting Louis XIV that were twenty times their annual revenue. King William, who was an unpopular Dutch import to the throne, ran out of credit and obtained more only by relinquishing the royal right of coinage to the newly established Bank of England.

As Renaissance governments turned to bonds, the favored method of dodging creditors during hard times was to suspend interest payments. From the sixteenth to the nineteenth century, France did so at least once every thirty years. During the nineteenth century, every Latin American government suspended interest payments, some as often as once every seven years. Max Winkler, a professor at City College of New York, wrote the classic study of defaulted bonds at a time when bank vaults were so stuffed with them as to resemble financial mortuaries, in the depths of the Depression in 1933. It was lugubriously entitled *Foreign Bonds: An Autopsy*. Professor Winkler wrote: "The fiscal history of Latin America is replete with instances of governmental defaults. Borrowing and default follow each other with almost perfect regularity. When payment is resumed, the past is easily forgotten and a new borrowing orgy ensues. The process started at the beginning of the past century and has continued to the present day. It has taught us nothing."

The mechanism of international lending in the nineteenth century funneled billions through the bond markets of Europe. They financed the new republics, their canals and their railroads, and the raw materials in the Americas and the Antipodes. The first wave of defaults rolled across Latin America in the 1820s, hard upon that continent's independence from Spain. The credit of Latin American nations was no good in European capital markets for another half century. The states of the new North American union, like the infant Latin republics, borrowed to raise money for investment that their primitive banking systems could not provide. The money developed new lands, especially cotton plantations. Raw cotton for European mills accounted for half of U.S. exports then. But after the speculation, panic and recession in the 1830s and 1840s reduced their revenues. New York, Pennsylvania, Maryland, Indiana, Delaware, Michigan, and Arkansas took the soft option and stopped paying interest on their debts. Florida and Mississippi formally repudiated theirs.

Sharp American financial practice became legendary in London. Even the U.S. Treasury was turned away from the London capital markets by angry creditors when it tried to borrow in 1842. Dickens' Ebenezer Scrooge has a nightmare in which his solid British bonds are transmuted into "a mere United States security." Most states later made good—except for Mississippi. The Council of Foreign Bondholders, organized in 1868 to lobby against defaulters raising new money in London, continues to this day to pursue that state to make good on 1831 Planters' Bank bonds and 1838 Mississippi Union Bank bonds. They have a total face value of almost $7 million. Perhaps this is the only organization that puts the Mississippi state government in the same class with such unnatural political bedfellows as the Union of Soviet Socialist Republics, the People's Republic of China, and other grand defaulting powers. The council wrote the Mississippi state treasurer as recently as 1985, but its latest report recounts laconically that "no reply, however, has been received. . . ."

Capitalist risks abroad yielded greater returns than British government securities of consolidated public debt ("consols" for short). Soames Forsyte's rasping admonition not to sell consols, as he passes to a greater reward, is the financial advice of a fuddyduddy solicitor. The lenders were the confident new bourgeoisie of Europe. The *belle époque* of imperialist expansion extended from the end of the Franco-Prussian War in 1871 to the start of World War I. An estimated $30 billion left Europe's capital markets to develop new countries, the equivalent of almost 300 billion of today's dollars or about one-third of current third world debt. The money carried no explicit government guarantee, although it certainly carried the blessing of the state. British investors favored North American railroad bonds, which put their country in a position to exploit cheap raw materials and gave their salesmen the inside track in selling locomotives, lathes, and similar capital goods turned out by what was then the world's industrial workshop. Almost half of Europe's investments came from the City of London. It was then the financial and commercial center of the world, as New York City is today, although its impeccable social foundations and therefore its dependable sources of wealth and savings differed radically from the financial paper chase that enriches and consumes the hip bourgeoisie of today's fin-de-siècle New York.

Thus, the suspension of interest payments by Peru in 1876 or Brazil in 1898 created mere hiccups in the flow of finance through London. A very occasional seizure, such as the imminent collapse of Baring Brothers when that great investment bank was caught holding too many Argentine bonds during the default of 1890, would be alleviated by injections of cash from the Bank of England and the British Treasury. The owners and managers (they usually were identical) of that or any other great investment house suffered little from their misjudgments; a Baring was sent out to Egypt as proconsul over that financially embarrassed country so vital to British strategic interests. He was later ennobled as Lord Cromer. A descendant, still suffering no disgrace, headed the Bank of England in the 1960s. His family and personal prestige were sufficient to raise a $3 billion international loan, the first of many, to support the weak currency of his declining country. This latter-day Lord Cromer also was dispatched as British ambassador to the United States. During a visit home, he invited a representative of the British Treasury, the same institution that had saved the family bank in the previous century, to a festive partners' lunch at its London headquarters. The civil servant noted that, of the twelve people seated at the table, he was the only one who did not carry the surname of Baring.

Financial institutions tend to be less enduring on the European continent, where money is a more political object. Germany under the Kaisers directed its investments to its own colonies and to other dependent trading partners in order to build an autarkic industrial base for the logistical support of conquest. They later lost all. The French loaned their savings to help cement the Franco-Russian alliance against Germany, a political investment of some $4 billion they were later to regret with particular pain when the new Bolshevik government repudiated all the Tsar's debts in 1918, citing a 1792 declaration of the French revolutionary government: "The sovereignty of peoples is not bound by the treaties of tyrants."

This freewheeling system of finance wrote its own epitaph in World War I, creating an overhang of dead-weight debt in the 1920s with pertinent lessons for today. To supply the means for their mutual slaughter, the governments of Europe had purchased both raw materials and manufactures in the United States. Some of the money was raised on Wall Street, in bonds, of course. The United States, for a century the recipient of loans that had enabled it to become a mature industrial power, thus was catapulted, unaware and unready, into the position of a creditor nation. Prewar flows of money had financed productive investment, albeit sometimes recklessly, but postwar arrangements were propelled almost entirely by political motives and were designed to repay the costs of war, the ultimate consumer of all.

War debts among the Allies left the United States a net creditor of about $9 billion. All other European countries except Britain were debtors. Under the 1919 Treaty of Versailles, Germany, with billions in reparations laid upon it at the insistence of the vindictive European Allies, became the biggest debtor of all—to them. Thus, an unstable money-go-round was constructed without widespread regard for its consequences. The victorious Allies in turn had to send enough money to America to repay principal and interest on their war bonds. The Allies thus depended on the reparation payments from Germany, plus whatever they could earn from foreign trade, to service their American debts. This still left a huge gap in the chain: the reparations were of such punitive size that the Germans could not possibly pay them without a drastic cut in their standard of living. Or, if that disciplined nation actually *did* decide to pay, the reduction in their

buying power would have left a huge hole in the
European economy.

The significance of this to the burden of today's
international debt may be read in a simple comparison: as a relative burden, the interest payments now
falling on Latin American debtors are at least double
the level of reparations that Germany found intolerable
in the prewar era that produced Hitler. Even at their
height in 1929, the annual reparations that Germany
had to pay to the victorious World War I Allies equaled
only 3.5 percent of its gross national product. In 1985,
foreign interest payments by Mexico, Brazil, and Argentina averaged 6.6 percent of their GNP.

These startling figures illuminating both past and
present, which have been discovered by Professor
Albert Fishlow of the University of California, recall
the prescience of Keynes. His famous tract, *The
Economic Consequences of the Peace,* written in 1919
at white heat after his resignation from the British
delegation to Versailles in protest at the Allies'
Carthaginian peace terms—proved chillingly accurate:

> Will the discontented peoples of Europe be
> willing, for a generation to come, so to order
> their lives that an appreciable part of their
> daily produce may be available to meet a
> foreign payment, the reason of which, whether
> as between Europe and America, or as be-
> tween Germany and the rest of Europe, does
> not spring compellingly from their sense of
> justice or duty? On the one hand, Europe
> must depend in the long run on her own
> daily labor and not on the largesse of America;
> but on the other hand, she will not pinch
> herself in order that the fruit of her daily
> labor may go elsewhere. In short, I do not
> believe that any of these tributes will con-
> tinue to be paid, at the best, for more than
> a very few years. They do not square with
> human nature or agree with the spirit of
> the age.

For Europe and Germany, we now may read Latin America.

That puritan internationalist Woodrow Wilson refused to admit that there was any connection between one side of the international debt ledger and the other. But in the 1920s, the Republican administrations took the initiative in renegotiating the size of the reparations according to Germany's perceived ability to pay. That left the U.S. government free to demand full service on the Allies' war debts. "They hired the money, didn't they?" said Calvin Coolidge. His Secretary of the Treasury, the hugely wealthy banker Andrew Mellon, encouraged Wall Street to hire out more money. Its bond houses already were eagerly doing so when he spoke to Congress in 1926: "America, with its excess of capital seeking profitable investment, must aid by making private loans to Europe for productive purposes." Three billion dollars was raised in New York by European governments during the 1920s, one-third of it going to Germany. One researcher estimates that Germany's total overseas loans actually exceeded by 10 percent the 33 billion marks it paid in reparations. But the American capital loaned to Europe was no more productive than the Saudi money recycled by New York banks to Latin America half a century later. Once postwar reconstruction was completed, the Europeans used the money, according to the Royal Institute of International Affairs in a survey of the financial wreckage in the 1930s, to build swimming pools, public libraries, and theaters, and, finally, to rearm.

Nor had the banks distinguished themselves by prudence. A 1932 Senate Banking Committee study found overimaginative bond prospectuses, bribed foreign officials, and overall "one of the most scandalous chapters in the history of American investment banking." By the latter part of the decade, American financiers turned to the booming stock market, again leaving a gap in the financial chain. When it broke irrevocably after the 1929 Crash, the inevitable defaults came, with Latin America in the vanguard. Germany followed as short-term money fled, both to cover losses in Wall Street and out of fright at the menace of the Nazi Party. High tariffs imposed by the United States prevented Europeans from earning the money to service their debts, and then they began retaliating against each other with barriers, breaking the link between trade and finance. In 1931 came a German declaration warning that "the limits of the privations of our people have been reached." Reparations finally were cancelled in July 1932, but too late. Six months afterward, Hitler came to power. Within a year, the Nazis stopped payment on all their loans, perhaps the least worst thing done by that gangster regime.

In Latin America, commodity prices plummeted, and on New Year's Day in 1931, Bolivia stopped payment on its bonds. Within two years, Argentina was the only country on the continent rendering full service on its foreign debt. During the Depression, there were fifty revolutions in Latin America. Argentina, which has an agriculture similar to Canada and during that era had an equivalent standard of living, submitted to a regime of technocrats that slowly dug the country out of debt under terms of a one-sided treaty imposed by Britain. It had to wait until 1943 for its revolution, which brought to power a militarist and populist regime pledged to restore national pride. This revolution imposed the Peronist political model, from which Argentina is only beginning to recover after forty years. Peronism did not even depend on an idea but an individual, and a demagogue at that. It bankrupted the country socially, politically, and morally by cultivating its quarrels and illusions instead of its resources. Financial bankruptcy was merely a symptom.

10

Both a Borrower and a Lender Be

The existence of huge debt implies the threat that the debtors may be unable to pay, or unwilling, which is worse because they then have no interest in compromise. The money then is gone forever. In a closed society, where we "owe it to ourselves," sanctions and remedies for default abound: debtors prison or bankruptcy court for those too unimportant to merit special treatment, bailout for Continental or Chrysler. But in the open and essentially lawless world of international trade and finance, imaginative instruments of credit have to be invented to finance the sale of goods to countries that cannot pay for them out of current and, probably in all honesty, future earnings.

This task, demanding financial imagination of unprecedented brilliance, became urgent after oil prices quadrupled in 1973, and many of these countries no longer could afford enough of the world's most widely traded commodity even to fire up their boilers. The huge, sterile dollar profits of Saudi Arabia and many of its fellow oil exporters could not be allowed to hibernate in their New York and London bank accounts. They had to be put to work or the world economic system would have seized up, like an engine starved of oil. These dollars were loaned at almost breakneck speed by the banks and resulted in a whole new pile of National Debts: $990 billion, including accrued interest, now owed to the industrial world by the authorities of less developed countries. About half is due to governments or international organizations like the World Bank, but the rest is owed to commercial banks. About $350 billion, or one-third of the total, is owed by Latin American nations, who have a long and honorable tradition of throwing in their hands and walking away from the game.

Third world debt is less menacing for its size than for its concentration. Sixty percent of American bank loans to less developed countries were made by this herd of lumbering financial giants, and 60 percent of all *those* loans were made to Latin America. When they stopped to examine their balance sheets after Mexico disclosed on Friday, August 13, 1982, that it had run out of money to pay them interest, the nine U.S. money center banks in New York, Chicago, and Los Angeles discovered, to their horror, and to that of the U.S. government, that Latin America held the power to destroy them. Together the nine had loaned all the countries of that mad continent the equivalent of 75 percent more than the banks' combined capital. Since then, they have been improving that ratio, but even the three largest debtor countries could inflict severe damage on them and the U.S. financial system. Mexico, Brazil, and Argentina, slyly christened the MBA countries by *The Economist* of London in honor of the thrusting new American business class that had managed this unprecedented disaster, still hold loans that represent one-third to one-half of the big banks' capital. Any one of these countries has the power to strike a grave blow at the banks and the financial system, but so far they have not. When borrowing and lending stop, so do the civilized relations between states.

The international debt crisis has been sputtering for so long that it now has been reduced to a problem, or, more accurately, a chronic disease. Its clinical history was too familiar for the warning symptoms to have been ignored. History also gives no guarantee that the worst is over. Quite the contrary. In the past, governments did not default immediately, but only after at least a year or two of depression convinced them that their situation was not just grave but terminal. Suspending interest payments was their escape hatch while they negotiated longer and usually cheaper repayment terms. Granted, governments always borrow. Only their stories differ: there is the mythical future of Brazil, black gold in Mexico, and the magic of supply-side economics. "If the stories are believed long enough, and they usually are," writes John H. Makin in *The Global Debt Crisis*, "the eventual result is one of the financial crises that punctuate history with remarkable regularity at intervals of about fifty years; two generations seem sufficient effectively to erase from mankind's memory the lessons of the past." This, too, is a tale of self-deception and greed, but it carries an unprecedented threat to the world's financial system because of the new role of the multinational banks.

This time around, the prospective borrowers in Latin America had an attractive new line that proved irresistible to banks flush with Arab oil money. After the first OPEC oil shock of 1973, the governments of all industrial nations also were eager to recycle the money so it could be put to work financing their export trade to the cash-starved third world. Without it, the 1974 recession that followed the quadrupling of oil prices during the previous year would have been worse. Latin American technocrats, the best of them trained at some of the same (or better) economics faculties of Harvard, MIT, and Chicago as the bankers, offered them a one-stop service. Instead of sending out costly specialists to evaluate individual projects, the banks left that to the local governments. They borrowed the money in their own name and parcelled it out to nationalized and private enterprises. They had been freed from the tiresome inhibitions imposed by traditional banking practice or the cautious analysis of official lending agencies such as the World Bank. The technocrats also offered their creditors the putative stability of military regimes that guaranteed a docile, or anyway repressed, labor force.

For the Latin American elite, the money was the realization of a dream: foreign investment without foreign control or a foreign lien on the profits. If their land was to be raped for oil, copper, tin, or other minerals that feed the industrial world, at least they could manage the operation and profit from it themselves instead of depending on the technology dispensed charily by multinational corporations. Everyone forgot that the most successful transfer of development capital in history had operated under the closest possible supervision and cooperation: the postwar Marshall Plan that rebuilt Western Europe at a total cost of $13.4 billion in grants and loans over five years, or just a few hundred million dollars less than the entire U.S. defense budget for only one year, 1950.

By the end of the 1970s, half the profits of the major U.S. commercial banks came from foreign business. Even in the crisis year of 1982, 20 percent of the profits of Citicorp, the world's largest bank, came from its Brazilian subsidiary. Not only was it profitable, it was glamorous, and more fun lending to a finance minister than chivvying along a $100,000 loan to a scrap-metal dealer in Cleveland. Ambitious young men armed only with an MBA, an alligator attaché case, and a profit target set by their superiors, were sent to third world capitals and told to prove themselves by making loans. The larger the spread between the wholesale cost and the retail price of credit, the higher the bank's profit. When the loans went sour a few years later, the young men had been promoted far away.

As seen from both sides of the ledger (although not from the bankers' boardrooms at the top), even the most appalling contours of this credit profile matched. Angel Gurria, a Mexican government financial official, recalled to Joseph Kraft what happened after Mexico struck oil: "All the banks in the U.S. and Europe and Japan stepped forward. They showed no foresight. They didn't do any credit analysis. It was wild." The Bank of America started out offering Mexico $1 billion in August 1979, but ended up with so many other banks clamoring for a piece of the action that $2.5 billion was raised for Mexico. In 1982, while I was researching in London for a story that we later called "The Debt Bomb," an experienced British banker sat back and reminisced: "The banks set up high-cost branches that had to meet specific profit targets, sometimes even monthly targets, and never mind the risk. Money was just raw material to be fed into the sausage machine. The local operation would just pick up the phone to New York and say, 'Send more dollars.' Business was available in such large lumps because money was being thrown at the clients, and no one ever sat down and calculated the concentration of risks in each country. They used to say, 'Why worry? Brazil will always be there.' But they never thought what might happen if Brazil ran out of foreign exchange and couldn't pay those dollars back, *in dollars*. Banking is not a business like any other business. It can't be, if you expect a safety net from the central bank."

Central banks had tried to slow the tide, with mixed results. In 1976, Arthur Burns, then chairman of the Federal Reserve Board, called in the nation's leading bankers and warned them of the risks of international banking. "They told me they knew more about banking than I did, and that no government could default anyway," he later recalled. "I told them they had forgotten history, including the history of our own country and some of our states in the nineteenth century." In fact, there was little he or any other regulator could do, even though the public might have to pick up the bill one day. America is a legalistic society, and any public official trying to limit private risk without specific legislative authority would be told to mind his own business, and not the bank's. By contrast, the Bank of England operates by tradition and guile. Bankers drop by the offices of the Old Lady of Threadneedle Street every few months for a cup of tea and an examination of their outstanding loans. As the bankers themselves describe their informal and effective method of control, any bank that seems too heavily concentrated in a risky area is so advised with a wink and a nod.

Only one senior government figure anywhere attempted actively and openly to defuse this Debt Bomb from the very start. In London in 1974, Harold Lever, a self-made millionaire speculator, warned the British

Labor government, of which he was then a member, that banks would collapse under the flood of oil money "just like a flood of water on the roof of a house." He tried to interest the Shah of Iran in a financial deal. Oil prices would be indexed to inflation in exchange for the oil producers putting their excess wealth into long-term investments in Western countries. (Their surplus would rise to $110 billion for the year 1980 alone!) Lever maintains that the Shah was interested, but that the U.S. government and his own were not. In Washington, the Republican Treasury Secretary, William Simon, told him, "Don't teach banks how to run their business." Simon's colleague at the State Department, Henry Kissinger, was not asked, but at the time he was interested in arming the Shah with costly weapons. How would America's Middle East policeman (as the Shah then was) pay for the weaponry if he was committed to depositing his excess cash in long-term bonds? The Carter administration was similarly heedless. It encouraged loans to the developing world because they financed U.S. exports and created American jobs. Through the 1970s, this entire recycling operation was accounted an outstanding success. Everyone pretended not to notice that the debtors' books balanced only because the Great Inflation raised their GNP and quickly eroded the relative value of their debt.

11

"The Children Will Have to Pay It Back"

The game changed radically in 1979 when oil prices doubled. Another, deeper recession slowed the industrial world's economies, dragging down the prices of commodities that third world debtors had to export in order to carry their loans. They earned less money to pay interest on their debt. Simultaneously, dollar interest rates climbed to panic levels; it was the Federal Reserve's way of attacking inflation under its new chairman, Paul Volcker. This was something new. In past recessions, credit always was cheaper because companies did not need it. But governments did. They borrowed for public works or unemployment pay, and that took up the economic slack. This time, money cost more, much more, and the cost was passed on to the customer through floating rates. It was like living in a house with a large mortgage—a floating mortgage—and suddenly suffering a huge loss in income. In 1974, banks literally had been giving away money at what economists call a negative interest rate. The real rate—interest rates minus inflation—was a negative 6.8 percent. In 1981, it climbed to a very positive and painful 9.5 percent. This historic turnabout in monetary policy was designed to squeeze out new debt and slow down inflation; this it quickly achieved. But Latin America already was locked in. It could not earn the dollars to pay the extra interest. Debt had promoted growth in the 1970s, but in the 1980s, the loans merely piled up interest and fed on themselves.

As bankruptcy loomed for their biggest foreign clients, the U.S. banks tried to save them in the only way they knew how. They loaned them more money and then hoped for better times. Because the banks had yielded supervision of their loans to the Latin governments themselves, they were able to turn a blind eye to what was happening to their money. As fast as the banks could wire fresh dollars to Latin American governments, the money was loaned to businessmen, after a suitable amount, of course, was skimmed off by venal civilian and military bureaucrats. The money in the bank accounts of both the businessmen and the bureaucrats quickly fled to safer havens, mainly in the United States. This mass flight of capital landed in Florida skyscrapers, New York apartments, and accounts in the most solid American banking institutions. It was not even necessary for the money to hide in Switzerland. The big American banks also maintained special departments that welcomed the money as savings, even though the lending officers in a different department had sent it to those same countries for supposedly productive uses.

In the autumn of 1983, I happened to meet the personal banking officer in charge of Argentine accounts at the Chase Bank in New York. Her job was to encourage wealthy Argentines to deposit dollars with Chase in the United States; as long as the banks loaned to Latin America, its citizens would deposit some of the money in New York. A former member of the Spanish diplomatic service, she was fairly new to banking, and she was troubled because she no longer was able to meet her quota of deposits from her carefully cultivated Argentine clients. Ever since Chase had stopped lending to Argentina after the debt crisis broke, she said, "We are not getting any more money back from Buenos Aires." She wondered if her superiors understood the reason for her predicament; I assured her that they most certainly did. Shortly thereafter, the bank no longer required her services.

By definition, an accurate count of flight capital is

impossible. But every specialist who has studied the phenomenon—from Alexandre Lamfalussy, the present general manager of the Bank for International Settlements in Switzerland, to Jeffrey Sachs, a Harvard professor who advises the government of Bolivia—puts it at between $50 and $60 billion. The calculations are not based on anything like detective work in Swiss bank accounts, but on a simple comparison of published figures specifying lending, borrowing, and the increase in banks' foreign deposits. They simply do not tally without the assumption that borrowed money was flying down to Rio (although more went elsewhere) and then coming right back, often in suitcases. The figures mean that about one dollar of every three loaned to Latin America by banks between 1979 and 1983 made that round trip.

This amazing ratio is more than just some book-keeping curiosity. It turns out to have been the slow-burning fuse on what bankers refused to admit was a debt bomb in their vaults. Except for the Philippines, where it is reckoned that the Marcos family spirited away billions, no such capital flight is evident in loans to the industrious countries of Southeast Asia. Among Latin borrowers, Brazil seems to have lost less than 10 percent to capital flight, partly because its tough military regime made sure that local investment in its huge riches was kept profitable by holding down wages. But 40 percent of Mexico's borrowed money leaked away, 60 percent of Argentina's, and every penny of Venezuela's. Like alchemists, the Latin American elite converted the debt of the public at home into their private assets abroad. When Mexico first disclosed in 1982 that it could not service its debts, the reason was very simple: it had run out of foreign currency. The money had fled, $11 billion of it in less than six months. Under any other circumstances, this would have been called bankruptcy. But because the banks, and not their bondholders, had been left holding the bag, it was like a guilty secret that could not be so declared. A moratorium on the $250 billion owed only by the three MBA countries would force America's nine biggest money-center banks to count the loans as worthless on their books, and curtail their lending. The federal government (for which read the American taxpayer) then would have to bail them out with backup loans.

From the beginning, the banks had the option of monitoring their loans and making the same calculations as the Mexicans did toward the end, but they did not bother. The reasons for this help to explain why the banks swallowed the bait offered by the third world to begin with. In the past, they would have served as middlemen for men of property who were used to paying for their gullibility by losing some capital when a few bonds in their portfolios turned sour. But banks now think of themselves as financial service industries or money centers, in effect, money changers. They are more actively concerned about how much they can earn trading money rather than lending it to countries, companies, and individuals they know. The latter get ground up in the sausage machine just like the former. This involved an emphasis on brokering that denies the very purpose of a bank, which is to lend other people's money on a balanced assessment of risk and prospects. In their new incarnation, as buyers and sellers of money in the marketplace, the banks took huge risks for huge profits and did the lending themselves. In doing so, they violated some principles of orthodox banking on a grand scale. They loaned short-term capital on growth investments that would have taken years to mature. There was no resale market like a stock or bond exchange to spread the debts around to speculators, who make a living taking risks, so the banks assumed it themselves.

The most outspoken proponent of this new view of bankers as businessmen was Walter Wriston of Citicorp. He at least is to be congratulated for superbly playing the banker's traditional role by suavely keeping up appearances after billions in Latin American debt turned sour in the summer of 1982. Publicly and privately, he assured all who would listen that there was no such thing as a day of reckoning and never would be, at least for sovereign governments. In a September 1982 article in *The New York Times*, Wriston blithely informed the borrowers that they need only adjust their economies and come back for more money to refinance their debts, just like the U.S. Treasury. This comparison between the world's worst and best borrowers (which no longer seems quite as ludicrous as it did at the time), occasioned a riposte from Britain's Harold Lever, who called Wriston "the Peter Pan of bankers, because he still believes in fairies." Wriston had no choice, however, but to declare publicly that the money-go-round was still in operation, even though it already had ceased abruptly. To have admitted otherwise would have been to invite a banking panic by signaling depositors that their funds were at risk.

At the insistence of Paul Volcker of the Federal Reserve Board, a rescue package of billions in public loans had been organized quickly to help Mexico keep up the interest payments on its $85 billion foreign debt. Without those payments, the banks would have been legally obliged to start declaring their loans worthless. The resulting profit squeeze on Citicorp and other lenders would have been the least of their problems. Credit throughout the United States and the industrialized world would have contracted. The bankrupt client would almost certainly have pulled his bankers down with him. With *them* would have gone the Western financial system, upon which even the government of the United States depends for credit. None of these risks had been foreseen by the free-market ideologues of the Reagan administration. Only a year before, Secretary of the Treasury Donald Regan would have been perfectly willing to declare Poland in default to punish its European banking creditors without giving a thought to the effects on the world financial system. "Boys, this is high-stakes poker," he confided to a group of journalists. As for Wriston, one of the main beneficiaries of the emergency bailout, he later published a book of his speeches and writings extolling the pleasures of commercial risk. He also complained that no one had foreseen that Volcker, in raising interest rates to bring down inflation, would "lock the wheels of the world." The new breed of banker does not applaud when someone stops the music.

When the music did stop, a quite different sound could be heard. A plaintive flood of speeches, Congressional testimony, interviews, articles, bank newsletters, and similar material of questionable objectivity attempted to share out the blame among the venal and the foolish. What they echoed, however, was a more crucial contest: an arm-wrestling match among Latin American debtor countries, their commercial bank creditors, and their governments over how to share the cost. At first, the debtors were forced into programs of economic adjustment that cut citizens' living standards to help repay their National Debt. IMF Riots, named in honor of the International Monetary Fund, which supervised the disbursement of the new credits in conjunction with the banks, became a new feature of the world political landscape. But, contrary to the Wriston promises, the loans in this decidedly less optimistic round were meager, less than enough even to help the debtors pay the interest on their loans. To earn the rest, they have had to curtail imports and thus pile up huge trade surpluses; for Mexico and Brazil, these turned out to be larger as a percentage of national income even than Japan's. Per capita income in Latin America declined 15 percent. The United Nations Economic Commission for Latin America estimates that in the four years after the crisis broke, countries of that continent sent back to the developed world about $100 billion more in interest and repayments than they received. This is an unnatural situation of the poor paying the rich that is politically unsustainable.

Through generations of misrule, the people of the Latin American countries know from experience who will pay in the end. In the brilliant Argentine film *The Official Story,* a voyage of discovery for the Argentine middle class into the horrors that had been committed in their name by the deposed military dictatorship, one honorable skeptic remarks, "It is the children I feel sorry for. They will have to pay all this back." They already are. The Argentine government cannot find $7 million to finish equipping a new pediatric hospital in Buenos Aires. Productive investment for long-term projects is drying up. Hundreds of millions in appropriations for university expansion, oil exploration, animal hygiene, road repairs, and railroad modernization were among those dropped from the 1986 Argentine budget. What cannot be stopped is work on white elephants like atomic or hydroelectric power plants. As Mario Brodersohn, Argentina's secretary of finance, explained to Bradley Graham of *The Washington Post,* "Their debts are already so large that you'd be making large interest payments whether you finish them [the projects] or not." This official works with a desktop computer that Citibank furnished him as a gift, rather like helping a man calculate the costs of his own funeral.

For half a decade, the debtors have tried to use the unspoken threat of mutual bankruptcy to squeeze better terms from their banks in rescheduling the time they have to repay their loans. The banks' only real punishment for default would be the same as it was in the nineteenth century: closing the financial markets to new credit for the debtor countries and thus blocking their trade. Governments can assist the process mainly by offering money directly or through the IMF. In 1985, the United States, through Treasury Secretary James Baker, proposed $29 billion in new loans to fifteen major debtors over a three-year period to assist their economic growth after years of austerity. The annual disbursements would at best cover one-quarter of their interest payments. The offer was to be matched by bank credits. The banks demurred for at least a year, until Mexico forced them to relent in 1986 and lend it a few additional billion so it could pay the interest on its debts. Now the money was round-tripping from the banks to Latin America and back in quite a different way.

Once the banks cut off the loans, and other sources of credit and trade began to dwindle, the balance between lender and borrower began imperceptibly to shift. Instead of allowing the banks to dictate repayment terms, the debtor countries started unilaterally limiting the amounts they would pay and stretching out their loans. Alan Garcia, elected president of Peru in 1985, announced that his country would set aside only 10 percent of its earnings from exports to settle its debts. "Either debt or democracy," he said in a United Nations speech. The banking community threatened to cut off his credit; Peru started conducting more of its trade through barter. Brazil and Venezuela called the bankers' bluff and discussed rescheduling before submitting themselves to an IMF regime. President José Sarney of Brazil told a barely attentive U.S. Congress that the debtor countries planned to "pay less [in interest to the banks] so they can import more." Slowly, the debtors began to play off the banks against their own domestic customers in the real economy. For them, the choice, as Sarney said, was either to send dollars back to American banks to help them balance their books, or to use the money to import real and productive goods from American factories. Every dollar less paid in interest means one dollar more in trade. In the long run, there was no doubt which choice was preferred by governments on both sides. Mexico, a model debtor until oil prices collapsed, suddenly needed between $7 and $9 billion to service its debts. "At $20 a barrel, the debt is my problem. At $15 a barrel, it is theirs," Mexican Finance Minister Jesus Silva Herzog said as he began negotiations for a new loan. He was fired in midpassage, but the agreement with the United States confirmed this principle: what the debtors repay to the rich countries is conditioned by what they earn from them, because what they earn can be recycled in real trade.

Such trials of strength are likely to continue for years. The decision by John Reed, who succeeded Wriston as Citicorp's chairman, to start unloading his predecessor's heavy legacy by realistically writing off at least a cool billion of third world debt, cost his stockholders only three months' profits and strengthened the bank's hand for the next negotiating round. The banks and their foreign debtors now are as inextricably linked as the social classes in the United States that share our National Debt. If the third world does not pay, their debt will become ours, unless we are willing to let our banks fail. We also are in a similar relationship with the foreign holders of the bonds and other obligations of what now is the largest debtor in the world, the United States of America.

12

Deeper in Debt

The United States is acting increasingly like a third world borrower. By persistent borrowing from foreigners to finance its voracious consumer appetites, the United States in 1985 became a net debtor to the rest of the world by the sum of $107 billion. This balance of assets and liabilities moved against the country for the first time since 1914, the year in which the United States became a creditor nation and, not coincidentally, one of the world's decisive powers. It succeeded England as the hub of the international financial system and banker to the world because it is the issuer and guarantor of the dollar, the world's favored currency for conducting trade and investment, and for holding the cash reserves of nations. In Latin America, debtors have recently found themselves owing more to the bank than they could manage, with drastic results. But never has the bank itself found its liabilities exceeding its assets. This gap is widening year by year.

Economics tells us this is not a cash flow problem, like that of the other $100 billion debtors, Brazil and Mexico, who followed the classic recipe for bankruptcy of borrowing in the short term to invest in projects that pay off only in the long term. The United States has not run out of cash to honor its debts. At least not yet. As the world's banker, the United States has the unique privilege of borrowing money in its own currency. The dollars that it sends abroad to honor its debts are accepted at face value. At least so far. Our political and financial credit—the two are not unconnected—have accrued in part through the personal magnetism of a President who is seen abroad as the most successful domestic leader in recent American history, whatever may be thought of his policies. His credit was guaranteed by the puritan figure of his bank manager, Paul Volcker, whose very presence was meant to assure lenders. Their continued lending depended on this double confidence, and for a time the two men, so unlike, were captive to each other. It was Reagan, however, who foolishly snapped the bond by refusing to express his public confidence in Volcker for his reappointment. As became painfully apparent when he was eased out by Reagan in favor of Alan Greenspan, a respected Wall Street consulting economist who long wanted the job, no successor was immediately available to construct an equivalent House of Mirrors for the broadcast of such confident reflections. George Bush, bidding to be the political inheritor of this problem, would do well to remember his own sage analysis of his erstwhile rival's "voodoo economics."

Once again, it therefore becomes appropriate to invoke the analogy of commercial finance. To understand why, remember the difference—and the connection—between deficit and debt. The foreign deficit records how the United States got from there to here over a period of just five years. A flow of money has drained into a swamp of debt by the country's annual purchases from foreigners of between about $50 and $100 billion more Mercedeses and Toyotas, Paris fashions, cheap Asian shirts, and package tours to Europe than the Boeing 747s, Caterpillar bulldozers, or bushels of Kansas wheat that they bought from Americans. The country could not manufacture and pay for all the things it wanted. That also included the greatest peacetime consumption of military equipment in history.

Like an entrepreneur exuding confidence, it borrowed against the future. Not to build a bigger business, but to buy a grander house and a bigger car, like some of the jug-eared Hollywood heroes of an earlier, more hopeful age. The future now has arrived in the form of America's rising debt to the rest of the world.

This state of affairs came about because the United States ran a kind of beggar-thy-neighbor policy with its Allies, not in trade but in finance, bidding for their money rather than for their markets. It operated through three channels: the federal budget deficit, the high interest rates that financed it, and the high dollar that resulted. It takes a bit of care and concentration to show how they interacted with deadly effect.

As an accident of the high interest rates first set by the Federal Reserve in the early 1980s to fight inflation and restore faith in the currency, the dollar became a magnet to foreigners. They were delighted to turn their spare marks, yen, and even their Swiss francs into dollars. In Madison Avenue terminology, high interest rates and a clear commitment to capitalism made the dollar the hot currency, the talk of the markets. Money flowed in from abroad. Bankers call such deposits "hot money." How long it remains in any one place is a direct function of how much interest it earns. Early in the decade, it came from Latin America, and it would have fled from there in any event, regardless of interest rates. But it was the high rates that kept the Latin billions in dollars, and soon they were joined by Europeans. From 1980 to 1985, American banks trebled their foreign deposits, to $350 billion. Exactly how much of that new money is "hot" enough to flow elsewhere at the drop of an interest rate, only its owners really know. But it must be a sizable proportion. At the start of the decade, liquid deposits held by foreigners in American banks represented only about one-fifth of their holdings in the United States. They now represent one-third. More sober investors sent their savings to buy stocks and bonds with a medium-term horizon. Foreigners with a longer view, and there were fewer of those, bought farms, factories, and Florida condominiums.

This worldwide taste for dollars drove up their price by simple laws of supply and demand. The Reagan administration, rather like Chanticleer greeting the sunrise, took this as a worldwide vote of confidence in its policies. It ignored the complaints of its partners and their warnings of the baleful effects to come. Chancellor Helmut Schmidt of West Germany, Europe's most distinguished statesman, complained in 1981 that his continent was being drained of investment capital by "the highest interest rates since Jesus Christ." German businessmen naturally preferred the luxury of earning 15 percent in a dollar bank account or a gilt-edged bond to the effort of investing it in their own uncertain economy. By their actions, they confirmed the truth of his complaint.

Within five years, the foreign assets built up during almost three-quarters of a century by patient American saving and aggressive investment abroad had been eclipsed by the pile of money foreigners had parked in the United States. By the end of 1985, foreigners owned an assortment of assets in the United States worth $107 billion more than what Americans owned abroad. Five years earlier, the position had been almost precisely reversed. U.S. companies, banks, and individuals were then $106 billion ahead. In the interim, under the most bombastically free-enterprise regime since the 1920s, the United States had committed the capitalist's unforgivable sin of living off capital.

In an earlier generation, when the nation was more commercially isolated, its domestic tastes less sophisticated, and its manufacturers the model for the world, America would have spent more at home. But this time, as money was pumped into the economy by the federal government's huge budget deficits, it leaked abroad to pay for foreign goods or foreign pleasures. Both had been made cheaper by the high value of the dollar. Anyone standing on the Champs-Elysées during the summer tourist boom of 1985 would have seen an amazing demonstration of this: lines of blue-rinsed ladies from the heartland of America being led by tour guides to the slaughter of French boutiques.

Since Americans were no longer just buying from

themselves, they also were no longer just borrowing from themselves. But to maintain the spending spree, the government had to bid for money to fill the black hole in its finances created by $200 billion budget deficits every year. Foreign investors filled it, but at a price. Attracted by high real interest rates, they loaned a larger portion of their savings to the United States. That maintained the demand for the dollar. Volcker did his part by limiting the supply; the Fed refused to print too much money lest inflation ignite again. That supply-demand mix assured the high price of the dollar. For other industrial countries, such as Japan and Germany, this meant jobs and profits. They either sold directly to Americans or underbid them in other markets where the dollar had made American goods too expensive. For Americans, it meant lost jobs and the prospect of more difficulty managing the heavy foreign debt in the future.

In retrospect, it was both economically eccentric and politically unsustainable for the world's richest country to import not only other people's goods, but also their money. Some of the billions were financially volatile when the loans turned into Latin American flight capital, then became morally insupportable as enforced payments of interest from Latin governments. The industrial countries of northern Europe, mainly Britain, West Germany, and the Netherlands, intensified their traditional investment in American companies. Their industrialists negotiated direct takeovers, and their pension and mutual funds invested through the New York Stock Exchange, where about 10 percent of all transactions now originate abroad. But the largest financial supporter of the American consumer boom was also its largest beneficiary—Japan.

In five years, Japanese savers, mainly through their life insurance companies, used their country's export profits to pile up more than a quarter of a trillion dollars of foreign bonds, mostly in dollars.

Not entirely by coincidence, their annual purchases were roughly equivalent to their trade surpluses with the United States. In 1985 private Japanese buyers bought $45 billion worth of dollar bonds, in 1986 $70 billion, and in the first half of 1987 alone, $60 billion. Then they took fright and stopped. Their central bank had to fill the U.S. deficit hole instead. Its reluctance to continue was one of the proximate causes of the 1987 crash. Almost half of Japan's private investments were U.S. Treasury bonds; most of the rest were gilt-edged bonds issued by U.S. companies. Like most life insurance companies, the Japanese also are putting money into real estate, except that the real estate is in places like New York, Washington, Los Angeles, and Dallas. In 1985, Japanese real estate investment almost doubled to about $1.8 billion, then almost trebled again in 1986 to an estimated $6 billion. The prudent Japanese saver (which really means the Japanese worker) found himself locked into symbiotic relationship with his American customer. If at some point he discovers he can earn more elsewhere and decides to stop lending the United States the money to buy his goods, the demand for dollars will fall, and so will its price against the yen. Americans will stop buying Sonys and Toyotas, but the Japanese will still have a lien on America's earnings through bonds, stocks, and real estate.

This is a less durable relationship than it at first appears, because it means that the United States has to appease the Japanese with interest rates high enough to attract their money. This used to be called Danegeld, after the money paid by the peaceful Saxons of Britain to keep away the marauding Vikings. The promises were often broken, and the brutal relationship between the two was what political scientists now would describe euphemistically as unstable. For Japan, however, it is not necessarily unpleasant or unprofitable, any more than the General Motors Corporation finds it tiresome to run its subsidiary, the General Motors Acceptance Corporation, to finance the purchase of its automobiles. As the bottom line now reads, Japan has replaced the United States as the world's largest creditor. Britain stands a surprising second, but this is not necessarily the result of praiseworthy policy. It is one result of Britain's following its historic investment route abroad and neglecting its industrial base, manufacturing gentlemen on the investment profits instead of tradable goods. West Germany stands third, but in contrast to Britain its foreign investments have been built to support its profitable export trade. The United States, as the world's largest debtor, has to face a profound and painful change. For even if the deficit stops flowing, and that will take quite some time, the pool of debt will remain far longer.

In 1980, American investments abroad netted the country a surplus of $30 billion. The money earned from foreigners increased the U.S. national income by slightly more than 1 percent. That advantage has been dropping steadily as foreigners pile up American assets. Americans have had to send more money abroad each year to pay *them* interest on their investments. The surplus is vanishing now. Americans will have to spend more of their time working to earn enough profits for the new owners of their factories, their bank deposits, and the Treasury bonds of their National Debt. Since the United States has been borrowing for today's consumption and not for productive investments that paid long-term dividends like the nineteenth-century railroads, it is the young who will have to earn the interest in the future to pay for the present spending spree by their elders. The transfer will be less obvious than the way in which they already pay part of their salary through the Social Security system to finance their elders' consumption. But the result will be the same. The children will have to pay it back.

13

Into the Swamp

Of all the uncharted journeys, one of the most eerie is wading slowly into a swamp of debt with the leading nation in the world. Adjusting to life in this swamp is going to be the single most important price that the United States must pay for living in debt. It leaves the country more exposed to shocks and more vulnerable to the financial leverage of its creditors. It makes the United States more like other countries; they have always lived in this swamp, which is the world as it is.

America will have to bargain with its partners over how much of its goods they will accept in settlement of its debts, and how much of their money it will borrow instead. This gives some option to the United States in the way it will lower its standard of living, but it will not come cheap. Failure to reach an acceptable bargain could force a crash of the dollar, leaving the debtors holding bales of devalued paper. That Samson-like threat is the major bargaining lever left to Washington, and it was used in devaluing the dollar almost 50 percent from 1985 to 1987. But be warned: England used the same strategy of weakness for loans to support its standard of living as the pound slid toward collapse in the 1960s and again in the 1970s. Eventually its bluff was called, and in 1976 the International Monetary Fund was ordered in as financial policeman for the country that once ruled the financial world. We will explore these alternatives, all of them unpalatable, and start with the most unpalatable, because it is not an alternative at all: estimating the final bill.

The process of slowly unwinding the high deficit-interest-dollar spiral probably will last until the end of the decade. U.S. foreign trade deficits will continue to mount, piling up more debt. Estimates vary, but the additional cost probably will add up to about $500 or $600 billion. For ease of calculation, and to make the high rollers comfortable, let us say a round half trillion. Assets such as real estate, or promissory notes such as bonds, are being transferred to other people just for underwriting our spending spree. No one, least of all the Japanese themselves, expects that they will suddenly sell the automobile plants they have built in Tennessee to produce for the American market, or demand cash for the Treasury bonds they have put away for their retirement. Or that the British and Dutch will throw their American holdings in Shell Oil or Lever Bros. on the stock market in a caprice of profit-taking and go home with their pockets full of dollars. If they did, the paper they received would have to be heavily devalued, and they did not come to America for a mere fistful of worthless paper. They bought the bonds, built the plants, and invested in the companies because they want to earn money from them.

Servicing our debts (which are their assets) means sending a creditor the money he expects. This is a matter of simple arithmetic, laced with some financial psychology. The figures presented here are conservative. Foreigners probably will start thinking about investing elsewhere if the return on their money slips too much below about 10 percent a year. That is why they sent it to the Land of Opportunity in the first place. That means sending them a regular $50 to $60 billion a year. This seems little enough in an economy that earns about four trillion dollars a year. But, in fact, it represents a gigantic swing of $150 billion in the U.S. international accounts. The balance sheet has to move from a minus of at least $100 billion, which is the amount we borrow to cover one year's current international accounts, to a plus of about $50 billion, which we somehow have to earn to pay the interest on what we have borrowed from abroad—even after the borrowing itself stops. Remember the 3 percent of our national income that we have been borrowing to pay for Mercedes cars, package tours to Paris, or, if you count consumption in a different way, the rise in the defense budget. The shift of $150 billion would reverse the flow of borrowing and add up to about 3.75 percent of America's national income. There's that 3 percent again—come home to roost with interest.

Short of turning America into a vast theme park and renting it to foreigners, which is what tourist countries such as England and Italy do in the summer, there are two ways to earn that kind of money. One is to produce goods that America's creditors want to buy. That is what the Germans and the Japanese have been doing. The other is to slash prices on what we already produce by cheapening the value of the dollar. In fact, it will take a combination of both, and we will look into this from a different angle later, when we examine the problems of productivity. But right now, let's just add up the accounts and look at the bottom line. It now takes about one million workers to produce $40 billion worth of output in the United States. Simple arithmetic tells the rest. About three to four million more members of the work force would have to produce items for export in order to earn the $150 billion needed to climb out of the hole and service the debt. Since American industry no longer has many monopoly items to sell, such as supercomputers or 747s, the quick way to compete is to cut prices on exports such as grain. That is already being done across the board by devaluing the dollar, but that has a price: a lower standard of living. What America sells earns less when the dollar is worth less; what it buys costs more. The deeper the debt, the steeper the fall in the dollar needed to balance the country's international accounts. Package tours to Paris will be off many a summer agenda.

To Americans, this may sound unnatural, offensive, and even something of an infringement on their liberties. But citizens of other countries that overextend themselves are used to such austerities. Sweden was a creditor country until the first oil-price shock doubled its energy bills. Rather than lower their living standards during the 1970s, the Swedes, through their government, borrowed about 3 percent of their national income from abroad. They soon built up a foreign debt equivalent to about one-quarter of what the entire country earns in a year. But in the meanwhile, the Swedes had closed down their unprofitable shipyards, streamlined their admirable high-technology industries for export, and devalued their currency twice. Their trade with foreigners now yields them a comfortable profit equivalent to about 3 percent of their national income. Virtually all that surplus, however, must be sent back abroad to pay interest on Sweden's foreign debt. The penalty for living on credit in the 1970s is that the Swedes have to pay their foreign earnings to their creditors instead of enjoying them for their own use now. This is the kind of challenge faced by the United States, which borrowed at about the same rate in the 1980s and can expect about the same proportion of foreign debt at the end of the decade.

But it is unimaginable for the United States to turn itself into a maxi-Sweden, populated by puritanical refugees from Bergman films working their neurotic way back to national solvency. Not because such a conversion is altogether implausible for our nation of workaholics, but because it would be altogether inadmissible to the rest of the world. The concern of the rest is not America's mental health but their own prosperity. The figures mean that the United States would have to shift into a trade surplus even larger than Japan's. Granted, it would pay the wages of three or four million American workers so they could earn enough to service the National Debt to the Japanese, the Germans, and the British. But those countries have no desire to export their employment to America so it can pay its bills. They want to keep those jobs for themselves. If the United States was that good at exporting, others could not buy our goods, because they could not earn enough money to pay for them. The U.S. economy is equal to about 40 percent of the rest of the industrialized world; our size almost puts us in a trap.

Then how will we earn the money to carry our debts, if not from the sale of American goods? A continued injection of foreign loans? From both. A combination of trade and loans, as has already begun to emerge from the somewhat different circumstances of Latin America, avoids too severe a disruption on both sides. Debtor and creditor are condemned to share the same bed with only one blanket. At first they will struggle over who stays warm, then realize that sharing it is the sensible way.

One alternative is another scenario known as the "hard landing." It is not impossible, but it has been so widely rehearsed that it is unlikely to happen, at least in the precise way that has been forecast. In the most homely terms, it means that the struggle for the blanket would end with the debtor on the floor, whereupon he pulls the creditor down with him. The first to propound it, in 1983, was Stephen Marris, an Englishman with thirty years' sad experience of watching governments stumble into economic crises at the Organization for Economic Cooperation and Development in Paris, from which he recently retired as chief economic adviser. Marris' scenario goes like this: Japanese insurance companies, British fund managers, and Swiss gnomes, unsatisfied with falling U.S. interest rates, decide to take their money out of Wall Street, precipitating a panic that sends the money fleeing into Swiss banks, German stocks, gold, and other boltholes. This rush for the exit pulls down the dollar, threatening the United States with a new dose of inflation through higher import prices. To entice the money back, the Federal Reserve Board has to raise interest rates in a swoop, plunging the United States into recession. The rest of the world then gets dragged down with its largest economy. That could be a very hard landing indeed for the world economy.

When this scenario first was mooted, it was deemed

inconceivable by traders on Wall Street, whose psychological capacity for self-absorption far surpasses that for their absorption of capital: where *else* could the money go? The huge rise of European stock markets in 1984–85, which was ignored by most of them, demonstrated the vanity of their question. But that had come as no surprise to another serious student of hard landings, Professor Lamfalussy, a Belgian of Hungarian origin for whom the anatomy of such monetary movements is bred in the bone. As general manager of the Bank for International Settlements, he is one of the world's premier central bankers, and he observes that, as usual, Wall Street misses the fundamental point. Money is fungible. Given the right price, it has a market anywhere, and not just on Wall Street. The mere threat that it might find a market elsewhere should be enough to give pause to the makers of U.S. policy.

Billions of dollars racing out of New York might, for example, land in the Frankfurt stock market, to nestle safely in the bosoms of sound German companies. The dollars would have to be converted into marks and soon would end up in the vaults of the Bundesbank, West Germany's central bank in Frankfurt. This powerful organization has an institutional horror of inflation, which it defines very simply as too much money chasing too few goods. It would very quickly have more dollars than it knew what to do with. Herr Helmut Schlesinger, the Bundesbank board member in charge of foreign transactions, whose financial outlook might most easily be described as high-button shoe, would then promptly call up Mr. Sam Cross, the soft-spoken chief of foreign operations for the Federal Reserve Bank of New York, which is the U.S. government's agent in such matters. He would sternly inform Mr. Cross of something he probably already was more than vaguely aware: the existence of unwanted billions of dollars in Frankfurt. Would Mr. Cross be interested in having these dollars back, and, if so, at what price would he wish to exchange them? There are, after all, so many dollars in Frankfurt, and the laws of supply and demand have not been suspended. So perhaps Mr. Cross would prefer not to take them back for the moment at a low price. The German banks that originally took them in from the Frankfurt Stock Exchange might be persuaded to hold on to them at a certain rate of interest. But it would have to be a very rewarding rate indeed. Yes, that would be costly, but would Mr. Cross prefer to have the dollars dumped back on the open market to see what they would fetch?

Of such events are deals quickly made, unless the U.S. government had already instructed Mr. Cross to turn down any such proposals. That would be a high act of state, because it would imply that the United States of America no longer cared what its currency was worth. The banker to the world would in effect be dishonoring its debts, because it would be ignoring the collapsing value of its banknotes. For the first five years of the Reagan administration, the United States actually held that cavalier position of not caring about the value of its currency. Administration ideologues boasted that the verdict of the free market was favorable, which was fine as long as the verdict was going their way and the dollar was rising, even if it exasperated America's lenders, such as Herr Schlesinger's constituent banks. After all, weren't their dollars worth more with each passing month? But once the dollar began to decline, it was preferable for the United States to try to talk it down gently, or have Mr. Cross buy up the odd hundred million or so on the days when its foreign owners threatened to make a rush for Frankfurt, Zurich, or other boltholes.

Of all international debtors, only the United States has this privileged option because its debts have been undertaken in its own currency, the dollar. The Japanese, Germans, and English, had turned yen, deutschmarks, and pounds into dollars under the confident spell of Ronald Reagan and the implicit guarantee of Paul Volcker. They are not prepared to receive their money back at whatever rate the United States chooses to make the exchange. On the docks, this is known as welshing on a debt, and punishment is severe. In personal life, it is called bankruptcy, and it used to be avoided. In commerce, it is becoming more common as voluntary bankruptcy or Chapter 11, after the section of the law that allows a business to suspend payment to its creditors and then negotiate with them how much of its debts it will repay. A company in voluntary bankruptcy has a peculiar type of leverage, the leverage of weakness. It derives from the threat implied by Mexico, Brazil, or Argentina that they might not repay anything at all. If the United States even hints at taking the last option, its pretensions to world leadership vanish.

14

Juggling and Levitation

The United States is the leader of the West because it serves simultaneously as the world's banker and the world's policeman and seeks the rewards of both roles along with their responsibilities. Retaining them will demand the coordination of an unprecedented financial balancing act with the traditional diplomatic one. Such juggling was never foreseen when America was a powerful creditor nation sucking in funds for its use. It is an ironic legacy of a President who boasted of reestablishing America's global political hegemony. As the financial turn was taking place, the diplomat and historian George Kennan wrote: "A country that has a budgetary deficit and an adverse trade balance both so fantastically high that it is rapidly changing from a major creditor to a major debtor on the world's exchanges . . . is simply not in a position to make the most effective use of its own resources on the international scene, because they are so largely out of its control. In world affairs, as in personal affairs, example exerts a greater power than precept."

How the foreign bill for the borrowing of the 1980s will be rendered, and at what price, is no longer a matter for mere economists and bankers. Relations between the world's newest super-debtor and its principal creditors in Japan and Germany will be a prime, if perhaps unspoken, topic during any political negotiation, like a ghost at a banquet. Who pays for the jet fighters in Japan or the troops in Germany? These conundrums have been on the agenda of the Allies for years, but never before with the United States as both *demandeur* and debtor to the same governments.

Money is power. This is such a trite lesson that it hurts to have to learn it again. In domestic policy, Japan and Europe will have more room for maneuver in deciding their own economic destiny as their banks pile up credits in dollars. That will enable them to finance their own growth without worrying unduly that anxious creditors will pull money out of the country and leave them stranded, as occurred when a new French regime tried a dash for growth on its own in 1981. On the contrary, it will be the United States, with balances of its own dollars borrowed from foreigners, that will have to think about a run on the bank. In the nineteenth century, the expansion of the American economy often was whiplashed by credit panics in London. High interest rates in London held money there instead of letting it flow to the high-yielding risks in the New World. That could happen again if Tokyo or Europe run short; as creditors, they will, after all, have first call on their money. How both sides handle these new relationships will help shape the political relationships of the industrialized world in the next decade.

Creditors dictate the terms in this world, not debtors. For the first time since the United States became a world power, its economic fortunes are directly tied to private and not to government lenders. To support the boom, the Reagan administration tapped the private market, which incidentally made it easier to ignore the tiresome complaints of the Allies. In 1985, private foreign buyers soaked up about one-fifth of the U.S. government's own debt, and moreover made it easier for the government to sell the rest of its bonds, notes, and bills to Americans. The foreigners took up 30 percent of the new corporate bonds issued on Wall Street. It is unprecedented for official American finances to be as delicately balanced as they now are on the fickle preferences of foreign private investors.

Imagine, then, that you are a fund manager in Tokyo, London, or Frankfurt. Only a few years ago, your bond portfolio was bare of gilt-edged American investments because American interest rates were so low and the dollar was so weak and unstable. During the past few years, your portfolio has become heavy with American Treasury and AAA corporate bonds. Perhaps they represent one-quarter to one-third of your fund's investments. If you are a prudent manager, you will occasionally think about diversifying your portfolio. Unless you detect some financial alarm signal, such as the gurgle of a big American bank strangling on its Mexican debt, there probably is no urgent reason to dump your American bonds and wire the money to Zurich. But you may think twice about putting any more eggs in that particular basket.

This is exactly what concerns the U.S. Treasury, because it must continue to find new money as long as it continues to run up new debt. When the prospective lenders do not automatically answer its call, it must sing more sweetly. It must maintain interest rates at a level higher than they otherwise would be, in order to attract more money. Interest rates seem to go into a kind of self-levitation, because it is not immediately obvious that what holds them up is a premium ordinary people do not see. The need to finance the intractable deficit keeps up the price of government credit and therefore the price of everyone else's credit. The international financial tail slowly begins to wag the American economic dog.

The Treasury rolls over some of its long-term debt every few months, scooping up $20 to $30 billion at a time from the financial markets to throw at the growing deficits. In May of 1986, Japanese investment houses went through a Kabuki dance with American wholesalers, first hinting yes, then hissing no, over whether they liked the 7¼ percent interest rates being bruited about. At the next auction, they nevertheless bought about $8 billion worth of ten-year and thirty-year bonds, or about one-third of the bonds on offer. In August, they bought about the same amount, but the U.S. government (and its taxpayers) had to pay more; the annual rent went up to about 7¾ percent for the right to use the money for the next ten to thirty years. In just one bond sale, the people of the United States thus agreed to send about $600 million every year in interest payments to the people of Japan, for periods extending well beyond the expected life span of a significant proportion of those Americans—although not, it should be stressed, the life span of their children.

For the United States, this is a burden; for the Japanese, a bargain. If the Japanese had loaned the same sum to their own government in their own currency, it would have paid them only the equivalent of about $400 million a year, and only for a maximum of ten years. The Japanese are the world's longest-lived people, and they are eager for safe and very long-term investments. But because the United States needs to borrow so much, it must offer them much better rates and terms than the Japanese can earn at home—in fact one-third better, or the difference between $400 million and $600 million. As one bond dealer told *The New York Times*, "The market will correct itself to whatever it perceives the preferred Japanese interest rate to be." That translates more roughly into the plain fact that Japanese savers are very close to dictating American interest rates. If the market does not give them what they want, they will save at home instead.

No wonder the Japanese are very dollar-conscious. The United States is at once their chief protector, customer, and debtor. Their banks, fat with the profits of Japan's exporters, hold more foreign assets than any other country. And they hold almost all of them in dollars, about three quarters of a *trillion* of them. If you happened to visit the Tokyo office of Mr. Toyoo Gyohten when he was the Director General of the Finance Ministry's International Bureau, you would have encountered an affable and uncharacteristically cosmopolitan Japanese who speaks idiomatic English from his days in graduate school at Princeton. He watched the dollar as if he had been posted as a lookout to signal the arrival of a *tsunami*. Behind the desk of the official who holds this very important position always stands a row of news tickers. To one side is the flickering screen of a financial monitor. From the ceiling hangs an electric sign almost a foot high, with illuminated numbers like a digital clock at an airport. They give the rate of the yen against the dollar, down to hundredths of a yen, at that very instant. One came away with the distinct feeling that if even the last two numbers (the ones on the right-hand side of the decimal point), were to vary unaccountably, Mr. Gyohten would pick up one of the many telephones in the bank on his desk and try to find out why.

There was a time, in the mid-1980s, that Mr. Gyohten might have given orders to the Bank of Japan to adjust the rate immediately if it began moving too high to make Japan's exports too expensive. Now he does not dare, at least not too much. The United States, through its Treasury Secretary, Mr. James Baker, hinted during a summit meeting, right there in Tokyo in the spring of 1986, in the presence of the President of the United States, that if he did adjust it, the United States might further cheapen its own currency, and make things even more difficult for Japan's bankers, exporters, and workers. The United States can do this by lowering dollar interest rates even though this risks the distaste of Japan's bond buyers when Mr. Baker's Treasury next needs money. Mr. Baker is a corporation lawyer from Texas with political forebears and political ambitions. Mr. Gyohten does not know if he is bluffing, but is not eager to risk finding out.

If the U.S. Treasury has to deal with its Japanese creditors at all, and it does, it is convenient to deal with Mr. Gyohten and people like him. Shortly after the 1986 summit meeting, he was promoted to Vice Minister of Finance. It was his ministry that permitted Japanese fund managers to start buying up huge amounts of U.S. debt in 1982 under pressure from Donald Regan, who then was the U.S. Treasury Secretary but never forgot that he fought the Japanese as a wartime Marine officer. Mr. Beryl Sprinkel, who then was Mr. Regan's deputy but behaved like the World War II tank gunner he once was, flew to Tokyo when the U.S. foreign deficit started rising, and stamped around Mr. Gyohten's office making demands. However westernized they may be, Japanese officials such as Mr. Gyohten feel conspicuous and uncomfortable in these confrontations, and Americans know this can be used against them. The terms and conditions of America's need for capital can be more easily negotiated with a society organized around consensus. If Japan's bond buyers were unhappy with American interest rates, something surely would be worked out through people like Mr. Gyohten, if he is treated right. But once again there might be a price. Whether Japan would ask for military, commercial, or financial advantages in exchange for being America's principal supplier of funds, it is impossible to know in advance.

Even this comfortable if costly relationship may not last. Mr. Gyohten would like his countrymen's banks to send more of their savings to third world countries. They would help fill the credit vacuum left by the withdrawal of debt-starved American banks and establish a commanding financial presence in the markets Japan must develop outside the industrial world. If Japan's trade surplus with the United States vanishes because the dollar and the yen continue to reverse course, the United States not only will risk losing its comfortable Japanese cushion of foreign lending, but it will be faced with a second wave of more diffuse and unruly exporters. Brazil, Mexico, Canada, and the thrusting Asian countries known as The Four Tigers (Singapore, Taiwan, Hong Kong, and Korea) together export about the same amount to the United States as Japan does, but they do not have the same amount of savings to recycle into American bonds. Without a supply of fresh savings from the Orient, the United States might have no recourse but to print the dollars to pay its debts, thus devaluing the dollar assets of Mr. Gyohten's banks even more and closing off more of his country's markets abroad. The day may soon come when Americans look back fondly to the time when they were better off playing a bluffing game with Mr. Gyohten, and when he was better off, too. For the present, both sides therefore prefer this kind of mutual self-levitation to a hard landing for the dollar and those who ride on it like a magic carpet. But this occult process demands the highest diplomacy, and it is very wearing on the nerves.

15

How to Go Bankrupt

It is January, 20, 1989. The President-elect, his face
still glowing a blush pink from a Florida weekend
but his eyes slightly pouchy after the previous night's
good-bye party for the Reagans, mounts the inaugural
stand in front of the Capitol to take the oath as the
forty-first President of the United States. It had been a
gruelling campaign against an ideologically confused
and divided Democratic Party, but he had run well in
the fading glow of Ronald Reagan. The outgoing President, never a strong party man, had surprised everyone by campaigning vigorously. Reagan had recognized
early on that the election of a Republican successor
would be his only remaining chance to imprint at least
some of his ideas on history.

As even Reagan had privately conceded in advance,
the Democrats swept Congress the previous November. But they lost the White House by a few percentage points of the popular vote. The Democrats'
ideological campaign seized California but split their
own party, committing Hari-Gary in the heartland (so
the pundits wrote). From the outset, it had been clear
to everyone that only the intervention of a seventy-
seven-year-old politician at the end of his career could
hold the White House for the Republicans. After eight
heady years under Reagan, the party had opted from
among George Bush, Bob Dole, and Pat Robertson
for a sober and unexciting centrist, who then ran

deeply in Reagan's debt. All were vulnerable to devastating remarks that never reached the mass of the country but percolated along the Bos–Wash corridor. They quickly reached the ears of the Wall Street nabobs who were invited regularly to the political and academic drawing rooms of Georgetown and Cambridge. For example, John Kenneth Galbraith, poet-laureate to the liberal establishment, passed on one deliciously wicked remark that George Bush was "the kind of man who reminds women of their first husbands."

With almost fawning loyalty, the candidate therefore keyed his campaign to the classic Reagan themes of self-reliance at home and military strength abroad. He repeated the 1984 Reagan campaign pledges never to touch Social Security or Medicare, and wisely distanced himself completely from the questions posed by the persistent budget deficits and rising National Debt. With George Bush's old phrase "voodoo economics" resuscitated as a Democratic campaign taunt, no Republican could address these fiscal questions while fighting to assume the mantle of the Wizard responsible for the wonders of Reaganomics. As for Ronald Reagan, he gloried in this one last hurrah before the electorate. He never tired of reminding his adoring audiences that they had escaped recession for six successive years, something that had never happened under any other Republican president in the twentieth century.

As a matter of fact, the economy had been just rocking along at slightly better than 2 per cent in 1987 and 1988. That was not enough growth to cut into unemployment, but not too much to reignite inflation, either. As the result of the devaluation of the dollar, prices started rising briskly only around the Christmas sales after the 1988 election, another economic time bomb that had been left by the Reagan administration for its successors. The economy had digested the huge deficits and was, in effect, bloated on them. Fiscal 1986, with its record deficit of $220 billion, turned out the last of the deficits that were supposed to stretch as far as the eye could see. Then the budgetary gap

began to narrow, but for the wrong reasons. Congress
had refrained from applying the full power of the teeth
in the Texas chain saw known as the Gramm-Rudman-
Hollings law. At the Capitol they preferred to remain
mesmerized by their own smoke and mirrors. For example, 1987 revenues included $2 billion from the sale
of Conrail, which was fine except that the same sum
had been included in the previous year's budget. Such
tricks were supposed to cut the 1987 deficit to the $154
billion prescribed by Gramm-Rambo, as Washington
skeptics called this ballyhooed if blunt budget knife.

A far more effective fiscal cleaver, however, came
slicing down from a totally unexpected direction: the
1986 Tax Reform Act. Millions of investors had rushed
to realize profits by selling stocks and real estate before capital gains taxes and other fiscal dodges were
phased out of the reformed federal tax code. Their
profits were thus taxed at a lower rate, but were
bunched into a single and, for them, more advanta-
geous year. Altogether, revenues rose 11 per cent,
providing a spectacular but unique windfall for the
Treasury and helping to reduce the deficit to $148
billion from the $175 billion that had been forecast for
1987. The President was so proud of the improvement
that he delayed the announcement for one of his rare
press conferences. He never hinted that the real reason was an unexpected—and unrepeatable—increase
in tax collections. But no one was fooled, least of all
those in the financial markets, where the government
had to continue borrowing to finance the deficit.

Apprehension mounted over the U.S. government's
voracious appetite for money "as far as the eye could
see" (as they were saying at David Stockman's new
employers, Salomon Brothers). Then a small earth-
quake on Wall Street was felt in Washington. True,
Black Monday merely rolled back stock values to the
still bullish levels of a year before. But it was enough
to force the representatives of the White House into
cautious communication with Congress on the deficit.
For four weeks they postured in sessions that a leading
participant, Senator Lawton Chiles of Florida, described
as "not the real world." They agreed to cut the deficit

by $30 billion in 1988, thus freeing politicians to do
what they like most, which is to prepare for re-election.
Lobbyists threatened dire punishment at the polls for
even the smallest increase in gasoline taxes or the
slightest delay in social security adjustments. The American Association of Retired Persons budgeted almost
half a million dollars for television spots during the
Iowa and New Hampshire primary campaigns. One
two-minute spot was ominously titled *27 Million*—the
number of members ready to punish any refractory
politician who might even think of touching their
monthly social security checks. Into the start of the
election year, as congressional conferees haggled over
the details of the deficit package, political courage
vanished totally. In order to gain maximum attention
for the image of shared national sacrifice, rangers in
Yellowstone Park were fired, and the officers' mess in
Fort Meyer, Virginia, was closed. But when people
with pocket calculators started asking just exactly what
the deficit level was supposed to be *before* the sacri-
fices, no one really seemed to know what was being
subtracted from what.

The deficit posed a politically excruciating dilemma
for the 1988 election year, because revenues turned
out to be the mirror image of the 1987 windfall. The
stock market crash had distributed its doleful share of
capital *losses* among investors, and as they filed their
income tax forms, they took them avidly. Revenues
declined by 12 per cent. As the presidential primary
season advanced, so did the deficit. When the books
for fiscal 1988 were closed on September 30, coincidentally in mid-campaign, the candidates of both parties greeted the figures with embarrassed silence.
Despite all efforts by Congress and the White House
to reduce the deficit, it actually *rose* as revenues fell in
the sluggish economy. For year 1988—electoral and
fiscal—the federal deficit added up to $164,534,000,000.
(The exact figure was $164,534,732,119.27, but in re-
cent years the Treasury has fallen into the habit of
rounding away the millions in its combined statement
in the same way that the ordinary citizen rounds out
the pennies on his income tax.)

The bond dealers had of course been following the numbers and fully understood them. They had already been asked to buy $15 billion in special zero-coupon government issues to bail out the Federal Savings and Loan Insurance Corporation and save up to 460 savings banks with "negative net worth" from bankruptcy and collapse. Nor did the bond market fail to notice the special farm subsidy appropriation of $6.1 billion rushed through Congress in the midst of the 1988 electoral season to make up for the Administration's overly optimistic estimate. In its proposals to Congress, it had actually budgeted a *decrease* of $6.1 billion in government support for bankrupt American farmers! There were other things. Nancy Reagan had finally prevailed on her husband for an extra appropriation for the war on drugs. The AIDS lobby, running a combined operation demanding funds through Hollywood and Big Science, proved irresistible to Congress. And of course there was the emergency grant for that Marine brigade which had been suddenly parachuted into Managua for "police duties." And so on.

Surprisingly, the financial markets took it all in stride. Another Dow-Jones "correction" of 267 points did take place on a summer Friday when most brokers had already fled to the Hamptons and the program traders broke loose. The swing was generally ascribed to Fed Chairman Alan Greenspan's half-point rise in the discount rate just before the Republican convention to demonstrate his political independence. Since the stock indexes had been heaving wildly through the year but generally settled sideways after each lurch, the drop was hardly noticed by the following month. The Fed had been trying to float the economy off the rocks by slicing away cautiously at interest rates. When government bond rates began approaching 6 per cent, that maneuver became too risky. During the later part of the year, interest rates crept slowly and steadily upward, propelled by the government's relentless demands for credit. The President diverted attention from the implacable deficit by continually threatening to veto any "bad tax" passed by the "spendthrift and irresponsible" Congress. He never told anyone what he thought a good tax would be, so hardly any were ever proposed.

The dollar was hovering around 130 yen, down to about half its value from the time when the administration had pointed to it as a sign of national macho (a point no longer made). Japanese goods were no longer selling briskly, and the Japanese trade surplus was declining rapidly. But the real reason for the improvement in the U.S. trade position was the slow growth of the American economy. Consumer debt had long ago reached its limits. Few families were willing to dig themselves into a deeper hole when it was hard enough to see out of the one they were already stuck in. Demand for Japanese VCRs, TVs, and the new mid-market sports cars was dropping sharply. As for the Germans, Mercedes had cut back its American dealer network long before the deutschmark strengthened. Along with BMW, it had such a lock on the market for high-performance sedans that it could sell all it wanted and still show a healthy profit for its American subsidiary, even at a lower margin.

With the American economy becalmed like a ship in the Sargasso sea, Ronald Reagan felt he must act. He did not want to go down in history as the third Republican president after Eisenhower and Ford to turn his office over to the Democrats by default because of a weak economy. He already had before him the example of Margaret Thatcher, who jettisoned ideology as elections approached in 1987, reduced income taxes for the middle class, and approved almost £10 billion in additional spending for education, health, and social services. More than 10 percent of Britain's workers were unemployed when she decided to seek a third term, so Mrs. Thatcher chose political discretion over fiscal valor in order to forestall the summary dismissal that the Tory Party ruthlessly reserves for defeated leaders. Not for her was the comfortable berth traditionally proffered to ex-prime ministers in the House of Lords, even under the fetching title of Baroness Threadneedle.

So in the closing days of the 1988 campaign, with both parties in a dead heat in the polls, the President and his putative successor devised a plan for a few innocuous election giveaways. Reagan himself could not offer them because that might destroy his anti-government image. So the candidate went on television to pledge that if elected he would offer interest-free college loans to any high school graduate with a combined SAT score of 1000 or better, and free medical care for everyone over the age of seventy with heart trouble, diabetes, arthritis, or other incurable ailments. "Nothing should be spared to ease the golden years of our senior citizens. Equally, we must not neglect the young, who represent the hope of America," he declared.

William Safire, called back for emergency duty as a campaign speechwriter because the Republican team had no sense of history whatsoever, noted that 1989 was not only the bicentennial of George Washington's inauguration but of the French Revolution as well. Safire wrote in a pledge for huge bicentennial fireworks displays in the major cities. That mixture of celebrations would play well in both the Brie and Bible belts. The cost would of course not show up until the budget for fiscal 1990, and people's eyes glazed over when the Democrats started talking *that* far ahead. On election night, the exit polls confirmed the wisdom of all these tactics. The Republicans took Illinois with the help of Chicago's Near North wards, and New York with a sweep of the Upper East Side and the middle-class suburbs of Long Island. The Democrats made one blunder that cost them dear. They had attempted to discuss Social Security reform during the campaign and were consequently wiped out in St. Petersburg, Florida, and Sun City, Arizona, as well as, of course, the Tennessee and Kentucky Bible Belt.

But with the election, the financial markets began growing restless. The bond buyers, both American and Japanese, finally had to face the imminent departure of The Old Actor, as everyone now referred to Ronald Reagan. The new President would confront an angry Congress with sizable Democratic majorities in both houses. The party's leadership was frustrated not only by the Democrats' narrow loss of the White House, but by their inability to reach an ideological consensus. In their frustration, they were determined to punish the new President.

The bond market heard the rumble as not-so-distant thunder: the angry noises of a continuing fiscal stalemate between a fractious Democratic Congress and a wimpish Republican president. The financiers had been content to keep lending to Reagan because they trusted him. They had meanwhile continued to hope that in the election the American people would deliver a clear mandate, either Democratic or Republican, on how to liquidate the deficit. But in this hope they were disappointed. In the Inaugural Address, the one thing that everybody heard was the dog that didn't bark. The new President never once mentioned the federal budget deficit or the National Debt.

With little time to spare as the government's credit demands mounted, the Treasury was already sounding out the bond dealers for its first quarterly auction at the end of February. It was selling a record $47 billion in notes and bonds. To make them especially attractive to the Japanese, the Treasury canvassed an offering of $15 billion in 30-year bonds at what seemed like a very attractive 7⅜ percent rate of interest. But the Japanese, who owned the world's largest banks with the deepest reserves of capital, remained more steadfastly inscrutable than was usual even for them. Just to be on the safe side, the Treasury raised the rate to 7½ percent.

In Tokyo, John Abbott, the chief U.S. Treasury representative, tried to sound out Toyoo Gyohten. He had recently retired with honor from the Finance Ministry and had been rewarded with the chairman's job at Nomura Securities, Japan's largest finance house. Gyohten conceded to Abbott that he was increasingly unsettled about the U.S. budget deficit. But with courteous if mock modesty, the Japanese also said he had never pretended to understand the mysteries of American politics even though he had attended Princeton. Gyohten then withdrew for several days of meditation at a Zen monastery near Nara that he frequented. Set in the folded, foggy landscape familiar in classical Japanese art, this establishment's chief monk is a native Texan who once worked for a Japanese advertising firm, then converted to Zen Buddhism, and now maintains an international network of contacts while strolling through the elegantly minimalist Japanese rooms speaking into a cordless telephone. Confronted with such perplexing cultural contradictions, the Treasury representative was wise enough not to pretend to a deep understanding of the Japanese character, even though he had spent two tours and almost a decade of his life in Japan. But he believed he knew an ominous financial signal when he saw one. Abbott tried to telephone David Mulford, the Treasury Undersecretary for International Affairs, but Washington officials of that rank rarely deign to return the calls of even senior civil servants. By the time Abbott's follow-up warning telegram reached Mulford's desk, it was too late to improve the terms of the bond offer. Auction day arrived. Officials at the New York Federal Reserve Bank made sure that the direct lines to the offices of Daiwa, Nikko, Nomura, and Yamaichi were in working order. Last year the big Japanese securities houses had been admitted to the inner circle of primary government bond dealers in recognition of the important role as buyers supporting the market.

One P.M., Tuesday, February 28, 1989. The deadline for the sealed bids. Officials slit open the envelopes. They lay the bids in piles, and start sorting out the highs and the lows. The highs are higher than usual, which is to say that they are lower in the way bond dealers do business. In fact, they are disastrous. Some of the huge American houses bid $1,000 to $2,000 less than the face value of the $10,000 bonds. But since the government still will have to pay $750 a year interest on the face value of each $10,000 bond, they would really be yielding between 8⅓ or 9⅖ percent a year, and not the 7½ percent sought that the Treasury wanted to pay. As the tally clerks watch the cumulative totals on their computer screens, the amounts also seem smaller than usual. It is soon evident why. The clerks peer outside. The private lines of Daiwa, Nikko, Nomura, and Yamaichi are unoccupied. The Japanese have stopped buying Treasury bonds. They no longer have surplus dollars, since they no longer are exporting as much to the United States; $15 billion, after all, was the trade surplus forecast for the whole of the coming year. They have precious little money to invest abroad, and the interest rate offered by the Treasury is not enough in their view to protect them against the risk of a protracted stalemate in American public finance. They have gone on a bond-buyers' strike.

Only about $5 billion in bonds have actually been bid for, and most of those at ludicrous discounts. Another $10 billion in bonds remain unsold. E. Gerald Corrigan, the President of the New York Fed, makes a few exploratory phone calls. The resident heads of the Japanese securities houses in New York are inscrutably unavailable, but everyone on Wall Street already knows that they have refused to buy any more Treasury bonds—and why. They swallowed huge losses as the dollar declined, and the Fed's attempt to keep interest rates down was the final insult. It now is obvious that Gyohten's move from the Finance Ministry to Nomura was the signal for a change in Japan's buying policy. Corrigan then tries the senior partners of the big American primary dealers. It is their responsibility to buy up the unsold government bonds and hold them until the market improves. But if the angry replies to Corrigan are any indication, not even the primary dealers will take them. Their refusal is unprecedented. Salomon Brothers' John Gutfreund, at once both courtly and blunt, speaks for the Street: "Mr. Corrigan, we feel keenly about our responsibilities to you personally, to the Federal Reserve, and to our country. But our country must also recognize its responsibilities to us, just as we do to our stockholders. We have more government paper on board than a garbage scow on the day after Christmas. If we take on any more, we'll sink."

Corrigan picks up the phone to the Treasury in Washington. A fishing companion and protégé of Paul Volcker's, he is a man without great intellectual pretensions but with a sound and prudent knowledge of how the banking system operates. During the week of the Crash, he played a key role in preventing a financial meltdown by aggressively supplying cash to the banks. Corrigan has good reason to recall remarks he had made to a banking forum at the New York Hilton in 1985. That was when the projections were first being made that the net debt of the United States to the rest of the world would total at least a half-trillion dollars by the end of the decade. He said then: "There is at least a question as to whether foreigners will be eager to continue to accumulate dollar-denominated assets of the amounts suggested at current, much less lower, rates of interest." On the other end of the line is Mulford. He in fact holds a joint Treasury portfolio in charge of debt as well as international finance; the two are not wholly unconnected. Mulford listens impassively as Corrigan gives him the news. A blow-dried banker who made his fortune in Saudi Arabia advising the sheiks where to invest their country's oil billions while they still had them, Mulford was not totally unprepared for Corrigan's call.

Mulford was frankly frightened. He had ten billion in bonds uncovered after the auction and nowhere to place them. Asking the Fed to buy them up would signal a new round of inflation. He would like to have been able to ring Michael Milken at Drexel Burnham in Beverly Hills and dump all the bonds on him. But since the Boesky scandal, the Treasury could not risk even rumors that it was dealing in the market with such operators, however unfounded such rumors might be.

The Treasury official dialed a number across the Potomac in Mount Vernon. A confident nasal voice, speaking with the remnants of a New England twang, barked out a name. "Is that you, Mr. Secretary?" Mulford still addressed his former boss and patron by his old title at Treasury, even though Donald Regan long before had moved on to the White House and then left government after the arms-to-Iran fiasco. Regan returned quietly to the million-dollar mansion he had bought for his retirement near George Wash-

ington's estate. But Regan, ever the aggressive salesman, could not stay idle for long. After a decent
interval to ensure there could not be the least suspi-
cion of impropriety, the former head of Merrill Lynch
returned to his first love, the firm he had turned into
the market leader in managing small investors' cash.
Regan became adjunct chairman in charge of developing the company's presence in the government bond
market. After the junk-bond scandal had tarnished so
many Wall Street insiders, a huge market share came
up for grabs. Regan often worked from his home
because, as he used to say when in government: "We
may be foolish, but we're not stupid." At the White
House he had been forced painfully to learn how to
avoid the trap of braggadocio and overexposure. Anyone really important now came to see him. In the
present financial climate, parading contacts like his
could be dangerously misunderstood.

Street-smart, Regan hardly needed to be told by
Mulford what had happened at the bond auction. "So
the Japs walked away from it and screwed you," he
said. "I always knew the little bastards would do it one
day."

"Yeah," said Mulford. "It's Gyohten. It has to be
him. He's paying us back for the way we screwed him.
But that was a long time ago. My problem is now. It's
three o'clock in the afternoon, and I've got ten billion
in thirty-year Treasuries uncovered. If I don't turn
them over fast, the press will sniff it out. The calls are
starting to back up already."

"Don't panic, David. It's all a big poker game, and
Gyohten holds a lot of the high cards. But not all of
them. No, sir. We,ve got some strong cards, and that's
what I'm here for," said Regan cheerfully, the quintessential salesman inside him reasserting itself. "Merrill Lynch can take all those bonds off your hands.
Right now. A yield of 10 percent guaranteed by the
government of the United States is what we need."

"Can you really move them all?" asked Mulford.

"Why not? This is a big market. Almost forty-five
billion in high-yield bonds were placed in the first half
of the 1980s. It was in 1986 that things really took off.

More than twenty-five billion were floated that year, but it was only a takeover market. Couldn't last. Now it's a different world: sheer survival, David. Sheer goddamn corporate survival. That's what we're here for."

When Donald Regan had a pitch that pleased him, there was no stopping him. He continued: "Drexel Burnham may have led the market then, but we were second in high-yield placings after them. You know what happened next. We've been building up a different kind of business ever since. You just can't beat the old Thundering Herd. No, sir. The size of the market now would amaze you—more than one hundred billion dollars. Fifteen billion in Treasuries wouldn't even be a strain on it now. They would give it real class."

Mulford winced, but beggars can't be choosers. The Treasury man had once been a banker, so he fully understood the dynamics of buying and selling government paper. A decade previous, part of his job had been buying billions from the Treasury on behalf of the House of Saud. He remembered wistfully that in those days, the Arabs had to buy them at par value. No discounts then. Regan meanwhile continued his presentation over the phone.

"We are lenders of last resort for the best blue chips in American industry when they need the money to stay afloat. That's what the high-yield market is all about. Why shouldn't I do it for my own country? I'm proud to. As long as the yield is good and the price is right, we have more than enough clients who will buy any paper, even ours. I mean yours." An embarrassed pause. "Excuse me, you know I didn't mean it that way. After all, we're in this together."

Mulford nevertheless knew exactly what he meant, but he sought one last bit of reassurance: "After this afternoon, I want to be clear on one thing. Are you absolutely certain you can make and maintain a market in Treasuries?"

"Absolutely. Over the years we've been moving Polish paper at 50 percent, and people buy it. Argentina and Mexico sell for 60 cents on the dollar, and Brazil and Chile for 70. Remember when our Somoza friends in Miami took a position in Nicaraguan bonds. They were a gamble at 10 percent, but when the Marines went back, the Contras made a killing. Now Nicaraguan paper is changing hands almost at par. For U.S. governments, the outlook *has* to be better than for all those other dogs. As a citizen, I certainly hope it is. Seven and one-half nominal interest is pretty low for high-yield paper in today's market. But I think we can move your Treasuries at 80 cents on the dollar, because people still think they're quality paper. I'll take them off your hands at 75. Of course you have to do your share in Washington and keep interest rates from going up, or that thirty-year paper will blow away with the rest of them."

"Done." Mulford hung up.

At 3:15 P.M. on February 28, 1989, the U.S. government had met its credit demands by flogging its Treasuries as junk bonds, a term that is disdained by everyone who deals in them. The Treasury worked through Merrill Lynch, a firm as American as apple pie, which had started moving aggressively to expand its share of the junk bond market in 1987. There was a certain poetic justice in doing the deal through the man who had sold more Treasury debt than any other Secretary in history. But the fact remained that Regan *had* helped to steady the market. This service did not come free to the taxpayers, of course. They had to pay an effective rate of 10 percent to move all the bonds quickly and spare the Treasury of the United States the embarrassment of the public failure of its bond auction. Through Donald Regan, Merrill Lynch offered to buy $10 billion in bonds at 75 percent of their face value, or $7,500 for each bond. At a 7½ percent interest coupon, the taxpayers would actually be paying 10 percent a year for the money that the Treasury finally received from the sale of the bonds at a discount. Regan reckoned that Merrill Lynch could resell the bonds to investors at 80, or $8,000 each, and make a profit of $500 on each bond. In future, if deficits continued rising, the taxpayers of the United States would have to pay even more to maintain the credit of their country.

*   *   *

This somewhat fanciful tale is only a slightly over-dramatized version of how the United States of America might avoid bankruptcy. It is fanciful, mainly, but not entirely, in the use of Merrill Lynch as an intermediary to raise money in the bond market. The Treasury's regular banker is of course the Federal Reserve System, but that relationship assumes that the public continues to buy the government's bonds. Throughout history, spendthrift governments have been forced to raise money through private bankers: the English kings to fight their wars, the prewar European nations from J. P. Morgan & Co., the MBA nations of Latin America from the New York and London commercial banks. In this story, the main buyers, who are the Japanese bond houses, have run low on dollars. They have finally decided that their own currency, the yen, is sounder than the dollar because of its ready acceptance abroad as payment for land, factories, and raw materials. People who are paid in yen, after all, can buy Japanese products. They can also invest their money in Japanese stocks, or simply leave it with the big Japanese banks, which in the mid-1980s replaced American banks as the world's largest. In our fable, the bond houses were frightened that if they decided to lend to the U.S. government the few billion dollars that they did have on hand, the value of their money might be further eroded by a new round of deficits that would eventually reignite inflation. The value of their Treasury bonds had already been cut almost in half when the dollar plunged from 250 to 130 yen. An interest rate of 7½ percent would not, in their eyes, have compensated them for the risk that the U.S. government might welsh on its obligations by inflating its way out of them.

But the United States, like Continental Illinois and the other money-center banks that tottered so dizzyingly back in 1984, is one of the world's few TBTF countries—too big to fail. There is, however, a price to be paid for survival, in this fable as in all others. The government has to turn quickly to dealers in junk bonds, which means selling bonds cheap, raising interest rates, or both. The alternative for Mr. Mulford would have been to revert to the dishonored tradition of instructing the Federal Reserve to buy up the unwanted bonds. But that is not something either side would wish to advertise, given the history of inflation. When a member of the public buys a Treasury bond, he pays for it with a check drawn on his own bank account, which represents a portion of his real wealth and savings. But when the Fed buys a $10,000 bond because no one else wants to buy it, it pays with a check drawn on the account of a Federal Reserve Bank. The seller of the bond, in this case the U.S. Treasury, deposits the $10,000 check in its account at that same Federal Reserve Bank. It then proceeds to pay its bills with the money, and the government thus borrows from itself to repay itself. If this exchange seems like a rather suspicious paper transaction, you have good financial instincts. That is how governments print money.

Once before in very recent times, a federal security had come perilously close to being a junk bond because of such fears. In 1980, in order to entice people to lend their money to the government for ten years or more, Treasury bonds had to offer on average the same return as the safest AAA-rated corporate bonds. Both paid between 11 and 12 percent interest during most of that year. During the month of February 1980, the government's credit actually was deemed by the marketplace a hairbreadth *worse* than that of blue-chip corporate America; in order to reassure nervous investors, its bonds had to yield 12.41 percent annual interest, while AAA corporate bonds yielded 12.38 percent. That was a frightening time. The U.S. government, which is supposed to be the safest borrower in the world, had to pay the same price for its money as companies that could have found themselves in bankruptcy court the next day. (In the recession that followed, a few of them actually did.) At that time, junk bonds had not yet been fully developed as financial instruments, but the future is always full of surprises.

A bankrupt is a man who runs out of credit. That is, no one any longer believes that he can pay his debts.

The sovereign nations of Latin America raised money to live beyond their means until their foreign bankers belatedly realized they had reached their limits. No one takes a country to court, because it cannot be hailed before a bankruptcy judge like an individual. Instead, the buyers and sellers of its promissory notes arbitrate its credit. As implied in the story of Mr. Mulford and Merrill Lynch, this had already begun to happen to the United States. It may seem sheer fantasy, but it is absolutely true that the promissory notes of sovereign debtors were being traded in mid-1986 at the deeply discounted prices cited in the story. Drexel Burnham, Shearson Lehman, and several other investment houses, large and small, do an active business in these dud loans, many of which pay reduced interest or none at all.

But, surely, buying a Polish loan must be some Polish joke. Not in the least. It can be profitable business if you happen to be an Austrian engaged in East–West trade. One of your most important clients, the Polish government, is eager to reduce its huge debt by buying it back, but Poland does not have the dollars or other hard currency to do so. So you sit in Vienna, buy a Polish promissory note at fifty cents on the dollar, and send it to Warsaw in exchange for a cargo of Polish ham, price negotiated in advance. Everybody profits. In Venezuela, where you may recall the government allowed every dollar it borrowed to fly to the safety of banks abroad, the government's oil company will accept its own promissory notes in payment for oil. How's that again? This might have taxed even the fertile commercial imagination of Milo Minderbinder, but it works. Like this: A small American bank, let's say somewhere in Louisiana, is eager to write off a bothersome $5 million loan it made to Venezuela in happier days, because nowadays the Venezuelans pay interest only on rare occasions. The Venezuelan government is just as eager to cancel the loan and the obligation that it entails to pay interest for years to come. Meanwhile, a small refiner in Louisiana is looking for cheap oil. The three get together. The Louisiana bank gives back the Venezuelans their

$5 million promissory note, which both sides agree to value at half-price, or $2.5 million. The bank still has a credit in Venezuela, but it is payable only in oil instead of dollars. Venezuela has plenty of oil; what it doesn't have is dollars. The refiner bargains with the Venezuelans for several boatloads of oil at even lower prices than he would have to pay in Texas, where they are already swimming in the stuff. But the Venezuelans are swimming in it, too, so they agree. When the oil arrives at the small refinery on the Gulf of Mexico, the refiner pays his local bank in dollars, and everyone goes away happy.

Some banks in Europe are buying up Latin American and East European paper—never was this financial term more appropriate—at deep discounts and putting it in cold storage for eventual sale at a profit to such potential customers as the Austrian trader in Polish hams or the small refiner in Louisiana. Some investment houses are trying to figure out how to roll the moribund Latin American loans into speculative packages for investors with strong nerves who are ready to bet that the MBA countries will eventually service their debts again with full interest. *Fortune* magazine christened this proposed financial instrument as The Ultimate Junk Bond. But it may not be necessary. Some Latin American debtors will literally sell off parts of their industry to foreigners in exchange for their outstanding debt. This also is not some surrealistic capitalist fantasy like Nathanael West's novel, *The Dream Life of Balso Snell*, whose eponymous hero sells off arms, legs, and much else to stay alive. So far, most of the countries are standing on their dignity (and their bargaining position) by insisting they will swap paper only dollar for dollar in exchange for shares in their factories, mines, or land. But that position is weakening, and cooking the books in such transactions to make them look like an even exchange is relatively easy.

Big American banks prefer not to publicize the losses they would have to declare if they engaged in such swaps. Instead, banks like Citicorp earn fat fees helping the little banking fish escape from the nets in

which the big fish entangled them in the first place; it
was the big New York banks that originally sold their
country cousins billions worth of shares in these dubious Latin American loans during the heady days of
lending. Like stockbrokers, the big banks make money
on the way up as well as the way down. Now it is the
Japanese who have started picking up the pieces and
putting them together: Latin debt, deep discounts, and
cheap factories. When the Nissan Motor Company
wanted to expand its automobile engine plant in Mexico, it bought $60 million in Mexican promissory notes
from eighteen small banks that were delighted to dump
the devalued paper at a discount, just like junk bonds.
Nissan paid the banks only $40 million for the pack-
age, which had been assembled by (who else?) Citicorp.
Nissan then sold the Mexican paper to the Mexican
central bank for the equivalent of $54 million—in
Mexican pesos. The Mexicans have more pesos than
they know what to do with, since nobody else wants
them. (Are you following this, Milo? So far, the Japanese have made a profit of $14 million in buying the
debt on the open market and selling it back to the
Mexicans for pesos.) With those pesos, Nissan paid for
a larger engine plant at a bargain price, simultaneously
increasing its equity and therefore its dominance over
its Mexican subsidiary.

There is no Catch-22 in any of this. It is all for real,
and it has been published in the newspapers. But
fantasy is always more intriguing, so let's turn the
clock ahead again. To 1990 this time instead of 1989.
The new President has been in office one year. Ronald
Reagan used to think of himself as a Calvin Coolidge
presiding over the prosperous 1980s; sure enough, his
woeful successor has inherited the mantle of the man
who succeeded Coolidge, Herbert Hoover. The President is powerless against the huge and rebellious Democratic majorities in both houses of Congress, who
refuse to accept the opprobrium for raising taxes to
control the deficit. The Mulford-Merrill Lynch junk
bond coup of the previous year has mainly borrowed
time, but not really a great deal of money. Although

Merrill Lynch has had little difficulty maintaining an active market in U.S. Treasury bonds as Regan had promised, supporting the market has turned out to be more difficult than he had reckoned. Treasuries have slipped and now are trading at fifty cents on the dollar, the same as Venezuelan and—ultimate humiliation— Polish paper. Interest rates on new Treasury issues have jumped sharply, and they now cannot be sold unless they pay at least 12 percent. The return of high interest rates has of course tipped the country back into recession. Sluggish economic activity has reduced federal revenues. Raising taxes in the middle of a recession would only make things worse. In January 1990, the President sends to Congress the first budget for which he bears full responsibility. With the economic outlook darkening, he has no choice but to forecast a horrendous budget deficit of $350 billion.

One year to the day after he received his first call from Mulford at the Treasury, Regan's phone rings again. It is breakfast time in Mount Vernon, and on the other end is Toyoo Gyohten, behaving with diplomacy and modest charm toward his former tormentor. Regan does a quick calculation and reckons that it is after dinner in Tokyo. From this he realizes that the call is both urgent and important. He displays far more patience in business than he ever did in government. He relaxes in an armchair and exchanges pleasantries, as he is perfectly capable of doing when he smells a deal. Japanese do not come to the point quickly, but in due course it emerges. After five years of buying and holding massive amounts of thirty-year Treasury bonds, Gyohten says Nomura is overstocked and would like to sell two billion dollars' worth. Can Merrill Lynch feed them onto the market slowly, being careful not to flood it and depress the price even more? Yes, replies Regan, that certainly can be done by a market-maker with his firm's financial muscle, but it might take a while. With the threat of inflation, not many people are willing to risk locking themselves into long-term bonds any more. It is getting to be a bit frightening again, like 1980, when the Treasury could only sell bills of one year or less. And then there is

going to be the problem of turning the dollars back
into yen. The exchange rate is beginning to slide . . .
An apologetic hissing comes over the phone. Unfortunately Gyohten has not made himself clear. If unloading two billion in bonds will unsettle the market, then
could Merrill Lynch start with one billion? And he will
be perfectly content to take dollars, in fact he *wants*
dollars, or as he lets on delicately, his client does. The
former Secretary of the Treasury needs no lessons in
financial etiquette when a deal of this size is at stake.
He immediately shifts to technical questions in order
to cement it.

If Regan had somehow managed to transport himself
to the bracing Pacific air of California's Monterey
Peninsula, he would have seen with his own eyes what
lay behind the Nomura proposition. At 8 A.M. that
very day, the president of Toyota, the world's seventh
largest corporation by valuation of the stock market,
and the president of General Motors, the world's tenth
largest by the same measure, tee off at the splendid
oceanfront Pebble Beach Club. It is fortunate that
nine holes of golf take a while, because the president
of Toyota has a lot on his mind. He would like to talk
about the joint venture that the two companies set up
in 1984 to produce the Chevrolet Spectrum by Japanese methods at a plant only a few hours' drive from
there, in Fremont, California. General Motors wanted
to learn how to adapt Toyota's high technology and
industrial relations, but when times got tough, one of
its first moves was to lay off thousands of workers.
Meanwhile, in Japan, Toyota was holding on to its
skilled workforce and retraining them to use new technology on the production line.

The president of Toyota did not stress such unpleasant contrasts, although he did point out that the two
automotive giants were supposed to be working together. Fifty-fifty basis. Ah, so. (First hole, long drive.)
The Fremont venture had proven successful; the plant
had even begun producing two models for Toyota to
sell in America. It has been working very well. Fifty-
fifty. Very satisfied. (Third hole, stuck in a sand trap.)
Yes, the president of GM agrees, his company has

learned important production techniques from the Japanese. (Chip shot back to the fairway.) And the president of Toyota also agrees that GM's marketing network has been most helpful. Very useful, yes, yes. (Fifth hole, birdie.) But . . . (Seventh hole, long drive to the green.) But Toyota would like to expand the engine plant, and it always feels more comfortable managing its own properties in its own way. (Putt sinks. Silence.) The president of GM points out that Japanese techniques have been invaluable, at least those that GM could adapt to very different American circumstances. But he stresses that GM could never enter into a junior partnership, even though Toyota is the larger of the two firms. Equal shares. That was the understanding from the start. (Eighth tee. Drive falls short. Hiss.) No, no, no. Toyota could never insult General Motors by asking the senior and more experienced company to place itself in a subordinate position to his own young company. The time has come for Toyota to stand on its own feet in the American market. (Vicious slice toward the sea. Splash.) The president of GM says he would be very sorry indeed to sever their working relationship. The president of Toyota says he will also be very sorry, but it will be better for all if . . . (Both sit down on a secluded bench overlooking the Pacific.)

The terms of Toyota's proposal to buy out GM's share of the Fremont factory are breathtaking. Four billion dollars in thirty-year U.S. Treasury bonds, and one billion dollars in cash. U.S. dollars, of course. The president of GM hesitates. He would prefer yen to what is rapidly turning into Treasury wallpaper. The president of Toyota (who had been telephoned by Gyohten shortly before leaving for the golf course) raises his offer to two billion dollars in cash. It will be paid one year after GM agrees to accept the Treasury bonds as a swap for full ownership of the plant. The face value of the bonds alone is equal to all of GM's profits in 1985, and those profits have certainly not increased since then. When the recession began in mid-1989, they slumped disastrously. For Toyota, which counts its profits in yen, the billions mean considerably less than what Toyota is offering GM in dollars. The president of GM accepts the offer of four billion dollars in bonds and two billion in cash. It was an offer he could not refuse.

These fables tell how America could go bankrupt without actually declaring bankruptcy. This is what could happen when a country deep in debt is also too big to be allowed to fail, but not nimble enough to shift its horizons. It is also what happens when a country lives for so long by selling paper promises that the holders of those promises eventually decide to cash them in for real things like factories. It is like a cloud passing before the summer sun, a slight chill only briefly noticed, when someone else becomes financial master of your destiny. By living atop mounting piles of paper that can hold us hostage to the interests of others, we are slowly allowing ourselves to become a third world nation.

PART II

AVOIDING DISASTER

16

The American Century

How did the United States turn itself from the master of the world at the end of World War II into its largest debtor exactly forty years later in 1985? This is an amazing reversal of fortune in such a short space of time. It came about by nurturing the illusion that America continued as the supreme power. It also came about by ignoring the country's fundamental values. The nation was created by cooperation between the individual and the community, not by the individual alone. By winning the war, the nation shaped the postwar world by consensus and cooperation, not by *diktat*. Adjusting to the reality of an America that no longer held absolute power paradoxically would have assured a comfortable and satisfactory dominance over others who were ready to accept wise leadership. Failure to adjust need not be irreversible. In other words, there is time to shake off the self-contradictory myths that the American government achieved its greatness without the active cooperation of the rest of the world, and that the American people prospered without the active participation of their government. Neither myth bears much scrutiny. Nevertheless, there is an occasional whiff of the rot of arrogance and isolation that ate away the Spanish Empire, which was built on New

World gold. Within two centuries after 1492, the Spanish had wasted their treasure on ornament and war and sealed off their adventurous energies from the intellectual discoveries that were animating the rest of Europe. Spain's successor empire was England in the nineteenth century, and its descent into a long, self-satisfied twilight was less dramatic. But both the Spanish and the English, the two empires that ran the world before we did, went under as they went into debt. No one yet knows whether toward the end of this century the weight of world power and nationalist pride will divert us, and the burden of debt tire us, as they did in England at midcentury.

The United States emerged from World War II as a conqueror unscathed. It was more powerful than the entire devastated European continent, than exhausted England, than humiliated Japan; more powerful and wealthier than all of them and their dependencies together. America, with less than 10 percent of the world's population, produced more than half its goods and owned 60 percent of its gold reserves. Its victorious armies in Europe were led by Dwight Eisenhower, a soldier-diplomat who would preside genially over a remarkable period of domestic and international tranquillity; those in Asia were led by Douglas MacArthur, a proconsul who would build modern Japan. With the death of Roosevelt, the awesome power of the United States for good and evil passed into the hands of an unappreciated Missouri politician named Harry Truman. To the surprise of many, this self-confident American original used that power wisely. Contrary to the now-fashionable nationalist myths of rugged individualism, the postwar political and economic system created by him, and consolidated by his successor Eisenhower, was based on domestic consensus and international cooperation. This man from Independence, where the wagon trains had set off to tame the West, never forgot his roots.

The West was won not by the gun but by the plow and the railroad. The Lone Ranger was an anachronistic invention of the entertainment industry, and Tonto was kept busy getting him out of trouble, anyway. The peace was kept by the federal marshal or the community posse. Like the Iron Horse and the Homesteader, they were nurtured by the state, whose role is only grudgingly acknowledged by the rhetoric of American capitalism. By knitting together the farms, industries, and cities of the continent in the late nineteenth century, the railroad served as the single most important multiplier for America's economic takeoff. Money came from bond buyers in London, Bessemer steel technology from England, immigrant labor from the disdained villages of Europe and China, and the original venture capital, without which the entire enterprise would have been impossible, from none other than the capitalist government of the United States. Western land was the form of investment capital most freely available to the young Republic. Between 1850 and 1871, Congress gave the railroads right-of-way land equivalent to the entire states of Colorado and Wyoming for "the safe and speedy transportation of mails, troops, munitions of war, and public stores." Set against this great enterprise, the people themselves seem almost a footnote, but they also settled the West on government land grants. In 1862, the Homestead Act offered farms to anyone who would settle and maintain a house on them for five years.

This combination of commercial enterprise and government support is the forgotten foundation of America. Its agriculture was made into the world's most productive by government finance funneled through farm price supports, federal reclamation projects that irrigated the arid West, and technology dispensed by the county agent. The airlines, like the railroads, owe their start to government subsidies for carrying the mail. The trucking industry, and less directly, the entire automobile industry, owes its growth to the 40,000-mile interstate highway system, which was an Eisenhower public works project worthy of ancient Rome; between 1945 and 1970, public spending on all highways grew one-third faster than the GNP. Highways supported autos, which supported steel. During the 1950s, when IBM was pioneering the commercial computer technology that still dominates the world, the company earned 40 percent of its revenues from the Pentagon. The Boeing 707, the world's first and phenomenally successful jet airliner, was a civilian adaptation of an aerial tanker whose development had been underwritten by the U.S. Air Force. Business and government, wrote Norman Mailer in *Miami and the Siege of Chicago* (1971), had been "locked in common-law marriage" for more than a generation.

This cynical epithet failed to comprehend the deeper governmental underpinning of the economy, which was strengthened in a never-again reaction to war and depression. It expressed itself in a postwar social consensus in America and Europe. In Europe, the welfare state needed to be more comprehensive because the terrible events of two European civil wars and their aftermath had shredded the social fabric. There was a common desire to rebuild on the basis of social cooperation instead of class conflict. In America, the government stepped in to promote the native sense of mobility, yet tried to square it with the desire for security that had been burned into the national consciousness by the Great Depression. The Veterans Education Act, known as the GI Bill of Rights, sent a generation to college and not incidentally upgraded its technical skills for the demands of a modern economy. The guarantees attached to the Federal Housing Administration's mortgages underwrote a huge stock of mainly suburban housing that encouraged worker mobility. Pensions for the old through Social Security, and a safety net through unemployment insurance, eased some of the worst insecurities of the competitive economy. Psychologically more than financially, they underwrote the postwar boom.

Most important to the ordinary citizen, but least visible to him, was the government's formal assumption of responsibility for the economy in the passage of the Employment Act of 1946. New Deal activists had proposed a "Full Employment" law that would literally legislate jobs by stipulating an annual deficit to stimulate the economy. The deficit would have been euphemistically called "investment," but simply would have meant printing money. This was deemed too radical, and the law as passed required that the president choose a Council of Economic Advisers and report to Congress on the state of the economy once a year. It wisely did not insist that he follow their advice. There had been numerous and dire forecasts of another depression. At its nadir in 1932, the Depression had left one out of four American workers without jobs and created an obsessive fear that it could happen again. But the specialists had overlooked a huge $44 billion pool of personal savings that had piled up when Americans saved one dollar out of every four they earned during World War II. As the money was spent, it created a boom in housing and industrial investment. Within eighteen months after the war ended, more than ten million demobilized servicemen and millions more former wartime workers had found jobs. Civilian employment was at a record, and production was 50 percent higher than in 1939. Growth proceeded under prudent finance. Truman was a balanced-budget man and vetoed tax cuts voted by a Republican Congress to embarrass him in the election year of 1948. "There is nothing sacred about the pay-as-you-go idea so far as I am concerned, except that it represents the soundest principle of financing I know," he said. Later, Eisenhower's interstate highway program was financed on a pay-as-you-go basis by taxing gasoline.

All this signaled the start of a new worldwide *belle époque* under strong American management. Its most formidable publicist was Henry Luce, founder and editor-in-chief of *Time* magazine. He called it "the American Century," with considerable justification as to genesis if not as to duration. The military underpinning of Pax Americana was as evident as the Royal Navy when Britannia ruled. But what made it work was an international arrangement by the industrial democracies to trade freely among themselves in goods and settle their accounts in dollars, which was comforting both to American ideology and to American interests. But it also suited their own: the rules of an open system of trade and finance tied together countries that had drawn themselves into economic fortresses in the 1930s and then gone to war. It was known as the Bretton Woods System, after the New Hampshire grand hotel where it was first outlined by the prospective victors in 1944. Keynes had argued idealistically for a supranational bank that would be able to create money for investment, but the U.S. Treasury vetoed that as a potential open drain from its vaults to bail out the rest of the world. He returned to England fed up with the stolid American worthies and their shiny, impassive municipal faces, which, he said, "looked like knees."

As usual, Keynes turned out to be right. No sooner had the spirits of Western Europe begun to revive in 1947 than it ran out of money for investment to rebuild basic industries like steel, coal, and railroads. Without a fresh injection of capital, Europeans would have had to retreat to the dangerous nationalism that helped cause two wars and to call for rescue from America. One by one, they also would have been picked off by the Soviet Union. Thirteen billion dollars was channeled through the Marshall Plan in a process that was not without its ironies. The canny Midwestern industrialists and Wall Streeters who ran the program from 1948 to 1952 insisted that the European governments produce concrete plans for spending the money before they would disburse it. These free-enterprisers thus inadvertently taught their European wards the value of national planning. But in forcing them to share the aid among themselves, they also succeeded in impressing on them the virtues of international cooperation. This eventually flowered in the single most successful international institution of the postwar world, the European Common Market.

With the rules in place and their policies coordinated perforce by increasing interdependence, the industrial nations of the world prospered at a rate and in a manner unique in history. Between 1913 and 1948, when the world's great nations were either at war or, as the European statesman Robert Marjolin once put it, "hardly talked to each other," their trade grew less than half a percentage point a year and their production by only about 2 percent. In the quarter-century up to the first oil shock of 1973, world trade grew by 7 percent and pulled production with it at a rate of 5 percent. Living standards followed the upward curve. Between 1950 and 1973, the average annual rate of real economic growth *per person* was 3.8 percent in the Western world's industrialized countries. That was more than three times the average for the entire 130 years of industrial expansion that began in 1820 after the Napoleonic Wars. The figures confirm the experience of anyone who lived through that era of prosperity. At an annual increase of 3.8 percent, living standards doubled in twenty years. That is precisely what happened to the industrial world as a whole in a single postwar generation.

In the United States from 1950 to 1973, living standards grew by 2.2 percent, which still exceeded the per capita growth rate of 2 percent during America's late-nineteenth-century industrial development. (At 2 percent a year, living standards or anything else take thirty-five years to double.) Because continental Europe had farther to go to catch up in technology and living standards, its annual improvement was in the range of 3 percent. In Japan, emerging from poverty, living standards grew by a phenomenal 8 percent. In the mid-1960s, for example, virtually every American household had a refrigerator, compared with only about half in France and three-fifths in Britain. But a decade earlier, fewer than one in ten British and French families had refrigerators. A major component of the boom was filling the desire for such consumer durables and catching up in the new technologies and assembly-line production methods pioneered in the United States. America made its profit by selling its techniques and investing abroad. Under the Bretton Woods System, everyone needed American dollars, and Washington's IOUs bought up and improved foreign factories. That was the era of The American Challenge, when the French publicist Jean-Jacques Servan-Schreiber warned, incorrectly, as it turned out, that the most powerful force in Europe soon would be the American companies based there.

No one foresaw that the springs of prosperity were

unique and eventually would dry up. The boom was
based on fulfilling material wants and social needs that
had their natural or economic limits. They were supplied initially by cheap energy, cheap raw materials,
and cheap labor. By 1951, 98 percent of the world oil
market was controlled by five American and two British companies. With the support mainly of American
military power, these Seven Sisters among themselves
regulated production and prices to the advantage of
the industrial consumers. Pax Americana held down
most other raw material prices, and agricultural technology did the rest for food prices. Wages were held
down by massive migrations from the land to the factory. Between World War II and the early 1970s, the
percentage of workers on farms dropped from 12 to 4
in the United States, 27 to 14 in France, and 23 to 7 in
West Germany. They could not stabilize at levels much
lower than that. Meanwhile, the fiscal demands of the
Welfare State began to outrun its capacity to lubricate
economic and social frustrations. Government payments for such benefits as pensions, health insurance,
and unemployment compensation more than doubled
in a quarter-century to one-fifth of national output in
major European countries, and doubled to one-seventh
in the United States. This began to approach the limits
of political tolerance.

The justice of this world system and its ulterior
political motives are not at issue here, and should not
be. While it lasted, it worked magnificently. No one
protested seriously enough to disrupt it except the
cosseted young, a phenomenon that had recurred since
Plato first described it in his *Dialogues*. However much
they may have resented American protection, some
Europeans knew how to make a strength of their
weakness by playing on America's fears. Raymond
Barre, a professor and perennial presidential candidate who somehow manages simultaneously to be one
of the most unctuous and outspoken figures in French
politics, recently remarked, "Without Europe, America ceases to be a superpower." Even when the postwar international system began to falter, it lasted long
enough to give the advanced nations of the world a

longer period of peace and prosperity on their home ground than they had known since the Roman Empire. But in both triumph and tragedy, people tend to be unable to discern what has cast them high or low.

The postwar system reached its zenith around the middle of the 1960s. The moment of truth probably passed virtually without notice—it usually does—when the United States proved itself unwilling or unable to subordinate domestic priorities to international goals. To maintain a stable dollar, it would have had to accept a slower economy and more unemployment, and presidents refused to do this within an electoral horizon that seemed to grow ever shorter. Although few realized it at the time, the reluctance of the United States to underwrite the system financially and defend it militarily reached its limits in Vietnam. The bills came due with a vengeance in 1973. In one year, the United States had to float its currency, risk a Constitutional crisis because its President might have to face criminal prosecution, withdraw the last American combat forces from Vietnam, and pay unexpected tribute to producers of oil who had been underwriting its consumer appetites with cheap energy. In history, 1973 probably ranks with the years of such pivotal events as the American and French revolutions of 1776 and 1789, the collapse of the world order into war in 1914, and the economic collapse of 1929. Each in its own way marked a permanent change in the world.

The New York financier Felix Rohatyn, with a weary sense of history worthy of his Viennese origins, has remarked that "the American Century lasted twenty years." Make it twenty-five: from the Marshall Plan to 1973. Thereafter, Americans had no excuse to pretend that their century could be revived, but they pretended anyway. The costs of illusion on such a grand scale are never inconsequential. Americans and their leaders tried any number of subterfuges to disguise their loss of absolute predominance in world economic and political power. Richard Nixon, in the face of military defeat and economic imbalance, boasted that America was "Number One." Still, Americans insisted on living beyond their means in the vain hope of bringing back the past, a process that both economists and psychologists call a failure to adjust. In the 1970s, inflation was the subterfuge that masked an international tug of war over raw materials like oil, and over markets like the Middle East and Europe, where America no longer had undisputed first claim. At home, inflation masked stagnant living standards. Families, industries, and the country suffered without fully understanding how it ravaged them, or even why. This reached its social tolerance at the end of the decade. High interest rates and unemployment restored financial balance, but that medicine proved too strong. Debt was the alternative method of escape.

For a country to live beyond its means, it can either print money or borrow it. In the 1970s, the industrial nations and the third world did both. European countries wanted to protect their industrial dinosaurs from the shock of high oil prices and save the workers' jobs. Third world countries bet that inflation would pay off their loans on agriculture, energy, raw materials, and their basic industries. But they weren't the only ones. Mexico based its loans on oil at $40 a barrel, but so did Texas and Oklahoma. Farmers in Kansas, betting that grain at $4 a bushel was forever, made the same mistake. What they all missed was that the price mechanism eventually works. After high prices call forth new supply, glut brings prices down. Worse, the huge new investments in grain land, metal production, and oil came on stream just as the world tipped into recession in 1982. The third world is stuck with its debts of the last decade, but so is some of the first world, which ought to have known better. The Hunt brothers of Texas tried to corner the silver market, which collapsed around their feet for a loss of a cool billion when the recession struck. Bunker Hunt shrugged it off with a memorable line: "A billion dollars isn't what it used to be." His brother Herbert told a Congressional inquiry that he was continuing to invest in oil, gas, coal, and precious metals as a hedge against inflation. But in 1986, the Hunts had to file for bankruptcy to prevent creditors from seizing the family oil company.

The Reagan loans date only from the 1980s. Almost by accident, Americans stumbled into something that had not been thought possible for a country as large and prosperous as the United States: borrowing enough money from others to maintain its high standards of consumption. This was the dubious achievement of Ronald Reagan. But a sound society has to learn how to live within its means. Runaway deficits are the sign that we refused to learn, and the National Debt is the most egregious evidence of all. If it is not curbed, something will snap. This is not a prediction, merely a declaration of financial vulnerability. Past is prologue. What follows is a historical account of how we approached that breaking point.

17

The End of the
Belle Epoque

The social and economic history of the United States during the past generation is opaque to many who lived through it. It is painful to come to terms with the limits it implied for even the most powerful nation on earth. The Vietnam decade, from 1965 to 1975, was a time of military defeat and social disillusion. Unexplained, these events led to political and economic disarray: they overlapped the second act, which became the Dreary Decade. It really began in 1973 with the rise in oil prices and ended with the recession of 1982. Its initiation by an improbable group of sheiks lacked the drama of the Crash of 1929, which helped produce the Great Depression and then the most sweeping social reforms in American history. The events of the 1970s amounted to a Quiet Depression. It created a society in which everyone had to fight to hold on to what he had. Calm was restored temporarily by borrowing that little bit extra to spread around.

The principal agent of the debility was inflation, often expressed in double digits. In one decade, prices by any measure doubled or worse. This cut the value of money in half. Although this social measuring rod had already undergone a full twist after World War II, the process of doubling the price level had occupied a full quarter-century under conditions of political sta-

172

bility and economic growth. Inflation had slowly facilitated social equity instead of suddenly distorting it. The initial symptoms were Vietnam, OPEC, and Watergate. But none of these events existed in isolation. With some historical perspective, they now can be assigned a general cause: the breakdown of the unique postwar social and international consensus. When it was seen to break up, people fought to obtain tomorrow's wage and tomorrow's price today, because an unconfident and uncertain polity could not assure them that when tomorrow came, they would receive even the same share as today. (And when inflation was all over, many did not.) The result was the most pervasive ailment of the age, an economic virus with the inelegant name of stagflation. It combined stagnant output with rising prices, and although economists claimed that the phenomenon theoretically was impossible, it nevertheless afflicted the entire Western world. As economic performance failed to measure up to the expectations nurtured in the unique period after the war, a process of defensive positioning gradually ended the *belle époque.* That was what inflation was all about.

Any government would have suffered from a comparison between hard reality and the first raptures of John F. Kennedy's New Frontier, with his promise to "get America moving again." But can-do courtiers foolishly promised that they could manage the defense of Vietnam as if they were running an automobile factory and could "fine-tune" the economy as if it were an engine. This set impossible goals for Kennedy's successor. Lyndon Johnson fell into the trap by trying to deliver more than the country and—as later became evident under Richard Nixon—more than the rest of the world was willing to pay for. From 1964 to 1968, Great Society spending for major social programs grew half again as fast as the federal budget, and kept right on growing under Richard Nixon, despite the cost of the Vietnam War. During the Johnson–Nixon decade, federal payments to individuals for retirement, unemployment, medical care, and public relief, expressed as a share of the national income, doubled from 5 to 10 percent. Both presidents also shared the cost of Vietnam about equally; the war cost $47 billion in the five years up to Nixon's election in 1968, and $59 billion in the following five years.

The ordinary citizen had come to see these social benefits as a right to which he was entitled, creating what the pollster Daniel Yankelovich has called an "entitlement society" that even Ronald Reagan later found impossible to dismantle. Social entitlements were cemented so solidly into the budget that each administration described them in bureaucratic jargon as "uncontrollable." In political fact, they genuinely were out of control. When the Vietnam War was over in 1975, defense spending in noninflated dollars had settled back to $68 billion, exactly the same as it had been a decade before. But the peace dividend that was supposed to be waiting was no longer there. During that decade, social payments to individuals, as expressed in constant dollars, had trebled to $121 billion. By far the largest proportion went to pensions and medical care for the elderly. The Vietnam dividend had already been spent without anybody having formally decided how. And it is not often noticed that these social entitlements were confirmed under Republican rule by one Caspar Weinberger, who served Nixon first as Secretary of Health, Education, and Welfare, and then as Budget Director. In both offices, he did nothing that was numerically visible to merit his nickname, "Cap the Knife." This may have been why Ronald Reagan chose him to manage an expansion of Pentagon spending whose only peacetime precedent had been the social spending of those years. David Stockman, Reagan's first budget director, claims that the Pentagon military buildup that later took place under Weinberger was actually larger in inflation-adjusted dollars than the Vietnam buildup, which destabilized the American economy.

When demands can no longer be satisfied either by the dividends of economic growth or by politicians earnest enough to levy taxes to pay for them, they have to be paid some other way. Nobody thought about debt then because the government was printing paper money instead of selling bonds. Without a clear consensus, the government under both Johnson and Nixon resorted to the classic expedient of printing money. Inflation and stagnation were the result of a political battle for the upper hand. Mark this closely. The schoolboy definition of inflation is "too much money chasing too few goods"—but that does nothing to explain why there is simultaneously too much of one and too little of the other. Inflation is a monetary phenomenon only on the surface, which is why simple monetarist cures of limiting the supply of money do not by themselves suffice. It is the result of a political tug of war among social classes in which democratic governments generally yield to the temptation to throw their weight on one side or the other. The process of inflation and its social consequences are best described by Keynes in a 1919 essay that begins with a famous piece of apocrypha.

> Lenin is said to have declared that the best way to destroy the capitalist system is to destroy the currency. By a continuing process of inflation, governments can confiscate, secretly and unobserved, an important part of the wealth of their citizens. By this method they not only confiscate, but they confiscate *arbitrarily* and, while the process impoverishes many, it actually enriches some. The sight of this arbitrary rearrangement of riches strikes not only at security, but at confidence in the equity of the existing distribution of wealth. . . . As the inflation proceeds and the real value of the currency fluctuates wildly from month to month, all permanent relations between debtors and creditors, which form the ultimate foundation of capitalism, become so utterly disordered as to be almost meaningless; and the process of wealth-getting degenerates into a gamble and a lottery.

In the 1970s, major interest groups such as unions were among the first to assert themselves in the strug-

gle to translate political power into purchasing power.
Nixon courted the construction industry hard-hats. Hu-
bert Humphrey and George McGovern courted the
public-service unions, such as the teachers. All of the
candidates, and their political successors, courted the
huge voting bloc of the elderly. All engaged in a
process of competitive bidding for political support.
Rarely did the wages or benefits of these muscular
political darlings seem to suffer. Occasionally, one
group such as the New York municipal workers had
the bad luck to find itself in the political line of fire of
the President of the United States, as when Gerald
Ford, acting on behalf of the city's bondholders, told
them to drop dead. More often, the bill was paid by
someone else in higher prices or taxes. In America,
the frustrations of Vietnam caused what no one dared
to call a class conflict. In Western Europe, the social
consensus fractured for different reasons. Two decades
of wage restraint collapsed under strikes on the continent between 1968 and 1970, and later in Britain under union pressure on a Labor government. After a
generation in which prices had barely seemed to move
at all, inflation in the United States and most of its
major industrial partners blipped for a time at about 5
percent. Worse was to come.

Beware of oversimplifications by robust partisans of
self-help. A generation ago, conservatives in America
were predicting the unravelling of society if the government's share of our national income went above 25
percent. Ronald Reagan continues to cite that figure
in the face of evidence to the contrary. But inflation
was not caused merely by some woolly-minded welfare
impulse toward higher levels of government spending.
During the 1970s, the Japanese, the Swiss, and the
West Germans all raised the share of the income they
spent through their governments by about ten percentage points. The first two spent between 25 and 30
percent of their income through the government, and
the West Germans spent almost 45 percent. Yet all
three ended the decade with the lowest inflation rates
and, not coincidentally, the most efficient production
techniques in the industrialized world. During the same

period, all government in the United States—federal, state, and local—spent roughly a steady 30 percent of Americans' income on their behalf, yet inflation rose relentlessly. Under Ronald Reagan, the government's share rose above 36 percent, but inflation actually fell.

Not big spenders but spenders by stealth are what cause inflation. As Lyndon Johnson said, "If I talk about the cost of the war, the Great Society won't go through." He didn't mean to leave a legacy of inflation, but it worked out that way because, as he also admitted, "I don't know much about economics." It is not the absolute level of government spending that boosts prices, but a suden change effected without a new consensus between the pleased new beneficiaries and the enforced donors, between the sharpies and the suckers in this unexpected social tug of war. Further proof lies in the experience of the 1970s. Those with lower inflation rates were Japan and the Germanic and Scandinavian countries, all of them organized around some notion of a social bargain among government, business, and labor. Inflation seriously afflicted the adversarial Anglo-Saxon societies such as our own. And it positively raged in the Latin societies of France, Spain, and Italy, whose citizens often feel they are living on the edge of anarchy. In Italy they actually were. Its rate of inflation is persistently the highest of any major industrialized country.

If the cracking of domestic social compacts had been the industrial world's only problem, the Great Inflation never would have merited its name. But the political ambitions of Richard Nixon for a massive and guaranteed reelection, piled atop the costs of the Vietnam War, combined to cut the last vestige of any international restraint on American policy. He destroyed the international monetary compact established at Bretton Woods. The kindly English scholar Austin Robinson had described it as creating "a world in which countries did not close their eyes to the repercussions of their actions on others." It had served as the rulebook for the *belle époque*. This does not mean it was a compact among equals; it was, after all, one of the things that signaled the start of The American

Century. But that made it a more workable compact than one in which too many weak countries would have joined in enforcing the rules, a situation that has helped doom the United Nations.

Political scientists have coined a word, hegemon, for the postwar role of the United States. It derives from the Greek word for leadership as well as from its English cognate, meaning political dominance. America had succeeded Britain reluctantly in the role. The precise moment probably was the day in 1947 when the British ambassador to Washington called on the State Department to announce that London no longer could help Greece fight back the Communist uprising. The wise economic historian Charles P. Kindleberger, who first learned about international commerce working aboard freighters during his college vacations, believes that the Depression of the 1930s might have been averted or at least limited if the United States had taken over Britain's nineteenth-century role as crisis banker to the world. Instead of hegemon, he prefers a simpler word: "I prefer to think of it as responsibility."

With leadership come privileges as well as responsibilities. Matching its military role as a superpower, America had the hegemon's responsibility of balancing the world's financial flows and economic forces, and it was to maintain that balance because it held the majority of the world's gold reserves and a virtual monopoly on the most efficient production processes. In return, it had the privilege of being the world's banker, which meant it could issue IOUs on its gold to settle its international accounts. Other countries would have to accept the IOUs of the hegemon. They were in dollars, the successor currency to the British pound and, before that, the Spanish doubloon. In earlier centuries, other countries willingly held both currencies in their reserves until both governments started draining the gold content of their money.

But the Bretton Woods System worked smoothly only as long as America's economic power was unchallenged, its policies remained prudent, and the dollar remained scarce enough to hold its value. By 1960, foreigners were regaining their prosperity and held more dollars than America's $19 billion stock of gold. In theory, they could have cashed in their dollar IOUs for gold and broken the bank. That threat was the U.S. allies' only leash on the policies of their hegemon; it would have been the equivalent of a mutiny in the ranks. The allies did not use this ultimate deterrent because they all realized they would have been worse off in a world without monetary order or, as a direct corollary, without the military order paid for by the country that also served as their bank. But once U.S. power shifted from absolute dominance to a mutual balance of advantage, America was more like other countries and other banks. The credibility of its banknotes depended on the plausibility of the use of its power, and not just its power alone.

Through the 1960s, the price of gold bubbled as the United States refused to sacrifice jobs at home or limit its adventures overseas in order to protect the dollar's value. It just kept printing more of them and inveigled its allies into holding more dollars in their financial reserves instead of demanding gold. Only Charles de Gaulle of France publicly refused; the French well knew the extent of America's quagmire in their old colony of Vietnam. Gradually the balance shifted. From holding half the world's reserves in 1950, the United States held only 15 percent in 1970 and 11 percent one year later. The others accepted America's dollars as IOUs because they could hold them as reserves. Commercial calculation made it convenient for the others to swallow dollars in vast amounts. Had they refused, the dollar would sink in value against their currencies, their exports would be more expensive, and they would lose jobs to American workers. Their dilemma was forcibly resolved by Richard Nixon in a way that, as he might say, made the Great Inflation great.

18

The Great Inflation Machine

Like most Republicans, Richard Nixon is commonly thought of as a hard-money man. In office, however, he ran a virtual money machine. During 1969, the first year of his presidency, he inherited a Vietnam inflation rate of almost 7 percent, highest since the end of World War II. He decreed a policy of "gradualism" in winding it down, like the war, to avoid the pain of a slump. Like the inevitable and agonizing military defeat, the slump came anyway. By 1971, unemployment was edging toward 6 percent, and the election campaign was less than a year away. The memory of the recession that had cost him the presidency in 1960 gave him an almost visceral fear of unemployment. He had appointed an activist ally at the Federal Reserve, Arthur Burns, an old-fashioned man who had made his career studying business cycles and then was Eisenhower's economic adviser. He parted his hair in the middle and had a voice with a confidential twang that sounded like W. C. Fields. A conservative by temperament, he nevertheless warned publicly upon taking office that, "in the event of a recession, I'll be a dangerous radical."

When recession came, Burns needed no coaching to apply the standard medicine. During the first half of 1971, the Fed doubled the rate at which it increased the supply of dollars. Even that did not fully satisfy Nixon and his palace guard, and Burns remained under relentless pressure from the White House, which had swallowed a quick-acting, harebrained monetary theory devised by an economist named Arthur Laffer. (This was his first Washington incarnation; he returned to influence again with the supply-siders who clustered around Ronald Reagan.) Billions of these newly printed greenbacks began fleeing abroad, and finally foreigners had had enough of them. Foreign central banks had to swallow more than three times as many dollars as they had the year before. By May 1971, the Dutch and the Belgians joined the French in turning in dollars for gold. They took out more than one million pounds of gold between May 3 and 12. West Germany and several other countries simply closed their markets for a week and would take no dollars at all. So much for the Almighty Dollar.

By August, in order to slow inflation and cut the trade deficit, Nixon and his advisers had secretly devised a program of import taxes and America's first peacetime wage and price controls. In one of his favored long-ball passes that confounded his opponents, the President had just turned his back on his anti-Communist upbringing by recognizing the Peking government. But his Treasury Secretary, John Connally, a Texas Democrat who was a boardroom version of his original mentor, Lyndon Johnson, warned Nixon privately that playing the China card could not in itself win him the 1972 election, while the economy could lose it for him. The decisions were shaped without consulting the public or the nation's allies in advance. Nixon and a small cabal of economic advisers left for Camp David on the afternoon of Friday, August 13, 1971, and came down from the mountain that Sunday in time for the President to announce on television what he called his New Economic Policy of wage and price controls. No one noticed until it was too late that this was the same title Lenin gave to his 1921 program after the initial reforms of the Bolshevik Revolution had failed.

Nixon feared he would be attacked for his most fundamental decision, that the United States would no longer exchange gold for dollars. Cutting that link formally demolished the Bretton Woods System and removed even the loose leash that America's allies had held on its economic directions. It meant that the United States could print all the dollars it needed to inflate its economy without worrying whether the Dutch, the French, or anyone else would try to recycle them back across the Atlantic for more of the treasure in Fort Knox. That would help lubricate the reelection of Richard Nixon with easy money to create jobs (a policy that, by comparison, really does make Watergate look like a third-rate burglary). If too many dollars landed abroad, well, the allies could go ahead and choke on them. That is exactly what happened.

Cooperation was replaced by Connally's bruising tactics, which spoke for a brand of economic nationalism that later was publicly acknowledged under Reagan. He was a man without vision and with principles on a level with Nixon's. This he implicitly acknowledged by lightheartedly comparing himself to a schoolteacher being interviewed by the local school board and asked how he would teach world geography: "Either way. I can teach it round or flat." Although he denied he meant to be a bully, one of Connally's battle cries in planning a confrontation with a stubborn opponent was, "Let's kick him in the nuts."

These highly effective tactics hardly made for durable policy. In the short term, they served Connally to negotiate a long-overdue devaluation of the dollar, which was agreed at a meeting of finance ministers at the Smithsonian Institution in December 1971. No one who was there will ever forget Nixon's bizarre appearance in the Great Hall, bathed in television lights under the historic airplanes hanging from the ceiling. The finance ministers and central bankers of the industrialized world had been restively corraled behind a velvet rope as a captive audience for the President to announce "the most significant monetary agreement in the history of the world." The Smithsonian Agreement, a sorry successor to the Bretton Woods System, lasted all of fourteen months before restraints were loosened completely and currencies were allowed to float freely, but the going was good before the crash came.

Throughout the election year of 1972, the Federal Reserve ground out 9.2 percent more money than in the previous year. Staff economists who questioned the rate were ridiculed by Arthur Burns, who became a victim of his own argument. Having led the argument for wage and price controls as a defense against inflation, he could hardly maintain that growth in money would reignite it. In fact, the controls merely delayed the day of reckoning until their removal. Nixon did his part by turning up the fiscal steam. With his budget already programmed for the second largest postwar deficit, the President ordered his cabinet to spend as much as possible in the first half of the year. Only the Pentagon hit its spending target, but they had a war on anyway. Even so, the best the entire administration could produce was a flow of red ink totaling $23 billion, pale by today's standards.

Nixon's pre-election spending spree helped propel more than $50 billion into the reserves of foreign countries between 1970 and 1973—creating more new reserve money, as the Yale economist Robert Triffin calculated in hyperbole worthy of Nixon himself, "than in all previous years and centuries since Adam and Eve." The recipients of this unwanted largesse had no choice but to lie back and accept it. No American gold was on offer anymore, except in the private market, and the price was rising. Any country that wanted to run a prudent anti-inflation policy by raising interest rates risked finding even more dollars on its doorstep chasing higher rates. This influx of money in turn would boost the value of its currency, making its exports more expensive and costing jobs. Resisting inflation thus had a negative payoff. And why shouldn't they lie back and enjoy it? It was the election season, and not only in America. From the summer of 1972 to the spring of 1973, West Germany, Japan, France, Italy, and Canada held elections. With the United States, they represented almost four-fifths of the industrial world's gross national product, and their leaders wanted that GNP to boom, baby, boom.

In the second half of 1972, the world's major industrial countries grew at a rate of more than 6 percent, and in the next half-year by more than 8 percent. The British Conservative governnnent of Edward Heath printed money in a dash for growth; it overflowed into inflationary real estate speculation instead of industrial investment and forced Britain to unpeg the pound from its Smithsonian value. When H. R. Haldeman, Nixon's chief of staff, brought him the news of this first crack in history's most significant monetary agreement, the President apparently couldn't care less. As Nixon said, "It's too complicated for me to get into." But the Italian lire might be next, warned Haldeman. Replied the leader of the Western world, "I don't give a shit about the lire." This characteristic episode is drawn from the Watergate tapes. By the following March, with the Watergate dam almost ready to break in Congressional hearings, it is hardly surprising that Nixon gave up on the dollar, too, and let it float.

With a little help from vengeful gods, the dollar flood spilled quickly into inflation everywhere. The unchecked boom jacked up world raw material prices by an annual rate of 25 percent in the second half of 1972, and 50 percent in the following half-year. By April 1974, they peaked 2½ times higher than they started in 1972. Food prices trebled in three years, pushed upward by the failure of the Russian grain harvest, a raid on low American stocks by Soviet buyers operating in secret, and, finally, by the sudden disappearance of millions of anchovies off the coast of Peru that would otherwise have made themselves available to be ground up into cattlefeed. But the biggest push to inflation was, of course, the fourfold rise in the price of oil in 1973. Altogether, these events raised the inflation rate in a rough but relentless mathematical progression into double digits within three years. From just under 4 percent before the 1972 election, it jumped to 8 percent in 1973 and a raging 12 percent in 1974.

Nixon liked neat, surgical strikes; as in Cambodia, he thought they would solve problems once and for all. Alas, they usually just created more problems, especially for those they were designed in part to help, like the unfortunate Cambodians. In his favored turf of geopolitics, Nixon usually understood what he was doing and deserved his reputation for sinister mastery. But in economics, he was an amateur who saw the subject as a mere handmaiden to electoral politics. In those years, I used to talk with a then unknown rhetorical operative named William Safire, who divided his time on the White House payroll between writing inflammatory speeches for Spiro Agnew and devising more sanitized economic hyperbole for the Big Boss. Having served early in his professional life as a Wall Street plunger, this ambitious Brooklyn boy was well trained for his job. Safire understood Nixon's economic thinking, to the extent that Nixon thought about the subject at all. Once Safire correctly warned me off a particular line of speculation by saying, "Don't always assume that we do everything here for Machiavellian reasons. Sometimes we are just stupid." That usually depended on whether the view was short term or long term. It is to Safire's official notes that historians will always be indebted for the most authoritative account of what happened at Camp David, published in his book *Before the Fall*. The dialogue makes it plain that in the serious economic subjects under discussion, Nixon fully grasped the essentials but applied the cynical techniques of short-term political management with Machiavellian finesse. Arthur Burns, then Chairman of the Federal Reserve Board, and Paul Volcker, then a senior Treasury official who would later occupy Burns' post, were both present at Camp David. Nixon instinctively knew, as they did not, that he could get away with breaking the link between the dollar and gold by blaming the whole mess on "international speculators" attacking "our dollar." The stupid part of the operation was that Nixon the geopolitician hardly seems to have thought at all about the long-term effects on the postwar international economic order.

What the President really wanted to have ligatured conveniently for the United States was nothing less than the financial discipline of the Bretton Woods

System. It forced governments to take prudent and often politically painful steps against inflation in order to guard the reserves of gold or foreign currency that stood behind their money. As the European author Luigi Barzini has remarked, Americans never realize fully what they are up to, and "the consequences of some of their actions are sometimes as surprising and shocking to themselves as to the rest of the world." OPEC did not just come galloping out of the desert on a camel. One of those who participated in the Camp David discussions, Nixon's chief economic adviser, Paul McCracken, reflected on its rueful effects just fifteen years afterward in the columns of *The Wall Street Journal*: "When the 1970s are finally seen with historical perspective, the explosion of inflation in that decade will be seen to owe as much to the removal of this [financial] discipline, with the collapse of the Bretton Woods system, as to higher oil prices."

19

The Revolution of 1973

The year 1973 should have ended national illusions about money, oil, our military reach, and our political virginity. Instead of engendering a sober sense of realism, it seems mainly to have produced scapegoats—Arabs, bankers, peaceniks, and Richard Nixon himself. The collapse of America's control over the world's most important and widely traded raw material was no more an accident than its lapses over the world's dominant currency. Money and oil have many similarities. Both are fungible, bankable, but potentially mercurial, and no modern economy can function without a secure supply of either at a relatively predictable price. Except for a volatile twenty-year hiatus between the breakup of John D. Rockefeller's Standard Oil Trust in 1911 and the assumption of production controls by the state of Texas in the Depression, the world price of oil has always been regulated. U.S. policy to ensure this was an important element of the postwar consensus, and this, admittedly, has always been one of the more unseemly aspects of the common-law marriage between business and government.

When the oil business went fully international after World War II, five American and two British companies openly managed the world market for oil. They were known to all as the Seven Sisters and reviled by populists with little sense of either past or future. It was assumed that without them, oil would be even

cheaper. The companies operated in a traditional if
occasionally sinister partnership with government, including the CIA when necessary to rid Iran of a regime that nationalized its oilfields in 1951. They had
already gained certain antitrust exemptions and tax
concessions just after the end of World War II, in
partial exchange for which the State Department declared that "American oil operations should be the
instruments of foreign policy in the Middle East." As
Anthony Sampson points out in his book *The Seven
Sisters,* these arrangements permitted the United States
to give overt political support to Israel while giving
covert economic support to the Arabs, a laudable piece
of hegemonic perfidy worthy of Victorian England.

When President Eisenhower wanted to stop the invasion of the Suez Canal by Britain and France in
1956, American opposition in the United Nations was
only the dignified but not the efficient instrument. The
two countries backed down under America's threat to
cut off Western Europe's oil supplies, an almost pitiful
demonstration that they had definitively become second-
class powers. After they fell in line, U.S. oil companies organized a supply line for Western Europe from
America's own oil reserves. Being a superpower meant
more than possessing nuclear missiles; Britain and
France soon had them pointed at Russia but it availed
them little. So powerful and confident were the oil
companies and their political masters that when Saudi
Arabia threatened the West with an oil embargo after
Israel defeated the Arabs in the 1967 War, the threat
went unnoticed. The arrogance that created Vietnam
had infected American business.

The key to the power equation in both oil and
money is a reserve supply. Try to imagine money as
well as oil circulating in a hydraulic system. Whoever
controls the hydraulic reservoir can control the supply,
and thus the price, as long as he is willing on occasion
to defer today's advantage until tomorrow. He simply
shuts down the reservoir to control the hydraulic pressure. This demands a bourgeois deferment of gratifica-
tion, which is the essence of capitalism in marketing as
well as investment. Nobody knew that better than

Rockefeller. In 1888, he said, "The dear people, if they had produced less oil than they wanted, would have got their full price; no combination in the world could have prevented that, if they had produced less oil than the world required." Spending dollar reserves for shortsighted political advantage weakened American hegemony; when the dollar floated, America in effect gave up its hydraulic dollar reserve. Ignoring the erosion of American oil reserves further weakened American power by opening the way for the Organization of Petroleum Exporting Countries to supplant the Seven Sisters.

Until 1970, there were enough idle U.S. oil wells to serve as a reserve equal to about 25 percent of national consumption. Less than 20 percent of America's oil was imported, so the threat of an Arab embargo could simply be shrugged off. But then OPEC began turning the screw. Populists would be surprised to learn that they had formed their organization out of resentment after the oil companies had actually reduced the prices they paid the producing countries. In 1971, OPEC was able to raise prices by one-fifth and sought a modest total increase of one-half over five years. By 1973, U.S. reserve capacity had slumped to 10 percent because of America's insatiable appetite for oil, both domestic and foreign. Thirty-five percent of the oil used in America was imported, mainly from the Middle East. The power equation had turned against the United States. Surplus capacity had evaporated under rising demand throughout the industrialized world because the companies preferred to draw their oil from the cheaper wells in the Middle East. They ignored until too late the political dangers to the security of their supply. American companies hardly prospected at home. The first wells in the state of Alaska were drilled not by an American company but by British Petroleum. With demand rising incrementally, their policy was still moved by historic fears of glut. In 1972, Frank Ikard, a former Texas congressman who was the oil industry's most important lobbyist in Washington, boasted to me: "The one thing the oil companies have done that certainly deserves full credit has been to assure secure oil supplies." Eighteen months later, that had a very hollow ring.

Like the British who thought the Egyptians would never be able to operate the Suez Canal by themselves, Americans in both business and government never dreamed that the desert oil sheiks, who in their minds seemed to have been typecast from the film *Lawrence of Arabia,* could organize against them. A White House oil task force saw little danger of a boycott in a 1970 report that, significantly, was dominated by free-market economists and defended by Secretary of Labor George Shultz, as he then was. (Just as the spendthrift Weinberger was put in charge of the Pentagon a decade later, the apolitical all-purpose Shultz was put in charge of the State Department. This says something curious about Ronald Reagan's sense of governance.) But the Arab oil countries saw the balance tilting. When American oil companies reluctantly granted their Middle East wards a price increase in 1971, George Piercy of Exxon was reminded quietly by Saudi Arabia's Sheik Ahmed Zaki Yamani, later to figure heavily in Western demonology, that Western oil supplies were tightly stretched. "George," said Sheik Yamani, "you know you cannot take a shutdown." The oil countries' frustration mounted with the devaluation of the dollar, which also devalued their revenues.

But when the shutdown came in 1973, the motive was essentially political retaliation against the West for supporting and supplying Israel in the Yom Kippur War. The embargo held, and the shortage set off a price panic. Fearful of losing their supplies, Western governments refused to cooperate in preventing the oil companies from bidding up prices, to the amazement of the oil producers. Even the Shah of Iran, who so enjoyed strutting his new power, later admitted candidly to Anthony Sampson that he had not understood until then how weak the Seven Sisters had been. Instead of coordinating policy with the companies on the nation's most important raw material, the administration had abdicated it to them. Like fat eunuchs, the companies had been captured by their suppliers. The vacuum of power, authority, and leadership could not have been more complete. When the Saudis announced their oil embargo on October 20, 1973, America was wallowing in Watergate. That was the same date as the Saturday Night Massacre, when Nixon fired the Justice Department lawyers who were pursuing him.

With money and oil floating, the hydraulic controls of the Western price system had been switched off. Nixon's resignation in disgrace coincided with the inflationary peak of 1974. But in fact his manipulation of the nation's finances and his neglect of its resources, both for political advantage, already had provided much of the power behind the Great Inflation. It was, of course, easier to pander to popular prejudice and blame OPEC's "oil price gougers," as some of the most distinguished organs of the American press called them in the prevailing hysteria. But they were hardly capable of masterminding any conspiracy, let alone one of worldwide scale, and in fact they had stumbled into their good fortune through Western, and specifically American, neglect.

Their mythical image, verging on racist caricature, is that of a group of hook-nosed men in robes sitting in a desert tent simultaneously carving up the world oil market and the world economy, while their Texas-trained underlings serve them cups of tea and plates of crunched numbers on world oil supply and demand. As anyone who has ever been near an OPEC meeting knows, the reality is even more ludicrous. Each oil minister would reserve a suite on or near the penthouse floor of a modern hotel, usually the Inter-Continental in Geneva or Vienna. Members of each entourage would shuttle back and forth from one hotel suite to another, bearing messages about what each minister thought the new, and putatively higher, oil price ought to be. Thus the bargaining would proceed in slow motion. Occasionally, an oil minister would descend to the hotel lobby, peer into the glare of television lights, utter a few sentences reeking of Koranic wisdom, and enjoy every second of his notoriety.

In its glory days, it was a political bazaar with economic chips: which country could be the most hawkish, the most daring? Through most of the 1970s, the palm was wrested from Libya by the Shah of Iran, who enjoyed telling the industrialized West that its day was done. As long as the low level of Western oil reserves handed OPEC an inflationary sellers' market, it operated as a rather disorganized price ring, floating from one luxury hotel to another. It never even faintly resembled a Rockefeller-style cartel that controlled production, because so few of its members were willing to try. When a farcical attempt was made briefly early in the 1980s under Sheik Yamani, a Harvard Law School graduate who matched Western and Arab talents for conciliation, the necessary benchmark production figures did not even come from the members of the price ring themselves. Since they did not trust each other enough to share them, the figures for their own production came from the international oil companies.

What was all this, really? A world caught in an international tug of war that no elected government was able to stop by acting only on the domestic level. That would have meant exacting the Arabs' full price directly from their citizens—and voters. The money could only have come straight out of wages. If the Bretton Woods System had been in effect, this is what they would have been forced to do. Such a quick adjustment would have been intolerable in the short run, but there are ways to borrow around these things for a little while. The eventual necessity of balancing international accounts, instead of letting them float, would have forced governments and their people to confront the dilemma instead of ducking it and eventually dealing with it through inflationary stealth.

The rise in oil prices had presented all governments with a conundrum. Its most obvious and immediate effect was inflationary. But it simultaneously acted like a huge tax that they were powerless to repeal. Among all industrial countries, it was the rough equivalent of a sales tax of two cents on the dollar. Like any tax, it slowed private spending—and the economy along with it. But governments got none of the benefits in balancing their books, because they were not the tax collectors. The revenues instead went to Colonel

Muammar Gaddafi of Libya, the King of Saudi Arabia, or the Shah of Iran. Some of them succumbed to a classical combination of megalomania and the touch of Midas, but that took time.

In the West, this led to a condition so new that no one had a name for it. By 1974, the oil shock created the worst inflation since the end of World War II, and the following year the highest unemployment since the Depression. The disease was worldwide. Economist Robert Triffin, a Belgian by birth, came up with an Esperanto-style "infession" from inflation-and-recession. Leonard Silk of *The New York Times* tried "slumpflation," which might have come from Piglet's nightmare zoo. What stuck was the term stagflation, which seems to have invented itself and which nobody liked any more than the disease. No one dared to cure it. In the style of Herbert Hoover, Gerald Ford, a former college football player, called summits of businessmen, academics, and assorted worthies. What came out of it was a rallying cry to "Whip Inflation Now!" WIN. Get it?

To no avail. For the rest of the decade, there were few winners. Until the inflation of the second oil shock, in 1979, made the policy intolerable, Jimmy Carter made good on his pledge to create jobs by running budget deficits. This is what presidential economists had been used to recommending for the previous decade. (Carter had five economics Ph.D.s in his cabinet.) Once again, the foreign dimension was last on the list. Carter's Treasury secretary talked down the dollar to increase exports until it lost 20 percent of its value and nobody wanted it. Instead of paying interest, Swiss banks demanded a fee from depositors to keep their dollars. King Khalid of Saudi Arabia wrote Jimmy Carter to warn him that unless his dollars stopped eroding, he would have to raise the price of oil again. Carter tried to mollify him on a trip to Saudi Arabia, and it became clear that the President was boxed in. Less than halfway through his term, he had to go on television to announce that he was raising interest rates. His rhetoric was no more credible than Ford's:

an energy policy was "the moral equivalent of war";
the country was suffering from a national "malaise."

Indeed it was. Look back at that Dreary Decade,
which ended in the apocalypse that wasn't. Remember
The Crash of '79, Paul Erdman's financial thriller about
the Shah of Iran and the money markets that didn't
come true? Or almost didn't? Trying to leapfrog the
oil sheiks by inflating the dollar didn't work. They
leapfrogged again by raising oil prices after the revolution in Iran cut supplies and OPEC got another chance.
Governments were powerless to stop their own companies from bidding up the price in 1979 and 1980.
Double-digit inflation, never far away in the middle of
the decade, returned at the end. So did gas lines,
lowered speed limits, small cars, and home insulation.
Shadows fell across the dollar as a world currency
when Iranian assets were frozen during the hostage
crisis. The gold price hit $850 an ounce after the
Russians invaded Afghanistan. And, finally, there was
the flight from financial paper into anything solid that
wouldn't go up in inflationary smoke. Oil, of course,
did best of all in the Dreary Decade. At an annual
yield of almost 30 percent, it did more than eight times
better than stocks and bonds. Anyone who had put his
money in 1972 into such exotic investments as Oriental
rugs, gold, and Chinese ceramics could have earned
on average at least four times more money during the
following decade than those who bet on the stock
market. Even silver, diamonds, and farmland did at
least three times better than the classic bourgeois investments. But at about 3½ percent return per year,
stocks and bonds increased at less than half the rate of
inflation.

In the redoubts of radical chic, it is no wonder that
they thought they were squinting into the twilight of
capitalism. Robert Heilbroner, the Norman Thomas
Professor of Economics at the New School for Social
Research, who once proudly wrote that his discipline
"has sent men to the barricades," now warned that the
economy was moving "beyond boom and crash," as if
it were a patient etherized upon a table. "The system
is crisis-prone," he wrote, "not because it cannot make

its subcircuits operate, but because the very act of successfully operating them creates tensions that make the economy vulnerable to breakdown." Remember the Club of Rome, which popularized the idea that the end is nigh? Publishing computer-generated charts that looked like fingerpainting whorls, the group warned that "population and industrial growth will certainly stop in the next century, at the latest," because the world was running out of everything, at exponential rates.

Even the sturdiest pillars of the Establishment began to tremble. Marina von Neumann Whitman, daughter of the man who invented the computer, first woman to serve as a presidential economic adviser, and later chief economist for General Motors, warned that unless the dilemma of stagflation was unraveled, it would mean the end of "a liberal and coherent international economic system." Gurus on Wall Street and in academe had no easy remedy to offer those directing the economy; many feared that inflation was destroying society, but that the cure, a recession, would be worse than the disease. On August 6, 1979, G. William Miller, the businessman who had failed miserably at his primary task of stabilizing the currency as Chairman of the Federal Reserve Board, attended the installation of his successor. Miller described the times as "the most distressing economic environment in fifty years"—a deliberate allusion to the Depression. "Inflation has struck at our nation's vitality," he continued. "If it is not checked, then it will threaten our democratic system itself." His successor was Paul Volcker, who happened to agree. Terming the nation's difficulties "unique," Volcker added: "And we have lost that euphoria that we had fifteen years ago, that we had all the answers. . . ."

20

"Stop Printing Money to Cover the National Debt!"

Few men change the course of history, and even fewer change it for the better. Paul Volcker did what everyone said could not be done: he manufactured a recession, pushed it to the edge by flirting with a world financial crisis, and finally sweated inflation out of society. He administered a purge that no elected official had dared. At the disposal of the Federal Reserve was only the blunt instrument of monetary policy, which offers just one lever. It can control the fuel for the engine of the economy by restraining or relaxing the availability of money and credit. Fiscal policy, which operates through the federal budget, can nudge the economy in various ways by adjusting taxes and spending money in areas that are deemed socially desirable or economically productive, or both. But monetary policy can go just two ways. Forward or backward, that's all. Volcker himself described his technique as "not very subtle: restraint, as consistent as we could make it." Backward.

Starting in 1979, when Jimmy Carter had lost credibility in fields far beyond the economy, and continuing through the first administration of Ronald Reagan, who then regained most of what Carter had lost, Paul Volcker and the six other members of the Federal Reserve Board, but mainly Volcker, made economic stabilization policy for the United States and the world. When dollar interest rates rose, the rest of the world was forced to follow, or risk losing its dollar reserves. Other countries may have preferred other weapons against inflation. But with the world on the dollar standard because no one else wanted the responsibility of managing—or mismanaging—the world's currency, others had to use the policies manufactured and exported by the United States. Nevertheless, when it came time for Reagan to reappoint Volcker chairman in 1983, Wall Street, London, and Frankfurt would hear of no other candidate. The financial markets hired him in the inflation panic of 1979, and they rehired him in 1983 as the only person they would trust. In clarity of purpose, mastery of detail, management of men, and dedication to the public service, Volcker's career and character have few recent equals. He is the son of the city manager of Teaneck, New Jersey, who imbued his children with the inflexible ideals of service inherited from the family's origins in the Bismarckian state. In modern American history, the figure Volcker most closely resembles is General George C. Marshall, selfless manager of America's armies in World War II and Secretary of State during the creation of the postwar system. Only events will determine whether Volcker's accomplishments are as durable.

Well before his arrival, the Fed had lost virtually all credibility as guardian of the nation's currency. By common consent, even inflation itself had been surpassed by the fear that it would get worse; the buzzword was "inflationary expectations." What was originally a game of social and international leapfrog had taken on a life of its own. Businessmen and workers had come to expect that the government would validate higher prices and wages by printing money. By the 1970s, demands had been stoked by the expectations of the *belle époque*, and no politician would risk saying how inflated these expectations had become. Hence the political predisposition to delay the day of reckoning by issuing at least a bit more money, even if it did not represent real wealth. When this became politically intolerable, it still was easier to operate at arm's length through the manipulation of the supply of money, rather than directly and painfully on the illusions of society itself by saying no to its demands.

Thus had risen to fashion Milton Friedman, one of those brilliant one-idea cranks who recur in American history, like Henry George and his single tax on land, or Mary Baker Eddy and Christian Science. Professor Friedman believes he has found an almost automatic formula for stabilizing the economy through the central monetary authority, which is what the Fed is. Through a lifetime of painstaking research at the University of Chicago, this prodigious scholar gathered masses of statistics through which he claims to be able to prove that the supply of money made available in the United States has historically been the principal determinant of the nation's economic activity. From this he concludes that if a relatively steady quantity of money is applied consonant to the economy's needs, all will be well, at least in the long run. As Keynes used to say before Friedman came on the scene, "In the long run, we are all dead."

Friedman's idea was a useful corrective to the system founded on Keynes. A child of paternalist Victorian rationalism, Keynes had been disgusted by the stupidity that had helped cause the world slump. He trained his formidable conceptual powers on the real economy of goods and services and determined that it could be revived by waving incentives at it. ("The engine which drives enterprise is not thrift, but profit," he said.) Friedman's accomplishment was simply to restate a few forgotten premises: there could be too much of a good thing, namely money. His problem is that he came to view his idea as a panacea, when all it amounted to was little more than a revival of the classical Quantity Theory of Money.

This had a timely implication for policy. Simply stated, the Quantity Theory implied that if there is too much money floating around, it will spill over into higher prices instead of serving as an incentive to the production of more goods. Further, it implied that if businessmen and workers could somehow be convinced that the supply of money is not inexhaustible, they would restrain their demands under the threat of going broke for lack of ready cash. (That is how the gold standard worked in the nineteenth century, and it produced some whopping financial panics when cash suddenly disappeared. But that was a different age with different politics.) The Quantity Theory can be boiled down to a patent-medicine formula: $MV = PT$. This truly sounds painless, indeed bloodless. If you reduce the quantity of money (M), the equation says that the sum on the other side goes down, too, especially prices (P). And in a time of inflation, P is what you're really worrying about. Nobody likes to talk too much about the other two letters, because if you are a member of the Federal Reserve Board and vote to reduce M, then T can also go down, and probably will. T equals the total amount of the transactions in the economy. When T goes down, that's a recession, buddy. And you're going to catch hell if you were the one who reduced T by turning down the dial marked M. No wonder the Fed moved cautiously.

When things don't work out quite the way Friedman and his disciples forecast, they blame changes on the velocity (V) with which everyone spends his money. Unfortunately, no one has figured out how to measure directly the speed at which money moves in a society where people are always promising that "the check is in the mail." And just what is money, anyway? Checks, cash, NOW accounts, savings? All of these and many others, in fact, including offshore animals like Eurodollars. A whole set of measures was developed to monitor different kinds of ready cash, depending on just how ready it is: M-1, M-2, M-3, and so on. Over in England, where Friedman gained some popularity with Mrs. Thatcher, the Bank of England discovered that as soon as it announced a new measure to guide its policy, that M would be distorted by money traders betting against it. All this has given rise to justifiable criticisms that the supply of money affects the real economic world of buying and selling, and hiring and firing, through some mysterious "black box," rather like what happens when your car starts making funny noises and you take it in for a checkup and the man says that will be $375 to replace that shiny black whoozit behind the transmission.

None of this criticism disturbed Professor Friedman in the least. In fact, he thrived on it. A small, bald, irrepressible man, he is a tireless polemicist and a brilliant publicist. He wrote unpleasant letters to his old friend and colleague Arthur Burns, complaining that Dr. Burns as chairman of the Fed had failed to maintain a steady rate for the emission of money. When I used to visit Dr. Burns at the Fed, he expressed occasional fears for his friend's emotional balance. Friedman campaigned for his money measures in Congressional hearings and in a highly readable column in *Newsweek*. Congress then passed a law making the Chairman of the Fed report twice a year on his targets for issuing money, but all the different M's made the law even easier to evade than the Internal Revenue Code.

Most of all, Friedman made converts on Wall Street. Why shouldn't money be what makes the world go round? Never mind that Friedman's friends in government, like Paul McCracken, once warned that his "cold turkey cure is not available in the modern world." The people who make their living dealing in paper money began to think it ought to be, because the alternative looked even worse. Get the Fed to turn off the tap, hard, with a wrench. Stop the party. Let everyone dry out. After all, something is very wrong when your stamp collection, your Oriental rugs, the paintings on the wall, and even oil in the ground are making you richer than the financial paper you trade every working day. Inflation is simultaneously shrinking the wages of the ordinary people Marx called "workers of hand and brain," and the value of the stocks and bonds you are selling them in exchange for their savings. When they wake up to it, they might start getting nasty ideas.

The Fed is like a Supreme Court of money. Formally independent of the elected government, it has great power within its chosen discipline but can exercise that power only when it moves with the tides in society. By the end of the 1970s, society had grown sick of inflation. Polls indicated, and politicians realized, that inflation was far outdistancing unemployment as the principal domestic worry. What the Carter White House wanted was a pillar of rectitude to reassure the financial community at a time of raging inflation. Volcker was not the first choice of the Carter White House, and the staff had no idea what a tough customer they were getting. Stuart Eizenstat, Carter's domestic policy adviser, concedes that "the President should have known, but he didn't." It was another nail in his political coffin.

Irving Shapiro of Du Pont, Reginald Jones of General Electric, and bankers including A. W. Clausen of the Bank of America, were among those canvassed. But none of these worthies from the private sector would have been as tough as Volcker, or as well known in both Washington and Wall Street. None of them would have been as technically knowledgeable and therefore as confident in command of the nation's monetary machinery. Nor would they have had the same moral legitimacy to do what he had to do. To move from the presidency of the Federal Reserve Bank of New York to the Chairmanship of the Federal Reserve System in Washington, Volcker took a deep pay cut, left his arthritic wife in New York where she was a bookkeeper, and moved into a small Washington apartment with wooden crates for end tables. A different appointee also might instinctively have been more solicitous of his lifelong comrades in the private sector. George Moore, chairman of the First National City Bank, had complained to Congress during a much milder squeeze in the 1960s, nervously mixing his metaphors. "It strips the gears when you go into reverse at fifty miles an hour and let the clutch out," he said. "Do not give the patient another bottle of castor oil." Repeatedly, the Fed had cocked an ear to such plaints, and even more so when they came from presidents of the United States and not mere presidents of banks. When the Fed raised interest rates to counteract Lyndon Johnson's first Vietnam boom, he summoned its chairman, William McChesney Martin, down to his Texas ranch, twisted his arm, and worked out a compromise.

Twice in the first months of Volcker's chairmanship, the Fed had already raised interest rates with little effect on the real world. This was the traditional way of influencing the availability of money and credit: by raising its price. Financial markets simply shrugged it off. Badly burned by inflation, people still borrowed, despite higher interest rates, in order to "buy now" before inflation raised prices even higher. Why not try the other way and restrict the supply of money instead of its price? The Fed does that by selling bonds and soaking up cash, which was what Wall Street had been begging for. Doing so would shake up the Street and get its attention, and that was what Volcker knew he really had to do. At an unprecedented news conference on a Saturday morning in 1979, followed by a radio broadcast, he announced that the Fed was changing its operating methods. From then on, it would ignore interest rates and focus only on the amount of money it supplied to the economy through the banking system. Milton Friedman redivivus.

But answered prayers are not always felicitous. Sheltered behind its money targets, Volcker's Fed pleaded no-hands as interest rates rose relentlessly so the Fed could sell bonds for cash. The prime rate rose above 21 percent at the end of 1980, just as Ronald Reagan was taking office. When they started blaming *him*, he suddenly developed a severe case of no-handedness and told people to talk to that fellow Volcker. Hardest hit always by the meat-ax of monetary policy are sectors that depend most on borrowed money, especially housing. Thousands of sawed-off two-by-fours, addressed to Paul Volcker, arrived in the mail at the Fed's marble building on Constitution Avenue in Washington. "Relief from high interest rates now," reads one anguished message on a wooden block that has been kept as a souvenir in the Fed's Flow of Funds Division. It sits on the office windowsill next to another that totally contradicts the first. It reads: "Let the free-market system work. Stop printing money to cover the national debt!" That was precisely what was already happening, but the sender apparently did not recognize the financial consequences of his own ideology. Answered prayers hurt just as much on Main Street as on Wall Street.

It took close to four years, from 1979 to 1982, to bring consumer prices down from their high of almost 14 percent to 4 percent. It also took two recessions, an unemployment rate that touched 10 percent, the highest level of business failure since the Depression, and an operational dilemma for the Fed, until it managed to convince the traumatized traders in Wall Street that it was in earnest about inflation. Persuaded as they were of the correctness of Professor Friedman's semi-automatic monetary theories, Wall Street traders waited every Friday afternoon for the Fed's weekly numbers on the size of the money supply. However they came out, up or down, the Fed was damned if it did, damned if it didn't. If the numbers moved down, that was supposed to mean tight money was here to stay, and likewise high interest rates. If the numbers were up, the traders reckoned that the Fed would have to tighten up even more on the money supply, and that would mean higher interest rates anyway. Fortunes could be made and lost in trading government bonds within these narrow estimates of high and higher; the episode came to be called the Friday Afternoon Follies.

So bemused was Wall Street that it lost sight of what actually was happening. Volcker had temporarily adopted Friedman's techniques because they were the only ones the financial community would believe, and their automatic nature helped shield the Fed from attack. In fact, little except lip service was paid to Friedman's monetary targets. (The Professor kept saying that if the Fed did it *his* way, the purge would have been administered more evenly, although it is hard to see how.) A close reading of Volcker's public statements during the entire period shows that his overriding concern was not with operational technicalities but with profound social and political phenomena; with expectations, behavior, restraint, sacrifice, continuity, persistence, patience. All these are his very own words, mostly offered in testimony to Congress. Despite his trademark cloud of twenty-five-cent-cigar smoke, Volcker rarely is obscure and always says precisely what is on his mind. What he does not say is what he proposes to do about it. He dare not, because he is one man with only one monetary lever against the markets, and part of his power is his ability to force them to outguess them.

What he was watching early in the 1980s was the effect of the recession that he had engineered, the worst since World War II, on the tug of war between wages and prices. Meanwhile, he was trying to steer the American economy with his single forward-and-backward tiller. Archimedes said, "Give me a place to stand on, and I will lift the world." Volcker did it, with his one lever, but he almost tilted it over the edge. When it became brutally clear in the early summer of 1982, just before Mexico escaped bankruptcy, that high interest rates were threatening a crash of the world financial system, the Fed suddenly relaxed the lever and turned the money tap back on. Professor Friedman's tactics had outlived their usefulness. Shortly thereafter, he warned that the Fed had not stayed the course, and he wrongly predicted a new outburst of inflation. But the entire operation had depended less on any one technique than on the eclectic skills, political will, and personal character of one man who not only carried it through but—like justice being done— had to be seen to be carrying it through.

Volcker had so won over the market that it could no more bear to lose him than a child its nanny. In Wall Street surveys he led all conceivable candidates for his job by margins of at least four to one. This was by no means an enviable position, and anyone visiting his huge, two-story office at the headquarters of the Fed was unlikely to come away with an impression of a man basking in worldly renown. Although the polls confirmed that Volcker was the second most powerful man in the country, a visit to the Fed is never like a visit to the White House, all pomp and guns. Burns used to come around from behind his desk, puff on his pipe, and confide political wisdom like a kindly professor, occasionally allowing tidbits to be quoted under the guise that he "tells friends" this or that. Volcker sat behind his long desk, sometimes with his feet upon it, his huge frame surrounded by piles of paper, files, and books of reference, the whole overlaid by smoke from his cheap cigars until he quit smoking. He peered through glasses that thickened over the years, asked questions, gave answers sometimes delphic and sometimes suprisingly direct, but wisely admitted he did not always have the answers, which made him a Washington rarity.

Under Reagan, the task of stabilizing the economy fell into Volcker's lap by default because the administration was locked in a debate with Congress over the size and function of government. It turned into a dispute over taxation and spending that dragged on for years and, by doing so, caused the deficit. The Fed coped with it by refusing to print the money to finance it. Throughout Reagan's first term the Fed navigated alone through crosscurrents of rising unemployment and interest rates and an overvalued dollar. It was left to Volcker to warn of rising debt and the other consequences of Administration policy. This hands-off policy suited the administration's free-market ideology. It left the active management to Volcker, so much so that when David Stockman was flirting with the idea of a gold standard, he suddenly realized that the country was already on a "Volcker standard," which was much to be preferred.

Even more, it conveniently suited electoral politics for Volcker to do the managing and take "the political heat," as Treasury Secretary James Baker has characterized it. But it was neither natural nor desirable in an electoral democracy for the single most powerful economic actor to be an appointed official, even one who is more than six feet six inches tall, like the legendary King Arthur, and every bit as incorruptible. The Chairman of the Federal Reserve Board can only help stabilize the currency; he cannot run the economy like some wise and disinterested Platonic guardian. Furthermore, the weapons available to the Fed are limited. The control of the currency is an important balance wheel for the economy, but not the steering wheel. The Federal Reserve Board can no more run the economy single-handedly than the Supreme Court can reform society unaided. If the Board were to try, it could well suffer the same over-reaction by easy-money politicians that was visited on the successors of the Earl Warren court by the zealots of the Reagan administration.

One man steering against the forces of the economy is never a strong enough defense, even when that man was Paul Volcker. Budget policy had atrophied as an economic tool because politicians dared not reverse it when it hurt. The burden thus fell on the thin whip of monetary policy, and in a recession Volcker's successor, Alan Greenspan, will be confronted with a terrible dilemma. Since the budget can stimulate the economy only by adding to the national debt, the burden will fall on the Fed. Its only lever is interest rates, and it can only lower them by printing money. Occasional emergency orders to the printing plant are both necessary and desirable, as they were after the Crash of 1987. But pressures to inflate out of debt were being applied by politicians and businessmen, and the Fed felt them. All that Greenspan and his board need do to please the men who put them in power, while avoiding the appearance of intervening in a presidential election, would be to leave the controls at forward speed and do nothing.

21

More Than Just Economics

The successes of the postwar *belle époque* persuaded the economics profession that its philosopher-kings had at last fashioned the key to the scientific management of the whole of society. As a group, economists tended to dismiss as almost medieval speculation the anxious questions of productive effort and just reward. Except to the degree that they could be measured, these were political questions and therefore tiresome. Their kind of economics was value-free; no choices were demanded among society's competing claims. This philosopher's stone was the gift that economists handed to politicians. To his credit, Ronald Reagan has made his values public: work, effort, reward. The economists who attracted him called themselves supply-siders, and they claimed to be able to remedy at least some of their colleagues' disdain for production and reward. But, like the others, the supply-siders also held out the hope of making hard choices easy. As their convert, they won over the first American president ever to have majored in economics, at the providentially named Eureka College in Illinois, which then had a student body of 250 and an economics faculty of one. The implication of this piece of biographical intelligence is not meant to suggest that Ronald Reagan is a rube.

Quite the reverse. He seems to have absorbed the sophisticated belief of his chosen academic discipline that it is a science, capable of predicting the future and therefore of mastering it.

But why is it that the professors who speak out most strongly in favor of job mobility, economic incentives, and the rigor of the free market always seem to have academic tenure for life? When they make mistakes, they go back to the drawing board. A businessman or a worker who makes a big enough mistake ends up out in the cold. A nation ends up in debt, as ours has. The President, and all of us, would have been better off heeding the advice of Samuel Goldwyn, one of the masters of his earlier profession: "Never prophesy, especially about the future."

Until he met up with the supply-siders, Reagan the political candidate was a disciple of the old-time Republican religion of purging inflation, mainly by a squeeze on money advocated by his friend Milton Friedman and endorsed by his erstwhile political leader Barry Goldwater. As late as 1978, Reagan foresaw unemployment and recession as an inevitable "belly-ache" of a cure for the nation's inflationary binge. This was not exactly the strongest platform for a presidential candidate. Economic education, political necessity, and personal experience seem to have made him vulnerable to the ideas of the supply-siders. They disdained the old-fashioned "root-canal economics" because its politically painful first priority was to cut spending. Instead, they proposed to cut taxes first. Not surprisingly, their program quickly found its way onto the Republican political agenda, was adopted by the Republican National Committee in 1978, and soon by Reagan, the first of his party's serious presidential candidates to do so. It was a populist idea whose time had come; its main proponent was Representative Jack Kemp, a former football player who demonstrated that a Republican could win 80 percent of the vote, blue-collar precincts included, in the dilapidated city of Buffalo, New York.

The supply-side idea was simplicity itself, especially as presented by a buoyant and unorthodox economist named Arthur Laffer. He demonstrated it with a theoretical curve so simple he could (and did) draw it on a table napkin in the shape of a bell. Like $MV = PT$, it merely stated a truism. At a tax rate of zero percent, the government obviously collects no taxes. At a tax rate of 100 percent, the government also collects no taxes, since no one wants to work anymore to make any money at all. Somewhere along the bell curve, as collections rise from zero to 50 percent and then fall back again as the rate reaches 100 percent, sits an optimum level of taxation. At some point, everyone will want to work harder, produce more, and earn more; therefore, the country as a whole would pay more taxes on the increased wealth even if every individual was paying less. Exactly where along the curve stood that point of revenue gain, Professor Laffer sayeth not, but he was certain of one thing. Wherever it was in the 1970s, it was too close to 100 percent. Move it down the curve, and tax collections would certainly go up. Reagan bought it and ran on it.

Imagine the attraction of this theory to Reagan, who in 1966 had said, "The entire graduated income tax was created by Karl Marx." He never tired of relating his frustrations as a movie star, when he discovered that after making only four pictures a year, he would be left with only nine cents of every additional dollar that he might earn for making a fifth. Trapped in this forbidding bracket of what economists call a 91-percent marginal tax rate, he preferred leisure to work and made no more films, or at least that's the reason he liked to give. Extrapolating from the fiscal experience of a movie actor to that of a blue-collar worker is the kind of discontinuity that economics is supposed to guard against, but caution is not in Professor Laffer's kit of tools. After all, he comes from California, too. Reagan would have found himself better vaccinated against such economic pseudoscience had he majored in literature. It assures any man of the theater a reading of the story of the mountebanks who promise gold to the greedy hero in Ben Jonson's classic comedy *The Alchemist*.

Nevertheless, the Laffer Curve became the theoreti-

cal justification for the Reagan tax cuts of 1981 that
were enacted on the premise that this fiscal Nirvana
would produce prosperity. We already know the doleful fiscal results of this Economics of Joy (the label
invented by the distinguished Republican root-canal
economist, Herbert Stein). So the immediate purpose
of introducing Professor Laffer, who earns a half million a year as an economics consultant and Pepperdine
University professor, is to point out that however his
professional colleagues may wish to disown him, this
hired gun is by no means an aberration among his
fellows. With the perspective of history, they now
should be able to recognize him as the precursor of a
zealous functionary in a different field. Arthur Laffer
was the Oliver North of Reaganomics.

In Washington, where about 15,000 economists live
and work, 11,000 of them are in federal service, and
perhaps about a thousand are in private consultancy as
"Beltway Bandits," so named because they scoop up
government research contracts inside the Washington
Beltway. All told in America, by the droll reckoning
of Dr. Stein, there exist some 100,000 economists who,
with their secretaries or assistants, earn an average of
about $50,000 a year, thus creating a $5 billion industry, "about the same size as the motion picture industry, which is, like economics, involved in producing a
combination of information and entertainment." Indeed, Dr. Stein's son Benjamin, a Los Angeles writer
who trained as an economist, combined the two by
playing the role of a teacher who bores his class silly
with a lecture on supply-side economics in the film
Ferris Bueller's Day Off. This not only sent the production crew into hysterics but also earned him con-
gratulations from the star and a senior studio executive.
As he later wrote in *The Wall Street Journal*, the house
organ of the supply-side movement, in Hollywood they
thought he was making it all up.

I first met Arthur Laffer long before Ronald Reagan
did. It was February of 1971, and already at the tender
age of thirty, he had hired out to the Nixon administration as the inventor of economic rationales for presidents to do what they want to do anyway. Laffer was

the chief economist for the Office of Management and Budget, working next to the White House under George Shultz, by then promoted to Budget Director. He had imported Laffer from the University of Chicago to work on a model of the U.S. economy, the first Laffer had ever done. Mathematical descriptions of the U.S. economy in those years had several hundred or more equations to track the relationships between, for example, taxes and saving, money and inflation, or investment and unemployment. Laffer produced one that had only three equations. And, like his bell curve of taxation a few years later, it had only one variable that mattered: the amount of money issued by the Federal Reserve Board.

With an econometrician's calculator on his desk and a blackboard behind him, Laffer explained with excitement that his most important equation made a startling forecast. For every dollar added to the money supply by the Federal Reserve Board, the output of the economy was guaranteed to increase by four or five more dollars *instantaneously*—that is the word he used—and it would remain at that higher level of activity permanently. That meant more jobs and, by implication, more votes. Even Milton Friedman dismissed this money machine, but the young economist was proud of his work, and in particular of its accessibility. He said, "Thousands of people work days and nights to get those other models out. He [Shultz] can't understand them, but he can understand this easily." That was too patronizing even for the impassive Shultz, and when it appeared in print, he cancelled a television appearance by his protégé. But it does not need even one equation to tell the central bank that if it lends more dollar bills to the banking system (or even if, as Keynes suggested, it buries them underground), people will spend them after they get them. What it does not tell the authorities with certainty is what they most need to know: whether the circulation of more money will draw forth more production or just more inflation. In the same way, no bell curve was needed to establish that lower taxes would leave more money in some people's pockets. What it did not establish was whether they would save it or spend it, work harder to earn more, or simply relax and spend a few more days at the beach. The value in economics as a discipline lies in its examination of the possible consequences of such decisions as printing money or cutting taxes. It allows those who are responsible for making them to consider what might happen next, even if they can never know with certainty.

The sole target of Arthur Laffer's 1971 calculations was Arthur Burns, chairman of the Federal Reserve Board. By adopting the Laffer growth forecast as its official target, the administration put the Fed on notice that it would come true only if the Fed supplied enough money, and that if it did not, it was clear who would be blamed. Thus, the Laffer forecast was meant to be a self-fulfilling prophecy. Burns fought back in Congressional testimony, and with technical staff studies showing huge holes in Laffer's logic. To no avail. Under such political pressure, the Fed had little choice but to step up its supply of money and make the prophecy come true. The rest is history, but it is more tragic than this farcical account (from my notes of the period) ever indicated at the time. As described in an earlier chapter, too much of the money then slipped abroad. The administration closed the gold window and ended the postwar international system, with pervasive results.

Washington economists will no doubt dismiss this bureaucratic farce as a one-night stand. But not in *two* separate administrations. Not with *two* presidents of totally different character. Academic economists will also disdain it as some rogue event. No; they themselves are Dr. Laffer's Dr. Frankenstein. He is what happens when social science tries to model itself on natural science and in the process loses its moral moorings. The self-interest invoked by Adam Smith to justify commerce did not imply the ruination of one's neighbor. He is quite clear about that. The object of work is not purely profit but status, respect, accomplishment, and the production of goods (a point worth stressing to those who justify corporate takeovers on the grounds of economic efficiency). The moral justification for the interplay of self-interest in the market is not that it makes any one individual better off, although it often does. The real beneficence of the Invisible Hand is that it balances human needs against physical goods, calls forth more of the latter by releasing the individual energies driven by the former, and makes everyone better off: "If I am not for myself, who is for me?" runs Rabbi Hillel's famous Talmudic question. Scholars, businessmen, courtiers, and presidents ignore his companion question at their peril: "If I am for myself alone, what then am I?"

22

Economics as Witchcraft

In the generations following Adam Smith, economics began simultaneously leaching out its moral content and his humanistic optimism. Malthus promulgated laws of population control through starvation, Ricardo the Iron Law of Wages. Other economists began constructing elegant mathematical models purporting to foretell the precise relationships between buyers and sellers in a theoretically perfect marketplace. Their discipline became the most rigorous of the social sciences because it alone was capable of ascribing to one otherwise amorphous aspect of human behavior an indisputable numerical value, that is, a price. What this rigor depended on, however, was the existence of a model human being governed solely by his economic needs. He was a person without tradition, law, family, or religion whose sole purpose in life was the maximization of utility, or what ordinary people call making the best deal possible.

Did such a *Homo economicus* actually exist? Certainly not—Adam Smith never thought so—but it would be wonderfully dignifying for economists to be able to postulate his existence and then predict what he would do next. Economics would then become a science because theory would model reality; its test would be the ability to predict events. From physics, we know science can do so; for example, the speed at which Galileo calculated that weights would drop from the Leaning

Tower of Pisa, or the energy that Einstein's equations correctly predicted would be released from the interior of the atom. Physicists can do this because the relationships of the physical universe are so unvarying as to be accounted causes. The law of gravity may be modified, but it will never be repealed.

But people are not brute matter, and the methods of economists are different. They operate by regressions, which means trying to judge what people will do in the future on the basis of what they have done in the past. The economics profession mistook the correlations of human behavior, which are the stuff of the social sciences or even literature, for genuine causes, which are the provable property of the sciences. Not surprisingly, this Faustian error began to be bred into the bone during the social certainties of late Victorian England, when individual behavior seemed as predictable as society itself. The profession might have heeded the sensible Victorian lady novelist George Eliot: "Prophecy is the most gratuitous form of error." If economics resembles any natural science, it is biology, which describes the myriad relationships among the species, their exchanges in food and territory, and their interdependence in what an economist might call the grand marketplace of life. The theory of evolution, which is one of the great theories of the natural sciences, classifies, describes, and accounts for patterns of development. But it has absolutely no capacity to predict the future. As George Eliot said, "Our deeds determine us, as much as we determine our deeds."

Like all social scientists, economists are products of their times and not of the discoveries of their predecessors. They do not "stand on the shoulders of giants," as Newton acknowledged he did, but face their peers across the disputatious history of ideas. The masters of the discipline recognize this. Keynes admitted that he threw some unnecessary mathematics into his magnum opus and presented it as a "general" theory in order to gain academic credibility for his ideas of putting people back to work in the worst slump in the history of capitalism. But he warned that there never would be enough knowledge of individual behavior to predict how people would react. An economist, therefore, could never forecast a return on a capital investment with any more certainty than the capitalist himself. If either could, they would be rich. "About these matters, there is no scientific basis on which to form any calculable probability whatever," he wrote in reply to critics of his *General Theory*. "We simply do not know."

Keynes had the learned man's ability to separate knowledge from speculation, which is why he was able to make his fortune on the latter. Operating every morning throughout boom and crash from his bed, equipped only with newspapers and a telephone, he took £4,000 of borrowed money at the end of World War I, and, by 1937, when a heart attack restricted him, had turned it into a fortune of £506,450. His advice is still timely: "The dealers on Wall Street could make huge fortunes if only they had no inside information." He beat them at their own game in the 1930s by investing in utilities, which the smart money was selling short because it was certain That Man in the White House would nationalize them. When it turned out that Roosevelt wasn't really a Red after all, utility stocks rose and Keynes made a killing.

But when Keynes' disciples brought his ideas to America, they fell victim to a feverish search for scientific universality, Much the same bloodless systematization also seems to have affected the imported ideas of another great European architect of modern consciousness, Sigmund Freud. He also studied the mysteries of human behavior without ever making the blasphemous claim that he had unlocked them, only that he had found one key. But something similar happened when the psychoanalytic movement roosted on the Upper East Side of Manhattan and when Keynesian theorems migrated from Cambridge, England, to Cambridge, Massachusetts. It may have been the need to gain acceptance and win over critics. It may also have been the obvious advantage that accrues to any man who can dispense certainties, especially when they are mathematically clothed: he is in a better position to charge his clients $100 an hour and up.

But there is more to it than that. Keynes is not so

far from Friedman; both share the assumption of the "symbol" tradition of economics that the real economy of work and worry can be managed through the manipulation of monetary incentives. Friedman is just not as wise in recognizing its limitations. For the correlations he has discovered between money and prices, he boasts an unvarying uniformity, which he writes is, "I suspect, of the same order as many of the uniformities that form the basis of the physical sciences." There seems to be something in the secular American bloodstream that wants to elevate science to religious dogma. No such outrageous claims are made by followers of either Keynes or Friedman in Europe. In England, those economists who serve up on demand the nostrums that their masters in business or government seek to imbibe are known by the delectable term "witch doctors." But in America, they are at daggers drawn. And to no advantage, according to one who is an authority in such matters, the business cycle theorist and former chairman of the Federal Reserve Board, Arthur Burns: "The argument between the Friedmanites and the Keynesians is a false argument about how well this or that group of economists can forecast the future. They cannot do so, and thank God they can't. If they could, a government could perpetuate itself in power."

Burns made that remark in private years ago when he was being harried by Arthur Laffer's forecasts, and when he himself was beginning to observe changes in the structure of the economy that made him dubious even of his own forecasts. Yet economics had just come through its golden age, as had society. It was no coincidence. Since economists forecast the future by looking over their shoulders at the past, they operate best in a period of social consensus, worst at a time of change. The first postwar generation was a time of great political stability. Social and even individual behavior was so stable as to be fairly predictable. There was a stable world order with a dominant political leader operating within a recognized set of rules. The dominant economic philosophy of Keynes—who had in fact helped to write the rules—was based on condi-

tions that existed in the real world: unused resources
that could be turned into the consumer goods everyone wanted and society agreed were worthwhile having. The Keynesian management of demand helped
create a steady market to underwrite the long runs
that made assembly lines profitable. The Keynesian
General Theory turned out to be the tract for the
times. Variations in the economy took place around
the edges, or "at the margin," as economists say,
which is the precise area where economic analysis
operates best.

All this changed in the 1970s, and economics had to
change with it. One result was the temporary rise of
Friedman, whose analytical tools were best suited to
the repair of an overheated boiler rather than Keynes'
techniques for stoking an underused one. But even his
tools served to fix only temporary leaks. Modern economics, Keynesian or Friedmanite, had been modeled
on nineteenth-century physics, which deals with tangi-
ble physical forces. It had created a mechanical model
of an economy rather like a huge power plant with
pipes coming out of it and economists as the engineers
watching the dials and tending the gauges. As long as
the pressures created by a consensus society were relatively steady, it was not hard to fine-tune either the
boiler or the economy. But by creating an engineer's
value-free technology, economists missed out on what
was happening in both the natural sciences and the
real world. Physics had begun to cross the line that
separated it from biology, and both turned their attention from the transmission of force to the transmission
of information, whether inside the atom or inside the
gene. By excluding politics, economists were unable to
tune in and adjust their discipline to major changes in
individual and social behavior. They had few analytical tools to work with and none to forecast political
explosions like the quadrupling of the price of oil and
its financial consequences.

Almost certainly, the most decisive change in Ronald Reagan's first term was the integration of the
world's financial markets through instantaneous satellite transmission, a technological event of surpassing

political importance that took place with frightening speed in the early 1980s. Not having integrated this information into their discipline, economists of all persuasions were thoroughly wrong. They misread how the distortions of the Reagan economic policy would interact with economic activity in the rest of the world, from the stratospheric dollar to the trade deficit, and on to financing the unprecedented National Debt through Tokyo, of all places.

But one variable was foreseen clearly by everyone except the supply-siders, and that was the growth of the debt. Daniel Bell, the distinguished Harvard social scientist, argues in a current essay examining the federal deficit that the stable economic relations of the previous generation had become "unhinged." But no more nor less so than changes in the relations within society itself, which hardly seem worth getting hysterical about. Economics promised too much by its scientific pretensions. It raised expectations that then had to be lowered, just as many other professions have done since the historic year of 1973, not excluding politics. In the field that should be called political economy, this opened the way for witch doctors to exploit the normal human desire for gain upon which the discipline rests. The main difference between the supply-siders and the rest is that they refused to admit that the debt mattered. Arthur Laffer, when he considered running for the U.S. Senate from California in 1985, insisted in an interview in the *Sacramento Bee* that the size of the National Debt was "not a crisis situation" and "by no means a reason to overturn Reaganomics." As if it had not already been overturned by events, the Professor continued in the great tradition of the Holy Fool: "It is far better to keep tax rates low and run temporary deficits than it is to raise taxes and destroy real economic growth."

Cast your mind back to the early months of the Reagan administration, when the Laffer ideas were being translated into political reality in the 1981 tax bill. Members of Congress received sacks of mail urging its passage at all costs, perhaps a national demonstration of the "greed" that a disillusioned David

Stockman found in the Congressional cloakrooms. The Democrat who was then serving as chief counsel to the House Budget Committee, a lawyer named Wendell Belew, felt that he and his political masters were facing a juggernaut they could barely slow down. The sacks of mail literally piled into Congressional office suites and remained there as a physical presence reminding the office-holders of public sentiment. But no rational or theoretical defense offered by the economics profession against the Laffer prescriptions had any credibility left. Belew recalls: "They figured they might as well buy that snake oil, because the old one certainly hadn't worked."

23

Reagonomics as Politics

What was Reaganomics? The period from its pro-
nouncement through its performance now totals
a Biblical seven years. From the 1980 campaign to the
1987 crash is an appropriate span to judge whether the
years were fat or lean, what had been wrought, and
whether Reaganomics even was economics. To answer
the last first: it was politics. That is not meant to be
pejorative, merely descriptive. When Ronald Reagan
ran for the presidency in 1980, he had to confront a
dilemma that was vexing every major democratic government in the industrialized world. Inflation urgently
demanded that government define the boundaries of the
state according to what citizens were willing to pay.
Governments that drew the line at the wrong place,
and nearly every one of them did, were summarily
ejected by the voters. The first of the new class of the
1980s was Margaret Thatcher, and she was followed
within two or three years not only by conservatives in
West Germany, Holland, Belgium, and Denmark, but
also by Social Democrats in France, Italy, Sweden,
and Spain. The nominal socialists prospered politically
by teaching their own conservatives the limitations of
the state, which they had already discovered in the
political wilderness. Almost all of them practiced what

the weekly *Economist* of London later called "Ronald Thatcherism." To govern is to choose. Borrowing postpones hard choices. As president, Ronald Reagan did both.

If Jimmy Carter had been reelected in 1980, he also would have had to convert to some form of austerity, and in fact he was already trying characteristically hard. Halfway through his term, in the budget he sent to Congress early in 1979, he began increasing defense spending, decreasing social spending, and projecting a lower deficit. He then acquiesced in the austere new monetary policy of Volcker's Federal Reserve Board. It was also under Carter's administration that the major initiatives were begun in federal deregulation of energy, trucking, airlines, telecommunications, and railroads. But, as so often happened with the maladroit preacher from Plains, he correctly divined the arc of the political pendulum but couldn't get out of its way. Reagan's heart was in the task of limiting the domestic role of government, and the public saw him as the man for the job. He knew what he wanted out of government, which certainly was less than it was already giving the country. He achieved a brilliant integration of personality and purpose, which is what makes a politician successful, and repeatedly outflanked his opponents. Now at the conclusion of his stewardship, we can see that he was not a political aberration, as his opponents would like to believe, but neither was he some divine gift to America. He was, as his ideological and political ally Margaret Thatcher likes to describe herself, a "conviction politician," and a man in the spirit of his times. A common mistake of ideologues is to believe that theirs is an ideology for all time.

America had never before been forced to take the medicine of limitation, and Reagan mixed it with his optimistic temperament and individualistic convictions. This made it far more palatable than anything offered by the lugubrious Carter, or by England's shrill nanny, who set stern limits on government borrowing in order to set limits on government itself. It is common for Reagan's acolytes, with their Adam Smith ties, to regard themselves as conservatives. They are no such

thing. Avowed conservatives carry a heavy obligation
to work actively toward conserving the social order,
hence their name. In England, such people classically
are styled Tories, and Mrs. Thatcher derides them in
her own Tory party as limp and "wet," because they
worry about the poor. (The best known American
Tory is the columnist George Will, who worries mainly
whether people *think* he worries about the poor.) Social Security was not created by socialists but by
nineteenth-century Germany's Iron Chancellor, Otto
von Bismarck, and the postwar European welfare state
was created mainly by conservatives out of social and
religious commitment that conveniently outflanked
the political Left. In that sense, Franklin Roosevelt
also was a conservative; the young Ronald Reagan
voted for him.

America's first conservative theoretician, Alexander
Hamilton, was an activist in government and would
incur debt, up to a point. Reagan, as he and his
ahistorical followers may be shocked to learn, springs
from a philosophical tradition more properly defined
as liberal, although he is not as radical a liberal as his
failed Robespierre, David Stockman. One has to return to the eighteenth century Enlightenment to understand their origins: the original liberals fought to
liberate themselves and society from the absolutist
rule of kings. Life as a philosophical liberal is not
easy, however exhilarating it may be when upward
mobility is crowned with success. The conservative
society has little tolerance for the energetic individual
who seeks to rise above his station. Instead, it offers
security and supposedly justice to the individual who
stays where he belongs; rich and poor remain in a
symbiotic and mutually supportive relationship. One
of the first liberal characters to appear in European
literature is Figaro, the manservant who is smarter
than his master, Count Almaviva; his dramatic creator
Beaumarchais later was a gunrunner for the American
revolutionaries. To many a European conservative,
liberal is still a dirty word because liberals are in-
grates. In its most fundamental goal, fascism in Europe was a reaction against liberalism; it attempted by

violence to turn back the clock to a more predictable order of society.

Jefferson, who learned his liberalism from the French Enlightenment, could afford to be a liberal. A paternalist landowner who was lord of all he surveyed, slaves included, naturally would prefer that form of government which governs so little that it later came to be called the Nightwatchman State. The most egregious of the liberal breed was the self-made man of the nineteenth century who insisted that while the nightwatchman must protect his property, he had no business interfering with the free market between masters and men, even if that resulted in child labor and the twelve-hour day. Their creed was a kind of Social Darwinism because it legitimized their survival at the top of the heap. Keynes was a liberal, but his genius for synthesizing ideas carried him far beyond its rudimentary law of the jungle. It is well worth repeating what he once said in a speech to those self-made and self-satisfied Social Darwinists in their intellectual base in the great English manufacturing center of Manchester:

> The political problem of mankind is to combine three things: economic efficiency, social justice, and individual liberty. The first needs criticism, precaution, and technical knowledge; the second, an unselfish and enthusiastic spirit which loves the ordinary man; the third, tolerance, breadth, appreciation of the excellencies of variety and independence, which prefers, above everything, to give unhindered opportunity to the exceptional and to the aspiring.

Like most European political ideas transported to America, liberalism had to be transmuted en route. Crucial to this was the relationship between the individual and the state. If a European stops to think about it, he will grant that he is a creature of the state. In Europe, the state makes the people. It is a legitimate expression of a homogeneous society whose traditions nurture the individual as part of a national family and, he hopes, will continue to do so. Much of his political speculation revolves around what his relationship to the state ought to be. But if Europeans acknowledge that the state made them, Americans reply that they made the state. And therefore, that they can also unmake it, or remake it in their own image. Once Americans had tipped George III into the dustbin of history, there was no absolutist state left for liberals to fight. There was only a prodigious Nature to tame, and that was what America was all about. The only real liberals were one step ahead of the state, on the frontier or in the new industries. Their Social Darwinist philosopher was Charles Sumner of Yale, who declared, "Millionaires are the product of natural selection." Once they settled down, they quickly turned to making the state their own creature. In California, they became Republicans who naturally paid lip service to the invigorating liberal principles of individual enterprise. But they hardly lived by them. They had turned themselves into conservatives who fought to preserve the established order because they profited from it. Through this century, most millionaire money in Los Angeles has been made in oil, which is a cartelized commodity; in land, which is profitable only when the taxpayers agree to build a road on it or irrigate it; or in aerospace, which feeds almost entirely at the federal trough.

The people who came to be called liberals in America early in this century actually were populists. In California and the Upper Midwest, they first called themselves Progressives. But they did not fight the state, either. After all, they created it. On the contrary, they demanded state intervention to redress the balance. Those who arrived at the statehouse too late, still wanted a share of development money or government protection for their commodities. A classic example was the Midwestern farmer fighting against high rates set by railroads that had been started with state aid; the result was the establishment of the Interstate Commerce Commission in 1887. Or take the farm support programs that began in the 1930s. Not surprisingly, many theoreticians of the New Deal programs were agricultural economists like John Kenneth Galbraith, who were shaped by public universities in California or Wisconsin, two centers of aggrieved yeomanry. But the Republicans, who call themselves conservatives because the state helps guarantee their economic security, are not particularly eager to give up or share the protection and subsidy they have already wrested from the state. So the fight between conservatives and liberals continues for dominance of the state that we Americans created.

When Ronald Reagan came to California, it was as a grateful wage slave for his motion picture studio. He later led the Screen Actors Guild in a strike involving Communist unions in the industry, which in due course gave him the additional distinction of becoming the only union leader ever elected President of the United States. Finally, he transferred his allegiance to management as a spokesman for General Electric, one of America's most institutionalized corporations. His personal history tugged in opposite ideological directions: a classical Jeffersonian liberal in rhetoric, a developmental Hamiltonian conservative in action. Yet he still regarded himself, and rightly so, as the defender of the ordinary man, whom he saw being ripped off by taxation and inflation in the late 1970s. Big Government had replaced Big Business as the populist villain. But the two had a long history of profitable alliance in the American consensus, and attacks on the former would surely affect the latter. This stored up contradictions for the future.

Reagan ran for the presidency on a more explicit economic program than any other candidate since the populist orator William Jennings Bryan espoused the free coinage of silver in the 1890s. Like Bryan, he promised a panacea and also presented his administration with the geometer's challenge of the squared circle. A pair of conservative economists, the respected Wall Street business adviser Alan Greenspan and Martin Anderson of the Hoover Institution in California, had drawn up what became the definitive balance sheet for Reaganomics early in the campaign. Of course, it featured vote-getting personal income tax cuts of 10

percent a year for three successive years, yet it promised a budget surplus within those same three years,
while simultaneously raising defense spending and
protecting Social Security benefits. How could this be?
At a speech presenting the program in Chicago, on
September 9, 1980, Reagan delivered the answer:
"Waste, extravagance, abuse, and outright fraud in
federal agencies and programs must be stopped. Billions of taxpayers' dollars are wasted every year
throughout hundreds of federal progams, and it will
take major, sustained effort over time to counter this."
For a Republican, this was amazing if he really meant
it. The principal beneficiaries of these programs were
the rich, the middle class, indeed the conservative
Republicans—precisely the people whose vote was being
sought by Candidate Reagan.

The most thorough chronicler of those early Reagan
days, Laurence I. Barrett, notes in his book *Gambling
With History* that Mr. Reagan's was not just another
idle stump speech but the definitive outline of what
was to become Reaganomics. Years later, Anderson
continued to send out copies of the speech and his
projected balance sheet, insisting that the supply-side
magic and smaller government was supposed to add
up to a surplus. There it was, *voodoo economics*—
right down to the effigies of the bureaucrats who were
having pins stuck into them. After Greenspan had
tried in vain to make the economic numbers add up, it
was no accident that when the budget-cutting began in
earnest Anderson could be a pitiless bully in dealing
with federal bureaucrats and their spending estimates.
Stockman, who describes Anderson's tactics with ap-
probation, genuinely believed that these public servants
had been mulcting the public of money that it never
wanted Washington to spend. This ex-divinity student
was to experience yet another conversion in power. A
purist, he actually reckoned on getting rid of all those
programs that his political master publicly reviled.

We will probably have to await Reagan's memoirs,
now being researched by a professional historian, to
know whether Stockman's master really wanted to get
rid of them or was merely looking for some ideologi-

cally attractive formula to pay for most of them while cutting taxes. To the degree that the President thought about the balance sheet at all, the evidence leads toward the latter hypothesis. His misplaced trust in supply-side alchemy is what plunged the nation so deeply into debt while he was finding out where his political ideology coincided with the public's and where it did not.

Reagan had gone through a similar debate over the role of government as governor of California, starting out advocating less, ending up paying for more, and in the confusion creating a fiscal backlash that left public finance in ruins. Under Reagan's leadership, the state budget jumped 122 percent, mainly because of wage inflation when Reagan was in Sacramento during the Johnson-Nixon years. California's early progressive leadership installed a tradition of public services, and the people who delivered them had to be paid or dismissed. As elsewhere, policemen, teachers, foresters, and others turned political power into purchasing power and won pay increases. Taxes accordingly rose under Reagan by the largest percentage in California history, borrowing being unavailable to states for current expenses, as it is to the federal government. The result was a tax revolt after Reagan left office. It became known as Proposition 13, a ceiling on property taxes that left localities starved for funds. So it is incorrect to describe Reagan as a child of Proposition 13. He really is its unwitting godfather, because he was unable to arbitrate between society's conflicting public and private claims and left the question to be sorted out in the political jungle. Since Californians could not assume operating debt, as soon as they decided to cut taxes, they got their bill in potholed roads and crippled schools. Once again, the bill for a confused fiscal ideology will come due after Ronald Reagan leaves office, but on a national level in the form of the National Debt.

24

How It Added Up

When the new Reagan administration confronted its essential task of shaping a coherent economic and fiscal policy in 1981, it had willed itself an abundance of ideological chaos. To satisfy all factions, the President had installed a divided team of supply-siders and monetarists. Alan Greenspan attempted to assert himself as chief of these assorted witch doctors as they settled in. He had served as Gerald Ford's chief economist and was a root-canal therapist of the old school. His strongest early intellectual influence was the libertarian novelist Ayn Rand, and he liked government spending even less than dentistry. The official who traditionally is supposed to resolve this sort of unseemly professional dispute is the Chairman of the President's Council of Economic Advisers. Divided, the administration could not agree on who he should be. It belatedly settled on Professor Murray Weidenbaum of Washington University in St. Louis, a former Nixon subcabinet official who had advised the Reagan campaign on his specialty of business deregulation.

A nonconfrontational personality, Weidenbaum had been warned by friends in Washington to refuse the job, but he was loyal to his President, his party, and his profession. He arrived to find the supply-siders focusing only on whether taxes would be cut sufficiently, monetarists focusing only on the supply of money, and Stockman focusing on the need for speed to complete the program as the economic underpinning for the first Reagan budget. When I later asked Weidenbaum what it was like adjudicating among the rival factions, he replied mildly, "Have you ever seen the movie *Rashomon*?" The optimistic document they all produced on February 18, 1981, was entitled "America's New Beginning," but it became better known as "Rosy Scenario." It had been so christened by a *Washington Post* headline writer over a critical account based on leaks by the supply-siders. Even the administration's ardent supporters in the economics profession found its optimistic projections incredible, and the program had to be taken back for repairs.

The fundamental flaw in Reaganomics was not that it set an overoptimistic goal of national recovery: lower taxes, slower inflation, a balanced budget, a stronger military, and a meat-ax to domestic spending. All this was designed to yield greater confidence in a leaner government that would give the individual and his ambitions more running room. These were not impossible dreams, and in any case the country needed a dose of hope at the time. But the conflicting ideologies of Reaganomics simply didn't add up. This was quickly evident to everyone except the public, which fortunately maintains a healthy skepticism about such matters anyway. There were essentially two massive miscalculations. The first equation involved how much of its own welfare the public would be willing to give up in exchange for a larger military machine. The second was more complex; it involved predicting the course of the economy, which could help solve the first equation by the rate at which revenue would be produced to pay for guns and butter simultaneously. Both errors were profoundly political.

In his Chicago manifesto early in the campaign, Reagan had committed his administration to raising the level of military spending by 5 percent. Carter was required by law to submit a lame-duck budget before leaving office, and he obligingly left behind an increase in military spending of exactly the percentage demanded by his sucessor. That would be one in the eye for the Russians, but it was typical of ideologues like Stockman that they believed it was intended to show up Reagan as a weakling. Carter's budget was by definition inadequate; the right wing had to be satisfied that more of the military's wish list would be fulfilled. For the administration's first full fiscal year, therefore, it proposed what Stockman called a "fix-up" package of military hardware that had first been designed by the Committee on the Present Danger, a wake-up-America group of reformed liberals. Cost was simply not an issue. Then Stockman and Weinberger, whose reputation for fiscal prudence should forever be scotched by what follows, met in hasty session at the Pentagon early in the evening of January 30, 1981, and agreed to increase the level not by 5 but by 7 percent. When Stockman started compounding on his pocket calculator, he failed to notice that the 7 percent had been piled on top of the fix-up package *and* Carter's original 5 percent. Or so he claims. But the Pentagon's computers carefully noted the agreement and clicked out a steady annual increase of no less than 10 percent for five years. Weinberger dug in and refused to cut the deal anew. By the testimony of young Robespierre's own memoirs, it took him several weeks to realize he had been guillotined by professionals. By that time, these astronomical numbers had become a political totem. The President told his staff that funds for defense were more important than a balanced budget because "what we're doing in defense must be seen as different than Carter."

This was spending for its own sake; worse, for public image and political illusion. It turned into a textbook example of the waste, fraud, and abuse Reagan had pledged to eradicate. In the U.S. invasion of Grenada in 1983, the only joint military operation actually undertaken by the Pentagon on his watch, different units of the armed services carried radios that could not communicate with each other, balked at tending each other's wounded, and attacked each other by mistake. Operating in the country's own backyard, an American force of seven thousand took three days to defeat fifty Cuban soldiers. By contrast, one year earlier, a British force of about the same size defeated

an Argentine garrison of eleven thousand and recon-
quered the Falklands, half a world away from home.

The errors in the joint budget and economic forecasts were based on similarly gross accounting errors,
and they were the product of ideological warfare. When
it was turned into an actual problem of public finance,
Professor Laffer's simple table-napkin curve became
more complicated. To square the circle of cutting taxes
while increasing revenues, the supply-side doctrine
would have to work like a booster rocket, providing
incentives for Americans to "work, save, invest, take
risks," in the words of the Treasury's policy economist, Paul Craig Roberts. In their own special kind of
seff-fulfilling prophecy, the supply-siders therefore forecast huge real growth and rapidly declining inflation, a
historically unprecedented combination. The monetarists argued, however, that the economy would mend
itself steadily if money was supplied at a much slower,
if predictable, rate. To make their economic numbers
match at the end, both factions had to forecast inflation falling from 12 percent to 2 percent in five years.
But that in turn forced their budget numbers into a
different sort of box. Low inflation means lower revenues, because wages stop creeping into higher tax
brackets and yielding higher revenue. Yet the forecasters still had to produce a balanced budget to fulfill
the President's goal of low inflation and no deficits. As
he told the American people in a television address
while his backroom economists were still struggling,
"We know now that inflation results from all that
deficit spending. Bringing government spending back
within government revenues is the only way that we
can reduce and, yes, eliminate inflation." That was the
speech that measured the National Debt as sixty-seven
miles high, or perhaps it now would be more precise
to say *only* sixty-seven miles high.

This presidential mantra (which ignored the fact
that the Fed under Paul Volcker had gone out of the
business of printing money to finance deficit spending)
may have sounded good to the business community.
But no economist and certainly no businessman would
believe in the economic boiler that the President's own

economists were building, and Weidenbaum knew it. He forced them to compromise on a target of reducing inflation from 10 to 5 percent, a figure that, he said, slapping his belly, came from "my visceral computer." That would provide sufficient inflation to add enough revenue while spending was being cut by Stockman's highly advertised salami tactics. Such was the basic arithmetic of Rosy Scenario. Michael Evans, an economist hospitable to supply-side ideas if taken in moderation, wrote that the administration was asking the economy "to perform not one but three unnatural acts: to expand output while the rate of monetary growth was contracting, to quintuple the rate of growth while the rate of inflation was being cut in half, and to help balance the budget while the government was massively cutting taxes and increasing defense."

Congressmen found that brand of snake oil hard to swallow, and their advisers found it even harder. One staff member of the House Budget Committee called his old professor, James Tobin of Yale, a Nobel Prize winner who had served in government. The aide was unable to understand or explain what seemed to be an estimating error of $80 billion. Tobin heard him out and said that was impossible; he was to go back and do his sums again because governments simply didn't make revenue-and-expenditure errors of such magnitude. This one did. Wall Street had no time for such illusions. Having already been burned by inflation too long, investors and lenders demanded record returns for renting out their money. This is called the "real" interest rate, the difference between what a bond pays and what a lender really earns after subtracting the rate of inflation. Since the Industrial Revolution, the real rate had been a remarkably steady 3 percent. With the prospect of huge deficits, the real rate soared to 6 percent and later rose even higher. On the publication date of the 1981 supply-side bill cutting income taxes by 30 percent over three years, market interest rates jumped two full percentage points.

After that, Reaganomics became dogma. Everything that happened in the real world followed the Law of Unintended Consequences. Instead of growing according to Rosy Scenario by more than 4 percent in 1982, the economy tumbled into the worst downturn in almost forty years. Volcker was putting it through a psychological wringer far worse than any devised by mere monetarists. That certainly slowed inflation, but at the cost of record postwar unemployment. Reagan did his part against wage inflation by firing the nation's striking air controllers and decertifying their union as the bargaining agent with the government. Yet another first: He was the only President to break a union that had supported him in his political campaign. By strict economic reckoning, the promised supply-side miracles never came to pass, even in the medium term of five years. After the deep recession and the preelection boom, economic growth resumed an anemic course of about two-and-one-half percent, lowest in the postwar period.

Instead of saving, investing, or risking their supply-side tax windfall, Americans spent it as fast as they could; they already were running just to stand still on the stagflation escalator. Americans saved only 3.5 percent of their income after the 1982 recession; the rate had been 5 percent in 1980, before all the tax incentives to save had been enacted. Private investment, after collapsing to 6 percent of GNP in the recession, returned during the 1984 preelection boom to the high of 17 percent it had reached in 1977 under Carter, but then it started dropping again. Even the things businessmen invested in were dubious seeds of future wealth. More than 90 percent of the growth of business investment in the first half of the 1980s went into office equipment (those ubiquitous computers), automobiles (which earned a tax write-off), and commercial buildings (which had even larger tax privileges and created a national glut of empty offices). Corporate profits as a share of national income never returned to the peaks they did under Carter. And goods as disparate as Kansas wheat, Caterpillar tractors, and Boeing jets now are struggling in international competition for markets that, having been lost because of the high dollar, will require more than just a readjustment of the currency to regain.

As for the federal budget, instead of reaching a surplus as promised by 1985, it continued in the deepest peacetime deficit in history. Defense, Social Security, and interest payments had put so much of the budget off limits from the root-canal therapists that they were forced to work in an impossibly small corner covering only 30 percent of the spending total. Senator Pete Domenici, the Republican chairman of the Senate Budget Committee, told the President to his face late in 1981:

> You can't get $100 billion in savings out of this little bitty piece that's left—the 30 percent part. You got money in there for feeding babies, for building roads, for cancer research, for the national parks, the FBI. We'll help you squeeze 'em, but we can't bleed 'em. You're just going to have to have some more revenue to make up the difference, to pay for all these things that we want or don't have a prayer of getting rid of.

The President was not amused. He insisted he would not buy "the same kind of talk we've heard for forty years," but in due course, his radicalism was blunted by Congress, his cabinet, and his own sense of political reality. The first round of Stockman's cuts was directed mainly against the working poor by tightening up on food stamps, Medicaid, and unemployment insurance. Congress supported them, but Democrats in the House then found support from centrist Republicans in the Senate. Good old-fashioned conservatives all, these Republicans could go no further without destroying their organic sense of the relationship between fortunate and less fortunate in society. This meant that if they wanted Reaganomics to add up, they would have to dip into the middle-class pork barrel: mass transit, roads, Amtrak, education, student loans. As Domenici warned Reagan, that deep they were refusing to go. Senate Finance Committee Chairman Bob Dole, who not only had presidential aspirations but also had military legitimacy in his visi-

ble wartime wounds, asked for more "compassion" for
the poor and refused to tear any more food stamps
away from them unless the Pentagon's rations also
were cut.

Inside the administration, pragmatists tried to persuade Reagan to propose new taxes in the budget he
would send to Congress early in 1982. White House
and congressional radicals argued against the need for
new revenue, shrugging off looming deficits. Describing their fiscal insouciance, Senator Daniel Patrick
Moynihan has remarked with characteristic bite that
"they are to conservatives as anarchists are to liberals." Reagan refused anyway, blocking, for example, a
proposed excise tax on beer lest it offend his Joe
Sixpack constituency, newly acquired from the Democrats. After a discussion in the Cabinet Room with
both his political troika (Baker, Michael Deaver, and
Edwin Meese) and his economic troika (Murray
Weidenbaum, David Stockman, and Donald Regan),
the President complained, "Why are we doing this?
We didn't come here to raise taxes." Weidenbaum
agreed, but in front of Reagan's own high command,
he reminded the President that "the problem is that
we haven't cut spending enough." The silence around
the table was broken only by the uncomfortable shifting of large bottoms in leather chairs; no cabinet officer had ever offered up any of his sacred cows for
slaughter, and that meeting was no exception. Neither
Reagan nor anyone else said another word until George
Bush diplomatically changed the subject. In fact, Reagan
stubbornly kept announcing his expectation that the
tax cuts eventually would allow the sagging economy
and the ballooning deficit happily to change places.
He cited the tax cuts that had helped Kennedy and
Johnson to balance their budgets. As though living in
another age (which to some extent he was), Reagan
refused to see the differences between the generations. In the 1960s, Kennedy had started with the
budget virtually in balance, a rate of inflation that was
virtually zero, and a pause in the growth of government spending until Johnson broke it by simultaneously
fighting a war in Vietnam and building his Great Society.

The Economics of Joy thus was converted into the Politics of Gridlock, and out of it emerged, by 1983, the $200 billion annual deficits "as far as the eye could see." Far from turning Reaganomics into a radical new policy, the President and his supporters, who once found Keynes a dirty word, owed their political survival to a vulgarized form of Keynesianism that generated deficits and boomed private spending just in time for the President's campaign for reelection in 1984. Professional politicians admired him even from across the sea. At the age of ninety, Harold Macmillan, whose studied insouciance earned him the prized nickname of "The Old Actor" when he was an energetic and highly successful Conservative Prime Minister of Britain a quarter-century earlier, realized exactly what was going on. Just after the 1984 presidential election, he told the House of Lords: "I rejoice at what Reagan is doing. He has broken all the rules, and the economists are furious. . . . I think I know how it has been done: it is because they have had the sense to make somebody else pay for it. In a word, Reagan, to reverse Keynes, has called in the resources of the old world to finance the expansion of the new."

Under the Law of Unintended Consequences, many things happened that neither Reagan nor his followers bargained for. One has to look at both the political and the economic ledger, but judging the President on his own goals, the first is as positive as the second is negative. What did he set out to do? More than anything else, to shrink the size of the minimalist American welfare state and change the priorities of government. The federal government would be there to defend you, all right, but otherwise you had better watch out for yourself. This, indisputably, he has accomplished. Defense spending rose from 22.7 percent of the budget in the year before he took office to 27.1 percent in the budget's estimate for the 1986 fiscal year. During the same period, the amount spent for what the Budget calls "human resources" dipped from 53 to 49 percent. Finally, grants to state and local governments, which is how Washington most directly helps education and law and order, were cut from 10 to 6 percent of the budget. These trends are projected to continue for another five years, at which time the figures will diverge even more sharply. Meanwhile, cities must fill the potholes; more than one third surveyed by the National League of Cities raised taxes in 1986, and half raised fees. The squeeze could have been worse; Congress chipped away at some of the grandiose defense plan that Weinberger euchred out of Stockman at the start, leaving military spending $50 billion lower than the $300 billion it otherwise would have been. But something more fundamental has happened than emerges from just comparing numbers. Reagan established a core consensus on the level of governmental welfare. He would say he has done it by holding fast to his principles, and his opponents would accuse him of using the deficit as a club to bludgeon them into submission. Neither is right.

The decisive deterrent to the expansion of government was a sublimely technical device tacked onto the 1981 supply-side tax cut by an obscure Colorado senator named William Armstrong. Any administration would have been ambivalent toward his idea, and Reagan's was no exception. Whatever its ideology, no government likes to have limitations on its margin for fiscal maneuver. Armstrong's proposal was the indexation of income tax rates to inflation. Every taxpayer knows about bracket-creep: he gets a raise, but inflation kicks him into a higher bracket and the government therefore takes a larger percentage of his earnings. This was manna for politicians; they could approve new programs and rest content that at least some of the money to pay for them would be there in the future because of inflation. Not any more. Since 1985, inflation has been factored out of tax levels, and this omission was cemented into the 1986 Tax Reform Act like a brick wall. The new boundary between the two brackets of 15 and 28 percent has been set around $29,000, just a notch above the average family income, in order to protect Congress from the wrath of middle class voters. Since the Great Inflation began, the government has been quietly slicing away a larger share of the average American's paper gains in his income. Now it will no longer be able to do so.

This is the real significance of tax reform. The loss of most deductions means that government no longer will be able to subsidize many pressure groups by backdoor handouts through the tax system, nor will it be able to collect the money through inflation. From now on, the costs of any new program will have to be voted formally out of real income. Any shift in the burden of taxation will have to be politically explicit instead of merely implied by inflation. Between the pincers of indexation and deficit, any rising revenues accruing to Washington are bound to be earmarked almost entirely for regaining fiscal stability. Instead of the citizen's being forced to hold his own by running up the down escalator of inflation, the government has been put in his place on the same treadmill. Any general tax increase, say, 1 percent across the board in each of the two new tax brackets, is almost certain to go largely toward deficit reduction. Reducing the deficit simply means changing the mix between taxation and borrowing to pay for existing domestic programs; it does not mean creating new ones. The tax cuts and the military buildup have starved the budget of revenue to prevent that. Government has had its allowance cut exactly as Reagan promised. When the public wants a new program, it will have to subtract funds from another one or vote higher taxes. And these would most likely be voted into blocked accounts for specific uses, following such models as Social Security for retirement or gasoline taxes for roads, instead of entrusting the government with the creation and management of any but the most essential of public goods, such as defense.

This is the classic liberal philosophy, and willy-nilly Ronald Reagan managed to put it into practice. He performed some absolutely necessary surgery on the inflated expectations of the body politic, but at the cost of a National Debt of crippling dimensions. Was no political strategy other than confrontation available to this essentially amiable man? What happened to the ideal of consensus that shaped his generation, and

mine? One sure result will be greater disparities in
society. There now is less money to transfer not only
from rich to poor individuals, but also from rich to
poor regions. This is a delicious irony now that Texas
is poor again, but it is not so funny to consider that by
starving states of funds, another burden of debt is laid
on future generations to repair roads and bridges and
educate the young. All are being allowed to run down
for lack of investment, because all available funds are
going to finance present consumption through the deficit. But what is not done now will have to be paid for
later. Government may be larger on paper, but it is
domestically weaker and more concentrated in the
military. Not a single major new government program
was created, and we can clearly see the design of the
fiscal pincers that will cut them off, especially transfer
programs to redistribute income. There is one argu-
able exception. Because of the National Debt and its
doubled interest burden over five years, there has
been a huge, unintentional growth in the transfer of
income from taxpayers to bondholders, that is, from
the poor to the rich, from the young to the old, and
from Americans to foreigners. These are among the
more enduring legacies of Reaganomics.

What we do not know is how long any of his legacies will last. The President must be given some credit
for damping down the social strains he inherited from
the years of the Great Inflation. He raised the country's spirits and he let Paul Volcker get on with his
job. But what we cannot know until the next recession
is whether the social peace will last. Has Ronald
Reagan's era of good feelings been just an illusion
bought by borrowing against the future? Or will society crack under the weight of the National Debt?

25

Downshifting the Great American Dream Machine

The social tug of war of the 1970s created both winners and losers by leaving the real incomes of most ordinary people stagnant while the society around them changed. That's not the way the Great American Dream Machine was supposed to work. Since governments began printing too much money, since OPEC began collecting its 2 percent sales tax, and since everyone started trying to get his own first, the purchasing power of average family incomes has barely changed by more than a few hundred dollars one way or the other. By some calculations, it even fell a few percentage points, but the numbers still come out pretty much the same, whether you take the mean or the median, whether you start in 1970 or 1973, or whether you finish last year or this. The indisputable point is that, after doubling in the previous twenty years, the figures abruptly stopped growing. They don't slope up, they don't slope down; they're flat. Average family incomes less inflation were $26,394 in the recession year of 1970, $26,500 in the transition year of 1980, $26,433 in the electoral boom year of 1984. The same weary twenty-six thousand dollars right straight through, turned stale, flat, and unprofitable. Those figures, from the report of the President's own Council of Economic

Advisers, proceed with slight variation through all administrations from Nixon to Ford to Carter to Reagan. It's a bipartisan calculation. The only difference is that the first three administrations maintained the money illusion by printing it; that's inflation. Reagan maintained it by borrowing; that's the National Debt. Whoever follows will still face the same problem of how to live in diminished circumstances.

Some Democrats prefer to start from the *annus mirabilis* of 1973, when average family incomes reached a temporary if record high of $28,167. This conveniently allows them to reckon that average incomes have actually fallen a few percentage points in the 1980s under Reagan. But 1973 was a Nixon political supernova, the causes of which we have already explored. Republicans look at the steady rise from 1983 to 1985, without conceding that the economy had just come out of a recession and had nowhere to go but up, and that the country is still stuck in that $26,000 range. However the numbers are reckoned, they add up to one simple fact: as a nation, and especially in the working class, we stopped receiving the kinds of raises we had become accustomed to, and a generation of presidents tried to conceal it, probably from themselves just as much as from us, by a money illusion we call inflation. Those who gained were those who got hold of anything that wasn't made of paper, like a house, and simply sat on it while its price rose toward the stratosphere. The precise gains are shown in the figures from Salomon Brothers included in the notes at the back of this book. But those profits do not arise from self-improvement by work and wage-earning, which is what the American Dream is supposed to be all about. Outside of polite society, where this type of activity is delicately known as portfolio management, it's called speculation.

If you count yourself as both middle-aged and middle class, try to remember how much money you reported for your family on your 1040 in 1973, the year it all began in earnest with OPEC, Watergate, and the rest. Multiply that figure two and one-half times for inflation. If that's about the money you're earning now, and chances are that it is unless something exceptionally good or bad has happened in your life, you're average and you've probably changed imperceptibly from being an optimist to a pessimist. Instead of believing that we live in the best of all possible worlds, you now probably fear that, alas, we already do. The green light at the end of Daisy Buchanan's dock has probably long since gone out. If you are young, you may still believe, as Jay Gatsby did against all evidence, in "the orgiastic future that year by year recedes before us." What we are trying to explain here is just how and why it still is receding.

Of course, if you got in on the ground floor, you are probably sitting comfortably on the value of your home. Just wait until you decide to sell it and move. If you're lucky enough to have bought it in the dear, dead days of the fixed mortgage, could you afford to buy it now? Wait until your children ask you to help with downpayments for their own starter homes. Of course, it could be worse. You could be a farmer, having been visited with financial punishments of positively Biblical dimensions. Real net farm income soared to a high of almost $26 billion in 1973, when American farmers joined in selling to the Russians in what became known as the Great Grain Robbery; it collapsed in precisely one decade to $5 billion. This left farmers with incomes lower even than their grandfathers' in the depths of the Great Depression; net farm income in 1933 was $6 billion. This debt problem isn't something for tomorrow; it's today and it's here.

Now really try to stretch your imagination: you could be an unwed black mother. You would then have replaced the poor rural tenant farmers and the aged at the very bottom of the heap with an average annual family income of about $10,500. This is less than one-third of the earnings of two-parent white families. Mind you, not all blacks did badly, which shows that well designed social engineering can work. The only family classification to increase its real income, even if only by about 4 percent, was that of black couples with children. It's obvious what happened. Thanks to civil rights legislation and government hiring policies—

20 percent of all public sector jobs are held by the black 10 percent of the population—stable couples got a chance at steady work, even if their income still fell below that of white families. As for tbe black mothers, if you were Charles Murray, the Reagan administration's favorite poverty investigator, you would probably argue as follows: the daughters of those Mississippi sharecroppers simply migrated to Detroit and Chicago, started having babies on welfare that was not available down South, and thus replaced their fathers as the chief inhabitants of the lowest income quintile. But don't blame social engineering for that, because the old were meanwhile being moved, indeed, catapulted, off the income floor by another social engine known as Social Security.

How we divide up our national income can be a matter of political choice if we want it to be, and that choice was made in accordance with the largest single voting bloc in the country, which is not poor and black, but middle-aged or retired. Because of rising Social Security and Medicare payments, the portion of the old living in poverty dropped from 15 to 4 percent during a decade that was hardly dreary for them. The proportion of children living in poverty (that unwed black welfare mother again) rose from 15 to 24 percent. While almost everyone else was standing still, the average income for families over sixty-five rose by one-quarter to $17,000. They have the votes. The thirty-six million recipients of Social Security are the largest single group of people in the country receiving money from the government; children don't vote. But someone has to pay, and by definition it has to be those at work, the majority of them young. They are waking up to the burden of the cost. Stand still and you may detect a movement underfoot like that of tectonic plates. It is the slow crunch of political ideals against economic reality.

Back in the *belle époque*, it was all different. Average family income rose 30 percent under Eisenhower, and another 30 percent under Kennedy and Johnson. Between 1947 and 1973, during which family income doubled, a new record was set every three years or less. Social reformers grumped (correctly) that the rich got richer, but so did everyone else. That was the rising tide that was; it lifted all boats. It really meant something to be the world's most powerful nation, to command the most advanced technology, to make things that people wanted, and to make them well. It meant that workers got their share, too. In real dollars, production and service workers' wages rose steadily by 2.5 to 3 percent a year. Not coincidentally, those percentages also equal the long-term increase in workers' efficiency, the output-per-hour measure that economists call productivity.

In 1973, everything changed, but it took a while to figure things out. Looking back, it's now obvious that the efficiency of the American economy had something to do with it. Like average family income, productivity almost doubled in the generation before 1973. It went limp thereafter and is still flat. Economic reward and prospects declined accordingly. Young people might stretch out their arms to pluck the future out of their parents' past, but it eluded them. In a charming book called *The Strawberry Statement,* James S. Kunen, one of the Columbia University student strikers against the Vietnam War in 1968, wrote about those great days of his life when he was only nineteen years old. Now he is divorced, bald, and writes for *People* magazine. His reflections are bittersweet: "All I wanted, I used to say, was to raise a family in a decent home and be able to spend a few weeks at the beach. That's all I want now, but I find these modest ends require massive means. It's hard to renounce materialism when materialism is renouncing you," Idealism comes more easily when economic expectations are growing; at the time of the French Revolution, the French peasantry was the most prosperous in Europe.

If astronomers can calculate the speed at which a star moves away from us by measuring something as miraculously precise as the apparent shift in the length of something as tiny as a light wave, certainly we should be able to measure the fading of the American dream here on earth. It needs a dynamic measurement of the scale of expectations in relation to material change, which is appropriate in a society where Becoming outweighs Being. This is no less difficult to measure than the red shift in stars. Two researchers deserve full credit for figuring out how to do it, Frank S. Levy of the University of Maryland School of Public Affairs and Richard C. Michel of the Urban Institute in Washington, D.C. By looking at incomes over a whole career, they have devised a method for weighing constant dollars against inflated dreams.

Imagine, as they did, that you were a man aged twenty-five during the good years from 1950 to the middle of the 1960s. The next ten years are the first real adult years of your working life, a time when the promotions come fast if they are going to come at all. On average, your real income would have risen about 110 percent if you had started out during that period of bobby sox, tailfins, and spreading suburbia. What an average paycheck then bought, would have slightly more than doubled in ten years. Like most people in what has come to be called The Best Years of Our Lives, you could plan to get married, save for a down payment on a house with several bedrooms and a garage, and start having children. Debt is something you can carry lightly, because as it matures, so do you, and happily. Now imagine you are a man of forty during that same period of the '50s and '60s. You've pretty much reached a promotion plateau, you have some seniority in your job, and you're comfortably anchored at home with a fixed-rate mortgage. If the world around you does well, so do you. Indeed, even though you may be stuck in the same job throughout your forties, the efficiency of your colleagues and the profits of your company are passed back to you in handsome gains in real income. On average, real incomes for men in that decade of early middle age rose about 30 percent. They were one-third better off.

That's where the rising tide took the country. Then it stopped, and the Great American Middle Class was caught in a backwater. Dreams were blocked for the young as economic expectations faded. From 1973 to 1984, the average real income of that once-eager and ambitious 25-year-old rose only 16 percent, instead of doubling as it had before. A man of thirty would be running to stand still for the next ten years; his income would go down by 1 percent. And the man who turned forty in that climactic year did not know it yet, but his real wage would actually *decline* by 14 percent during the coming Dreary Decade. Anyone who took on sizable debt during that period watched it go up in inflationary smoke for a few years, but when the rest of society wised up and started charging him the real cost of the money—in a variable-rate mortgage, say—he got burned, not the mortgage.

Mobility was severely straitened. Don't imagine it was easy to uproot and move from the Rust Belt to the Sun Belt. And consider whether those who did so are better off today. Frustrated hopes spread a fear of the risk that has always been part of an American's personal engine. When the general economic tide was rising, a blue-collar worker in steel or auto manufacturing could be laid off, find a lower paying job in a service operation like a garage, and still reasonably expect that within several years his personal standard of living would grow back to its former level along with the economy. Not anymore, when wages are stagnant. Almost three-quarters of a million workers produced automobiles in the peak year of 1978; now, about 150,000 fewer people operate the plants at peak production. What happened to those laid off as the recession hit in 1979? Seventy percent went back to work for one of the auto industry's Big Three, but almost half of them had lost all their savings. Fifteen percent were still unemployed in 1984. The same proportion found work elsewhere, but at one-third less pay and with few if any of the fringe benefits, which meant a pay cut of about half. Throughout all durable goods manufacturing, which provides the steadiest and best-paid blue-collar jobs, workers who lost their jobs and found new ones had to accept a pay cut of one-fifth. Not surprisingly, most of those who got pushed off the middle-class raft were of low seniority. That is, they were young.

These calculations are not limited to men for any sexist reasons, but because census and other data for women are limited. Average real earnings of women who worked full time, age notwithstanding, followed the general pattern. They rose 24 percent in the 1960s, then dropped 3 percent in the decade after 1973. The reasons for limitations in the earlier data are grounded in history. In earlier years, the family wage that mattered was essentially the man's wage. Feminists may decry this, but once male wages started dropping, they and their sisters were sent to work to maintain living standards. We will examine what happened to them in due course.

In the confident aura of the postwar Baby Boom, parents could hardly imagine that they would send their children into a world of limited opportunity. But demography is destiny, and it holds many of life's surprises. How many of those who grew up in the Depression could foresee their own material comfort in the postwar world? By the time their children went out to work, the world had changed again. In the 1950s and 1960s, there were never more than 17 million workers of between the ages of 25 and 34. And in a growing economy, there was plenty of room for them. Because of the Baby Boom (officially comprising the 76 million Americans born between 1946 and 1964), there now are 30 million workers in the post–25 decade, all of them with the bad luck to be competing for pay, security, and promotions in an economy that has been stagnating, indebted, or both. No wonder they job-hop. Pillars of corporate life accuse them of being disloyal to the society, but the society has been disloyal to them. They have to grab whatever they can get to raise their earnings to the best possible level before attaining middle age and its economic plateau.

Now peer again through the wrong end of their two-way telescope of diminished expectations. Consider a high school graduate from an average blue-collar home who goes out to work. In his mind, he remembers his father's salary as a personal measurement of success. In the 1950s and 1960s, his Great American Dream would have been fulfilled quickly. By age 30, the son would be earning almost one-third more than his father's salary had been when the young man left home about a decade before. There was nothing uncomfortably Oedipal in this, no sinister or tragic hint of the son replacing the father on the scale of economic power. On the contrary, he was merely catching up and taking his rightful place as a mature, wage-earning adult. In the interim, his father's salary would have been increasing, too, albeit more slowly because he was older. One reason for this upward spiral was the expansion of the economy, but another was personal and related to the first: education. The young blue-collar worker would have finished high school; the chances were about two to one that his father had not. This gave the son the ability to deal with technology at a higher level, feeding back into his firm's production capability. This generational advancement defined the American consciousness, but it stopped in the 1970s. The largest and, until then, the best educated generation the country had ever produced, collided with a stagnating economy. For a time in the late 1970s, the salary premium commanded by educated workers dropped. This shows up statistically, but everyone knows about the physics Ph.D. who went to work for the electric company and the honors graduate in history who had to drive a cab. Now the blue-collar worker has turned 30, but he earns 10 percent less in real dollars than his father earned when the young man went out to work, and the son lives considerably worse.

This is not something that can be cured by transferring income through the tax system. The money isn't there anymore for the Great Society or similar solutions. For the foreseeable future, any extra revenue will go to running down the deficits. What little equalization in income that has occurred during the postwar era, has already been voted through the Social Security system, and it has already reached political limits. Redistribution to the poor has been limited by two Reagan referendums: he won the presidency twice. The problem, say Levy and Michel, is "a growing inequality of *prospects*—of the chance that one would enjoy a middle-class standard of living with a house, children, cars, retirement—the whole package. Those who already had it were largely able to retain it, while those who didn't have it, saw their prospects dim."

Consider the college-educated son of a blue-collar worker, for whom the American Dream has turned into a nightmare of downward mobility. He is aptly described by Ralph Whitehead, a political scientist at the University of Massachusetts, as a "new-collar" worker. A member of the postwar Baby Boom generation now aged from about 20 to 40, he is a footsoldier of the uncertain service economy, earning at least a bit more than $15,000 a year, more likely around the average income in the high 20s, but in any case, an absolute maximum of $50,000. There are about 25 million workers in this class. Unlike his father, the new-collar worker can no longer count on lifetime security in the big battalions of an American manufacturing plant. Can he and his wife have three children, live in a single-family house, save something for retirement, and do it all on his own salary? Like his father did? You must be joking. He works with little security and fewer fringe benefits in a service job, something like a Federal Express driver or a manager in a car rental office. Or, if he prefers a spot of poorly paid glamour, perhaps as a salesman in a computer store. That is the sort of occupation for which his education at some undistinguished community college fitted him. His wife, another badly educated victim of the post-Sputnik boom in American higher education, has to help pay the mortgage. She may find herself working in a job that is part-time, temporary, or both, as a file clerk or a saleswoman. This new-collar couple has a very simple, bread-and-butter agenda. Housing, which costs too much. Child care, essential for a family that must hold two jobs. Good schools, because they know education still is the only way out. But none of these simple demands can be satisfied by the society with any certainty. How did these people get into such a fix? Read on.

26

The Two-Tier Society

Examine the new conditions of housing, marriage, employment, and even consumer spending. The young especially are squeezed. Even the yuppies suffer: their feverish behavior is an attempt to break free. An unexplained pattern of wage inequality has arisen since the mid-1970s, along with an intergenerational tug-of-war that Social Security was supposed to turn into a truce. In America, we are on the verge of creating a two-tier society. Knitting it together into a new consensus will be a task demanding more than the political genius of a Ronald Reagan. This is not just some East Side-West Side divide that gets healed when Blacks and Jews make enough money to move across the park. By affecting salaries, expectations, and indeed dreams, the economy set generations and classes apart that traditionally have been knitted together by hope.

Nothing is more intimate to the individual and at the same time more fundamental to society than marriage. It is the most important nexus of the public and private. The young have been delaying marriage in droves. Since 1973, the average age at the first marriage has increased by two years, to 24, highest since the new immigrants of the early 1900s were settling in the United States and searching out suitable mates. Buying a house at inflated values and high interest rates presents them with a struggle their parents never confronted. In 1985, an average 30-year-old who bought a median-priced home would have had to pay 44 percent of his earnings in carrying charges. (At that rate, he either bought a cheaper house, sent his wife out to work, or both.) In 1949, his father would have paid only 14 percent of his salary for carrying charges, and in 1973, just as the dam burst, an older brother, say, still could have gotten by nicely by paying 21 percent of average earnings for his mortgage. A house in Levittown, the Long Island model for postwar suburbia, cost $7,990 in the 1950s, or just 2½ times an average worker's annual wage. There was no down payment on a GI loan and carrying charges were $60 a month. Now Levittown houses go for about ten times that price, or "in the eighties," as the real-estate agents casually say. In that range, the only option for most young couples is to seek help from the family. GI financing now stands for "good in-laws."

At mortgage rates of 10 percent, only about 30 percent of American families can afford an $85,000 house in the suburbs, and even that would be on a 30-year mortgage with only 10 percent down. That demands an annual income of about $34,000, or just about twice the average earnings of a 30-year-old. No wonder wives go out to work: six out of ten house buyers are two-income families. Any new house will also probably be smaller. Less than half the houses built are single-family detached houses, and the percentage of those with two bathrooms and a garage is declining, along with their size in square feet. Many prospective house purchasers simply could not make it into the first tier of homeowners at all. One out of every three new homes sold in the United States in 1985 was a mobile home. They were shipped mainly to the states of the Old South, Appalachia, and the edges of East and West Texas, which are the areas of the country poorest in income, education, and public spending. Anyone who has driven across that part of the country knows that these homes, although nominally "mobile," have already left ugly stains that will be hard to rub out of an already washed-out landscape.

It is the income of mothers that preserves family

living standards, even at that stale and flat $26,000 a year. In 1973, the percentage of all women at work and the percentage of working mothers was the same, 44 percent. By 1984, 53 percent of all women worked, but 62 percent of mothers did. These working mothers are not just divorced, unwed, or chic single mothers-by-choice. Three-fifths of all mothers who live with their husbands go out to work, and because more of them do, their average earnings have risen while their husbands' were declining in a stagnant economy. Women contribute 20 percent more to the average household budget in two-parent families than they did in 1973 because more of them work, not because they earn more than their husbands. Quite the contrary. The Lord Himself told Moses to value a man at 50 shekels of silver and a woman at 30 (Leviticus 27:3–4). Working wives in two-salaried families still earn about the Biblical rate, 57 percent of their husbands' salaries. The typical occupations are not those of the flat-chested lady executive with the ruffled Brooks Brothers shirt who dresses for success; at least she does in the full-color ads. The Census Bureau says a typical working couple consists of a man on a production line or in craft or repair work and a woman in "administrative support." That means a pink-collar clerk, bookkeeper, or secretary.

This is a historic change from the Norman Rockwell image of father supporting mother and two towheaded kids at home. Since the 1950s, the proportion of such families has gone from typical to most untypical, dropping from 60 to 20 percent. Feminists would say this *Saturday Evening Post* stereotype deserved to end up in a Norman Rockwell museum (as in fact it has) out of total revulsion and not mere social revolution. One wonders. The greatest increase in the proportion of working mothers has taken place in the one group that would seem to have both the least need and the least desire to work—those who live with their husbands *and* have children under the age of three. Two-thirds more of them work than in 1973. Surely it is not that they want to leave their babies; they need to. Lest any doubt remain, when *The New York Times* polled working mothers it found that 71 percent of them had taken jobs primarily to help support their families. Other motivations ("something to do," etc.) were so far behind as to be barely visible.

The creation of new jobs has been the proudest boast of the Reagan administration and the Carter administration before it, even if both did it by pure Keynesian budget stimulus, and Reagan vulgarized the process in the extreme with his deficits. There were seven million new jobs during Carter's four years despite a punishing inflation, followed by five million during Reagan's first term despite a recession, and one million more every year thereafter. Starting again from our Year Zero, they added up to more than twenty million new jobs from 1973 to 1985. Europe created none because of its lack of mobility; its sense of security and social consensus was its undoing. But those with jobs contributed heavily to the social insurance premiums that preserved a decent if minimal standard for those without. A sense of social solidarity avoided the worst in all countries except Mrs. Thatcher's Britain. But for the Americans, it meant working more and enjoying it less; they had to price themselves into jobs at lower wages. These new jobs were hardly high-paying, high-tech positions. Probably nine out of ten of them were low-tech or no-tech, what are indelicately known to professional statisticians as hamburger jobs. Pass under those Golden Arches and look around. Only one-third of all new jobs in the United States went to men; the rest went to women. Since the start of the 1980s, the balance has become even more skewed, with men being hired for less than one-fifth of the new jobs. There were a few hundred thousand more miners and overpaid construction hard-hats, but durable goods industries, such as autos and appliances, created no new jobs, and nondurables like textiles actually lost 400,000 jobs.

The new jobs all appeared in services, and fully one-quarter were in retail trade. There is nothing demeaning about serving behind a counter except the paycheck, which keeps on shrinking as more people compete for jobs to maintain family living standards.

After all, that's capitalism. In 1970, retail jobs paid a respectable two-thirds of manufacturing wages. By 1985, they paid less than half, or an average of $9,220 a year, which is below the poverty line. The rest of the new jobs were in health services, local government, transportation, finance, and real estate, where only the doctors, the bankers, the brokers, and, on occasion, sad to say, the mayors get rich. Take careful note of some of those classifications, because they are unlikely to continue expanding: Costs of medical care have reached limits and are being capped stringently, and public spending curbs are likely to hold down local government employment. The Bureau of Labor Statistics forecasts that during the coming decade, low-tech or no-tech will supply all of the new jobs in the ten fastest-growing occupations, the demand being headed by more than half a million new cashiers, whose present pay is exactly half the average factory wage.

The boast of the American economy is that its loose job structure offers flexibility in responding to change. The American entrepreneur is the hero of the hour because, by rough estimate, 16 of those 20 million new jobs have been created in companies employing 200 people or less. Fortune 500 companies, pressed by international competition to become leaner and more productive, have actually shed labor and by some estimates have permanently lost about a million jobs. This is an economic plus, but it may also prove to be not only an individual but a social minus, because it means insecurity. About one-fifth of all jobs in the United States are part-time, which suits many wives and students but not women and the young with ambition. Others are temporary, and together these jobs are technically known as "contingent," which means they offer no security or even certainty of tenure and pay, no fringe benefits, and no prospect of promotion. Audrey Freedman, a respected labor economist at The Conference Board, a research organization supported by corporations, estimates that as many as one-third of the workers in the United States hold these jobs; i.e., they hold onto them by the skin of their teeth. Once restricted largely to women, minorities, and the young, they now are spreading to full-time male workers. That's what you call a hamburger job.

Even in steady employment, a two-tier structure is becoming institutionalized in union contracts. New employees are hired at lower wages and continue at a lower scale for the rest of their careers, which has frozen the workers on and off the middle-class raft in industries as diverse as airlines, construction, trucking, and of course the retail trade. Wage inequality has begun to show up as a long-term trend. Through the boom of the 1960s and even into the 1970s, the pay spread between people in the same job narrowed steadily. In 1978, it suddenly started widening. The gap has opened to the size that existed a generation ago, and it is not just some sudden ghetto phenomenon. It affects men, women, whites, workers, and professionals. In short, it squeezes the middle class and especially the young, who are hired later at lower pay scales. International competition, deregulation, and competition for jobs are among the factors, Barry Bluestone and Bennett Harrison, two professors of political economy who charted this evidence of rising inequality for the Joint Economic Committee of Congress, refreshingly expressed themselves at a loss to explain it fully. But they found in a follow-up study for the Committee that more than half the eight million jobs created from 1979 to 1984 paid less than $7,000, and that two-thirds of them were part-time. Splitting up jobs into part-time segments saves companies fringe benefits, lowers wages, and provides the jobs that wives must take to supplement the family income.

Such statistical observations are straws blowing in a weatherman's wind. The number of middle-income families (defined as the $18,000-30,000 income bracket) fell from 27 to 23 percent of all families during the Dreary Decade. And the wind seems to be blowing toward polarization: The number of lower- and lower-middle-income families rose 40 percent, and upper-middle- and upper-income rose by 70 percent. Another short straw: the Federal Reserve Board reports that from 1977 to 1983, while the number of households grew by almost one-tenth, the number owning stock fell by one-quarter. This doesn't just mean that some of them simply dumped all their dogs on a sick market. It means that the new arrivals could not afford to buy in. Another Fed survey indicates that about one million more young families had no liquid assets, a technical way of saying that they had no savings to fall back on. Not surprisingly, it also showed an additional million families taking on installment debt.

Figures like these have provoked a lively debate over whether the middle class is actually declining, or just being squeezed, perhaps into a different shape. Since membership in the middle class is also a state of mind, it matters little which is correct. They do show that staying on the middle-class raft is a struggle, and climbing aboard is harder still. This is one result of a harsh and demanding economic environment, and the personal frustrations inevitably will exact a price in social friction.

27

Fault Lines

Like its more traumatic ancestor of the 1930s, the Quiet Depression left scars on society, albeit more subtly because inflation masked its transfers between savers and spenders and between workers and speculators. But people somehow knew. Is it any surprise that the birthrate suddenly fell during the 1970s? No doubt the Pill made it easier, but just as in the Great Depression, the economy also made it essential to have fewer children. The children of the Baby Boom must have sensed the shift under their feet (demographics usually start tracing such shifts long before the demographers do), because in 1972 they suddenly delivered a Baby Bust. In that year, 900,000 women reached childbearing age, but they had 300,000 fewer babies. Throughout the 1970s, the rate of 2.1 births per couple needed to keep the population steady, dropped until it leveled off at 1.8, which means population decline. There now are 27 percent fewer children in young families than there were in 1973. In the 1950s, with wages rising, husbands and wives who themselves were children of the Depression could confidently indulge themselves in a huge bet on the future—children. Caring for a child to the age of eighteen costs more than $80,000, the Urban Institute reckons, and more than $100,000 when education at a public university is added in. Private colleges now are acting as their own banks, like the auto companies, in order to market their wares. "Most people can't pay for education out of current income any more than they can purchase a car that way," an official of the University of Rochester told *The New York Times* in 1986. The yuppies have done their sums and they know the answer, principal and interest: A BMW costs less than a child.

As a media phenomenon, yuppies are hard to beat: the self-centered Baby Boomers of the 1960s and 1970s who have matured (or immatured, if there were such a verb) into the selfish young adults you love to hate. Unfortunately, there aren't enough of them to make it worth the energy, and marketers have awakened belatedly to that fact. The money isn't there. If you define a yuppie as someone between the ages of twenty-five and thirty-four, almost certainly college-educated, living in a metropolitan area, working as a manager or a professional, and earning about $30,000 if living alone or $40,000 jointly with a roommate (the trendy euphemism is a statistical necessity), then only between 5 and 8 percent of their age group qualify. A marketing group that issues *The Lempert Report* worked overtime on the back of its envelope and discovered that about 36 percent of the age cohort earned less than $10,000. It decided to call them "yuffies" (for Young Urban Failures) and calculated that there were four times more of them than yuppies. In between, the marketers found the majority "working hard to earn a decent living between $10,000 and $30,000. . . . Dare we call them 'Yammies' for Young Average Americans?" The marketers are returning to the mass rather than the so-called class among youth, because after the condo, the car, and the payments on the student loans, *The Lempert Report* reckons that there isn't much discretionary spending power left once Ma and Pa Yuppie become a threesome: "Raising a child in the manner to which Yuppies are accustomed means boarding school, computers, a big backyard, and Oshkoshes in every color."

Before this goes too far—although it can never go far enough to rein in some overimaginative politicians—we might follow the marketers and examine changing consumption patterns from the 1970s to the 1980s that demonstrate the squeeze on yuppies, yuffies, and yammies alike. Over the decade after 1973, studies by the Bureau of Labor Statistics show that fuel and utility costs for all young families rose by one-half and gasoline by two-thirds. There's that OPEC tax; the Arabs extracted a cool $1,000 from their average incomes. Together with higher mortgage costs or rent, that meant young couples had to set aside about 6 percent more for these necessities. In the Baby Boom generation that came to maturity in the early 1980s, young couples gradually had to devote more and more of their income to basic necessities, and the proportion rose from two-thirds to three-quarters. Consumption accordingly declined. Young families spent 18 percent less on home furnishings, 32 percent less on clothes, and 15 percent less on personal care. Contributions to charity were slashed by one-third: When savings stagflate out of existence, it becomes more blessed to receive than to give.

This is the generation that not only will have to carry a doubled National Debt, but also carries its parents on its shoulders in style, an unprecedented income transfer from the young to the old. At present, polls and political analysis confirm that the young are relieved that the care of their elders has been socialized. It's better than having them around the house (especially a small one), and it increases the absolutely essential mobility of the young. But at what price? The rise in maximum Social Security payroll taxes, from a minuscule $60 in 1949 to $5,710 in 1986, is a major factor in the rise in the total average tax rate for young households from 10 percent in 1960 to 23 percent a generation later. The 1986 Tax Reform Act will affect this only marginally; the already legislated rise of the employer-employee payroll tax to a staggering $8,690 for Social Security by 1990 will affect it more. All evidence indicates that workers bear a major share of their employers' contributions in the form of lower wages, and this tax bite is one of the important factors overlooked in the squeeze on yuppies, yammies, and the rest.

The myth of Social Security, which helped protect it from its antediluvian opponents who thought Roosevelt was a Red, was that it was a government-sponsored insurance plan. That's why everyone had his own numbered individual account. But Social Security is no such thing. It is a huge mechanism to transfer money from the young to the old, rather like the office coffee pool on a grand scale. Today, every 10 retired parents are supported by 34 working children. That is one reason why politicians were able to raise the purchasing power of Social Security benefits by almost half from 1970 to 1985. But by 2030, when young people now entering the labor force will be retiring, the Baby Bust will explode on them with full force. There will be only 20 working children to support 10 of them. They are likely to be living longer, enjoying it less, and wondering well before then who will need them and feed them when they are 65. Anyone retiring now can actuarially expect to receive back from Social Security three times more money than was put in on his behalf. The young are transferring the money to him through Social Security. Even as early as 2010, when today's yuppies will be preparing to retire, benefits will be considerably less than today's. Under the 1983 reform, which supposedly put the Social Security system on a sound basis, an average wage earner will receive at best only what he or she put in, and in most cases only 90 percent of it, because ther will be fewer young people to put the money into the coffee pool. The social-insurance myth will long since have been exploded.

Simply to maintain current benefits, payroll taxes would have to rise from their present 14 percent up to anywhere from 25 to 40 percent, depending on which actuary you listen to and what his crystal ball tells him about the state of the economy over the next half-century. In America, payroll taxes at that level seem politically untenable, but not in other countries, where they seem to get value for money. Payroll-tax contributions may already seem astronomical in the Welfare States of France or Holland, where the government receives the equivalent of two-thirds of an employee's wage, or merely onerous in West Germany, where it receives one-third. Admittedly, such rates leave less money available for wages in cash, but they do purchase a wide safety net (some call it a security blanket) that includes retirement, unemployment insurance, and, above all, medical care. As a matter of fact, many large American corporations have quietly woven similar security blankets to protect their employees at about the same proportionate cost, mainly in private insurance premiums. The Fortune 500 company I work for, while relatively generous but not untypical, boasts that it contributes about 30 percent above my salary for these supposedly fringe but actually basic social benefits, as they are regarded in every other Western industrial democracy. The difference is that the blanket is not public; it is wrapped mainly around those who have been taken into the bosom of corporate America. That's what happens in a two-tier society.

Several deepening fault lines are exposed here. The gap between parents and children is situated in an ambivalent emotional area that the Japanese call "the darkness of the heart." With understanding, it can be broached in social and civilized discussion. If the nation regains its sense of family and community, priorities can be reordered and money reallocated. Another fault line occurs between those who made it into the middle class while the going was good, and those who came along later and didn't. This could result in something never seen before in America, a barely discernible line that may have begun delineating social classes permanently.

The new-collar worker's agenda is a classic program for upward mobility. Better schools for his children, which cost more tax money. Day care so his wife can work, which costs *him* more money. Better housing, which means lower interest rates so he can afford a higher mortgage. All seem to stand out of reach across a financial chasm created only partly by a generational fault line. Half the federal government's social expenditures now are mortgaged to the 11 percent of the population that is over sixty-five; so defensive are they about their benefits that they have been called the third rail of American politics. Education, income support for the poor, and welfare all must come out of the other half of the money left for the remaining nine-tenths of the population. Somehow, that darkness of the heart probably can be penetrated and that third rail crossed. But then the agenda confronts the iron laws of compound interest on the National Debt, and these are not subject to negotiation.

Cheaper housing will be one result of lower interest rates, but that demands a smaller federal deficit to lower the cost of borrowing money. Higher spending for education means a choice between spending less for the elderly and enlarging the pool of federal money devoted to social spending. Congress is already cutting the military budget, so higher taxes are the obvious answer, but they also have costs. They may solve the problems of both housing and education, but they also slow down the economy that provides the second family job and the money for child care. This is not just some jokey merry-go-round. It is the runaround, in which the young aspirants to the middle class are caught. In the course of time, the rising burden of past and present consumption, levied through payroll taxes and the interest costs of carrying the National Debt, will start dragging down the economy by squeezing first the young, then families, and then everyone.

Largely unnoticed by politicians, the structure of the engine that powers America's consumption has changed. From the mid-1970s to the mid-1980s, the demand for goods has been propped up by the earnings of working women, but that is approaching its limits. There are not many more women available outside the labor force, unless granny-power is pressed into service. At the other end of the demographic scale, the once-chic idea of Zero Population Growth, which at first protected the standard of living by delivering fewer mouths to feed, is becoming a drag on the economy. Fewer children means fewer consumers, which means lower demand to power the economy. Gradually, the economy starts running out of gas and stagnates. Lower growth means a lower standard of living for young and old. That would turn American political and social institutions on their head. They were founded on a radical economic notion that the next generation would be richer. It was also a notion bred into the bone by the early experience of this country. There was free land for the taking. Resources, like the oil first drilled in Pennsylvania, were literally oozing out of the ground. When we willed a National Debt to our children after World War II as their share of the price for defending liberty, it was in the full expectation, which proved correct, that they would grow rich and strong enough to carry it. Such expectations had also been the foundation of Social Security: that the young would earn enough to care for the old and still have enough left over to enjoy themselves. But that expectation is no longer the certainty it once was. In a steady-state economy, the morality of passing debt from one generation to another is destroyed.

This may signal another, deeper fault line of history. 1973 was the year that our national power came under serious question, and that was the year that a subtle stagnation of hopes set in. Is it possible that 1973 was this century's equivalent of 1893, the date that the historian Frederick Jackson Turner proclaimed the physical closing of the American frontier? Awakening to the implications of that physical fact took almost two generations. The illusions that persisted through the 1920s collided with reality at the end of the decade, and the disaster of the 1930s forced reform. Times move faster now. We still do not know whether the economic disruptions that followed on 1973 will turn out to be fundamental and permanent. At the climax of his popularity, Ronald Reagan joyfully proclaimed that "America is back," but in twilight of his presidency it began to appear only halfway back. We now may have to contend with a more careworn American character, but it would lack the hard-won historical stoicism that now sustains Europe. In due course, a more tempered American imagination would certainly emerge to create a different American ideology. No one knows what it would be, but it is a safe bet that it could not depend too heavily on the kind of expectations that once made the country "the last, best hope of mankind."

28

Beat the Yankees

Our 40th President's favorite president used to say that the business of America is business, so why shouldn't the businessman be able to pull the country out of this slough of debt? Service jobs certainly can't be the answer: the foundations of American wealth and power would be shaky indeed if they were built on millions of women workers taking in each other's washing. To be fair, the decline of American business as the world's most productive and competitive far antedates the arrival of Ronald Reagan. His policies, like those of his predecessors, only failed to arrest the trend, although he may deserve credit for accidentally doing something about it. The deep recession in 1982 and the stratospheric dollar combined almost willy-nilly to awaken American business to the first laws of economics. Not the numerical laws that flash out of some MBA's pocket calculator, but the basic laws of organizational behavior observed by Adam Smith.

That wise Scotsman's masterwork, *The Wealth of Nations*, does not start from his accountant's bottom line but in a pin factory. There he discovered the division of labor among a handful of specialist workers: "One man draws out the wire, another straights [sic] it, a third cuts it, a fourth points it . . .," and so on, until they produce more than forty-eight thousand pins a day, whereas one man working alone might have been able to make "perhaps not one pin in a

day." That is called improving productivity. It is not a
question of working harder, but working smarter, rather
like inventing a three-handed man. Mark that it also is
more deeply rooted in local teamwork and social cooperation than Adam Smith's disciples in the jungle of
individual competition would ever dare admit. The
American refinement of Adam Smith's division of labor is historic, and that is not too strong a term. It was
the installation of the first assembly line at the Ford
Motor Company plant at Highland Park, Michigan.

Until September 1913, the famous Ford Model-T
was bolted together by what had seemed a perfectly
sensible process of wheeling the parts to a central
point, where the labor of one man, standing still in
one place, was needed for 840 minutes, or fourteen
hours, to assemble the chassis. In a stroke of genius,
an engineer named Charles E. Sorensen turned the
process on its head. Each assembler stood in an assigned place, but instead of the parts being brought to
him, the emerging chassis of the car itself passed in
front of him on a slowly moving, chain-driven belt. As
it passed by, each worker, like his ancestor who had
drawn, straightened, cut, or pointed the pin, would
add his specialized part; first came the axles, then the
frame, the springs, and so on, one part per man. Thus,
by April 29, 1914, after a suitable trial period, it
needed only an astonishing ninety-three minutes, or
slightly more than an hour-and-a-half, of the labor of
each man on the factory team to assemble the chassis
of an automobile so it could roll out the front door for
a test drive. As described the following year in *Factory*
magazine, "The Ford motor and chassis assembling
methods are believed to show the very first example of
minutely dividing the assembling operations of so large
and heavy a unit as an automobile." The process cut
the working time—and the putative wage cost—by
almost 90 percent. The increase in efficiency enabled
Ford to sell the car more cheaply and therefore opened
up a wider market. Far from firing the supposedly
redundant men, Henry Ford hired thousands more of
them at the then unprecedented wage of $5 a day and
taught them the social skills of the modern factory.

Business is an expression of society and therefore changes with it; important organizational changes were made throughout the whole structure of companies. A seamless administrator named Alfred P. Sloan, Jr., reorganized General Motors by instituting a system of checks and balances for his managers that consisted of centralizing policy through rigid profit targets and responding flexibly to the market through divisional autonomy. GM's share of the market more than doubled in the mid-1920s. Henry Ford, the innovator who believed that "history is the bunk," ran his company into the ground by maintaining iron control and battling his workers with hired goons. After the war, his grandson had to rescue it from union-busting thugs with a pistol in his pocket. Sloan set a standard for competitiveness by which GM dominated, cartelized, and dictated the market to such a degree that it identified the nation's interests with its own in the unspoken American tradition of cooperation between government and business. "What's good for General Motors is good for the country," Charles E. Wilson, president of GM, ingenuously told Congress in 1953 upon being examined for his fitness to run the Pentagon; the ensuing uproar in no way prevented him from quickly being declared fit.

With a huge market to support long production runs, the assembly line and the divisionally organized corporation were the mechanisms for the interchange of wealth and goods that created the consumer society in every industrialized country during the next half century. They were to mid-twentieth-century economic development what railroads were to the late nineteenth. The social apparatus of the corporation combined with the political mechanisms that opened up international trade to apply the mass of technological discoveries, from electrical power to chemical dyes, to the production process. This increased efficiency and living standards at rates undreamed of in previous history. During the century following 1870, the average worker in an industrializing country increased his output almost *fourteen* times. The United States was just below the average with a twelvefold increase. European countries improved their efficiency faster than that—except for the British, who had begun ahead of the rest as the founders of the Industrial Revolution. The Japanese worker, literally emerging from feudalism, improved his productivity by a factor of twenty-six!

But when you examine these amazing numbers on charts that cover a century, what they show is not some dynamic race but a kind of equalizing Second Law of Thermodynamics. Countries that adopt similar methods tend to converge toward similar rates of output, and thus toward similar standards of living. Those that started out richer and more efficient in the nineteenth century, like the British, improve relatively less, while others, like the Japanese, catch up. God is not an Englishman, but he is not an American, either. The evidence of this comes before the eyes of any traveller, but the mechanism is less obvious. The more that countries trade and invest among themselves, the better they learn and adopt each other's production techniques. Modern communications speed the process.

Contrary to popular myth, neither America nor the rest of the world has been deindustrializing. The actual production of manufactured goods in the United States has increased in step with total output, remaining at about one-quarter of GNP throughout the entire postwar period. This proportion also applies to most of Western Europe. What has been deindustrializing is the worker, and this is what has been helping to create the two-tier society. In the 1920s, blue-collar manufacturing workers made up one-third of the labor force; in the 1950s, they made up one-quarter, and now they constitute only one-sixth. Industry is continually confronting its problem of how to produce more with less; the problem of competitiveness for America resides in the fact that some countries have been doing a better job of solving it than the United States. (This is quite different from the social problem American industry has handed over to the rest of us: what to do with these dethroned blue-collar aristocrats and their disenfranchised children? In earlier years, economic growth re-employed the former and education enfranchised the latter. As we have already seen, the only answer devised so far has been the unsatisfactory one of sending their wives out to work.)

Examine international competitiveness since the 1960s. A generation ago, the American industrial machine was the most competitive in the world. It had for itself about 30 percent of the export markets in the industrialized world. Japan and West Germany, our two biggest competitors, shared 20 percent between them. The positions now are precisely reversed, and they are beating the Yanks at our own game. While increases in U.S. productivity are stuck at around 2 percent a year in manufacturing, theirs is rising at 4 to 6 percent a year. We should not complain. To assist their recovery after the war, we gave them a low exchange rate to promote exports, licensed our technology to their companies, and even sent a specialist named W. Edwards Deming to Japan to teach the Japanese about producing quality goods for mass consumption according to methods of his own that had been rejected by American industry. Now full of years and equally full of honors from the Japanese, he is the single most important person, aside from the Japanese themselves, responsible for the fact that "Made in Japan" now is the hallmark of industrial quality that "Made in USA" once was.

Consider the manufacture of what now is at best a low-technology product, a standard room air conditioner. On the production line, for every single Japanese air conditioner with a defect, 70 American air conditioners must be fixed before they leave the factory (that number 70 is not a misprint). Obviously, not all of them do get fixed. Under the first-year warranty, one out of ten American air conditioners has to be fixed in a service call, compared to fewer than one out of a hundred by the Japanese. There is no magic in this; it consists of careful quality control and consumer testing, feedback on the reasons for failure, and sophisticated techniques of engineering design for reliability in Japan, which in America are used only by the aerospace industry. These are the results of a study by David Garvin of Harvard Business School published in its review under the appropriate title "Quality on the Line."

To help understand what has happened to America's relative position, Roger Brinner, chief economist of Data Resources, offers the analogy of the New York Yankees, the greatest baseball team of all time, participants in 33 World Series in this century and winners of 22. Like the United States, the unflappable pin-striped athletes cleverly exploited a huge local market with wise leadership and canny management (note the deliberately tortured syntax employed by both Casey Stengel and his contemporary, Dwight Eisenhower). Then other teams improved their coaching and training techniques, organized good scouting, and learned Yankee technology. All benefited from the player draft, which was designed to equalize the contest. They knew their business would fall apart if their competitors could not field presentable teams. Likewise, the United States drew up the postwar "rules of the game," giving its allies a sporting chance precisely because they were allies. As an obligation of world leadership, America opened its markets to its competitors. The prosperity of one benefited the prosperity of all by increasing trade and political stability. Naturally, with more volatile leadership, uncertain of its public goals, neither the team nor the league is all that it used to be.

The international system and the American machine began to wind down in the latter part of this century, and more markedly in the hinge year of 1973. It is not easy to measure the slowdown in domestic efficiency, since it usually is judged only by results. The standard measures compare the number of hours worked—like those on the Ford assembly line—with the value of what the workers produce. Counting all factories and offices, and smoothing out the jolts of the business cycle, all American workers were about 3 percent more productive each year from the end of World War II to 1965. This is no small change: anything growing at that rate almost doubles in a generation, and that is roughly what happened to the gross national product, the wages of an average worker, and the profits of American corporations. In the late 1960s, the trend declined to 2 percent, and from 1973 onward, productivity on average for all workers has increased less than one percent, in fact closer to only half of one percent. This is the management side of the unpleasant things that started happening to workers' wages around 1973. Corporate profits after inflation have also been going nowhere fast on that same flat slope. There is a certain rough justice in this. If you work dumber, you earn less. Whether it is your fault or the boss's—usually it is a combination—it is the society that will suffer as living standards decline.

The reasons for this decline have been the subject of prodigious study and analysis, and absolutely no one yet knows what they are. Among the likely villains are inflation, by distracting management from running the factory to following the gyrations of the financial markets; oil prices, by making energy-gulping machines in the factory costly and obsolete; capital investment, by not providing workers with more efficient machinery; the tax system, by discouraging investment and individual effort; the Baby Boom, by tilting the balance of the work force toward less experienced workers; research, by concentrating its resources on the military and space instead of marketable ideas; education, by failing to train workers to understand even simple instructions; and, lastly, the figures themselves, which are subject to large margins of error. Manufacturing traditionally performs better and services worse; factories, because they lay off people while increasing output, and service industries, because they then hire them at lower wages but find it as hard to improve their efficiency as to locate a three-handed barber. That is why haircut prices move up with inflation. Automobile prices don't have to move up, especially if the Japanese, for example, figure out more efficient ways to produce cars than Ford.

The largest productivity gains, and some of the largest losses, have, not surprisingly, been recorded in America by industries in transition. Under pressure of Japanese competition, the automobile industry has marginally increased its efficiency. So far, it has done this mainly by firing people, but soon it will do so by automating factories, or so its managers hope. With imported steel inexpensive because of the high dollar, integrated American steel mills laid off enough unnecessary workers to produce a ton of steel in 7½ man-hours, or three hours less than in 1982. Computers and telecommunications allowed about twice as many stockbrokers to do five times as much business in the stock and bond markets over the past decade.

Competition does not necessarily result in more efficiency or better service. When you have to wait in line longer at the bank to cash a check, the bank, struggling to cut costs in deregulated competition, is increasing its productivity at your expense. The airlines increased productivity by more than 6 percent for almost forty years by buying planes that could carry more passengers; in a regulated market, they felt they could risk the huge investments in more efficient new machines. The industry performed only about half as efficiently after deregulation permitted all comers to increase the number of aircraft seats. They did so faster than they increased the number of passengers who would pay full fare for them. Waiting longer at airports is one price you pay for cheaper seats, as the airlines try to make up their losses by cutting corners. But it also is the price you pay for lower taxes, since the government is skimping on its traffic management. Productivity in the telecommunications industry increased at an absolutely steady 6 percent or better for about thirty uninterrupted years right through 1983, thanks largely to the regular diet of technological innovation fed to it by Bell Laboratories in a steady business environment. No reliable measures of efficiency are available since the breakup of the Bell System. The busy signal on your phone, however, is a raucous reminder that the free market usually makes things work cheaper, but not always better or smarter.

29

More Than Just Business

A little more than a decade ago, these questions of production and competition would have had little of their present urgency. What other countries did to the United States was about as disturbing as what chimpanzees do to elephants when they ride on their backs through the jungle. We did not owe them money then. Through the early 1970s, Americans paid foreigners only about five cents of every dollar for their manufactured goods and sold them about the same amount. Now, about one-quarter of all the manufactured goods sold in America come from abroad and three-quarters of U.S. industry is subject to foreign competition. The United States may still be an elephant in comparison to its competitors and allies, but it is an elephant with a much smaller margin for maneuver, and maneuverability is not that great beast's normal advantage. The United States now owes huge debts to these same competitors, and it must earn money to pay them interest by producing goods they want to buy. Meanwhile, it is also banking on them to finance its continued prosperity. We have already explored what could happen if they—or their fund managers in Tokyo, London or Frankfurt—start losing patience.

Worries about international competitiveness predate the high dollar of the early 1980s, although it made matters worse. VW Beetles, Hondas, and Toyotas have been seen on American roads for more than a decade, and, as a socially observant lady of fashion remarked a while back, "There are altogether too many people nowadays walking around in Gucci shoes." Even through much of the 1970s, when the dollar was mostly below the Plimsoll line, imports sailed into American markets twice as fast as domestic manufacturers could sell television and hi-fi equipment, industrial chemicals, semiconductors, cameras, and machine tools. These are the high-technology goods in which the United States once led the world.

More than one-quarter of our machine tools and automobiles, and more than half of our consumer electronics, are imported; the United States may be on the frontier of technology, but it no longer stands there alone. Furthermore, by concentrating on a service economy at home, the country risks losing its manufacturing base. It would be nifty to tear down all those smokestacks in Ohio and convert the slag heaps into ski runs, but no one would be able to afford new skis (especially if they are Rossignols imported from France). When industry goes abroad, service industries like banking and insurance go along and take jobs with them; the Brazilian subsidiaries of Citicorp have a few American managers, but the clerks are not imported from Brooklyn. Meanwhile, engineering technology atrophies. Men in white coats can't just sit alongside Boston's Route 128 and send diagrams in the mail down to dollar-an-hour workers in Mexico. The newest thing in consumer electronics is the compact disc, which is being manufactured in Japan and by Holland's Philips, but not in America. Just another gadget that converts Cyndi Lauper into binary arithmetic? Not exactly. Its technology is similar to that of optical-disc computer memories, and any company that knows how to manufacture rock music on a compact disc has a running start on the next generation of computer floppies.

We have to work smarter because they do. There are shortcuts to that, but, like most shortcuts, they have risks. We have already taken one shortcut: firing workers to make companies lean and mean, in the latest management jargon, and letting somebody else worry about improving their productivity when they go to work in a hamburger job. The real accomplishment would be successfully organizing everyone to work smarter, not just leaving fewer workers on an assembly line to work harder. The other shortcut would be to continue devaluing the dollar so that the United States would become one big international discount store for foreigners, a kind of coast-to-coast Hong Kong-Taiwan-Singapore bazaar specializing in cheap merchandise regardless of quality. There is no doubt that the dollar was overvalued in the first half of the decade when compared to what it would buy in the countries of Western Europe, but that was fixed by a correction of about one-third in 1985. Moving it farther downward meant that American companies in international competition had their profits protected. But workers paid the price in lower living standards because things from abroad cost more. Both these quick fixes were necessary to help balance our trading accounts, but they did little to help realign our society. They only made it poorer.

So far, American society does not seem to have figured out how to make American business work for it, rather than the reverse. The evidence is still largely anecdotal, but nevertheless telling. Until the early 1970s, the American textile industry was a declining victim of low-wage imports. Now it is profitable, but its productivity is not exactly an American success story. Improvements came through importing technologically advanced looms from West Germany, Switzerland, and Japan; laying off one worker out of every six; and paying those that remained at the low end of the manufacturing scale. American mills now undersell the world in cheap cotton and polyester cloth because they are supported by a huge home market and are near their raw material supply. However, the high wages are earned not by the American textile workers but by the skilled foreign mechanics who make the looms. The blame, of course, lies not with the textile manufacturers, who are not running their business as a charity, but with the part of American industry that went right on producing obsolete looms. But the textile manufacturers are not blameless, either. If you walk into a shop in the shadow of a North Carolina textile mill, as I did a while back, and ask for some cotton thread of a particular color, you will be directed to a magnificent display of many colors—made in Switzerland. If you ask the woman behind the counter why, she will reply that the mills in her area are interested only in making cheap, easily produced parachute cloth in large quantity. That's productivity, of a sort, but not the kind that produces jet transports and high-skill jobs.

It is not surprising that workers are resistant to change. A study reported by *Public Agenda* found that only 9 percent of American workers thought they would benefit personally from improved productivity, which means either they did not understand what it meant, or, more likely, they understood all too well. No doubt there remains in the collective unconscious of labor the memory of the original efficiency experts with their stopwatches timing the duration of a sparkplug installation. They preferred the euphemism of "time and motion study," which their guru, Frederick W. Taylor, systematized into a book that he called *Task Study* but that sold better under the reassuring title *Scientific Management*. In the front office, they have their own reasons for cynicism. Studies by researchers at Morgan Stanley, the Brookings Institution, and MIT were unable to find any measurable results in the improvement of white-collar productivity over the past twenty years from the billions spent on office computers. Some bosses still may be empire-building huge entourages: one-third of the payroll jobs in manufacturing are not on the production line, up from one-quarter a decade ago, in the 1970s.

Patience. The computer revolution will take time to pay off. Every major discovery does, from gold in the New World to gene-splicing in the laboratory. Although the assembly line was invented in 1913, American productivity remained stagnant until the 1920s, when corporations were reorganized and efficiency increased by half in less than a decade. It took both

Alfred Sloan and Henry Ford to make the Roaring Twenties roar. It takes time for an economy and a society to invest in and then absorb, digest, and adjust to historic changes. During the 1980s, General Motors, Ford, and Chrysler spent hundreds of millions of dollars automating factories; executives of all three firms admit that learning how to operate the new systems will take much longer than they had planned. Individual workers have to change their machine-minding habits, groups have to reorganize the flow of orders and information, and managers must design new methods of gathering feedback from below. After twenty years of talking about the-office-of-the-future, it was only by 1983 that each information worker had at his disposal an investment in computers, telecommunications, and copiers that was larger than a production worker's stock of lathes, forges, or presses.

This new technology seems to be reaching critical mass. But whether it provokes an explosion of prosperity or implodes on its owners and managers, depends on whether they understand and can adjust to the changes that have been taking place in the world economy. It is almost a commonplace to say that the future lies in seizing the advantage of the "knowledge-based" industries. But this was true of the past, too. After the Chinese mandarins ignored their own best invention, Renaissance Europe prospered on the premier information technology of its day to spread the latest knowledge. This information technology was called printing. The trick is knowing what to do with the knowledge. In the nineteenth century, it consisted of applying huge amounts of energy—first steam power and later electricity—to convert raw materials such as iron ore or bauxite for human use as steel rails or aluminum pans. Since everyone now can do that, there is not much money in these process industries, and corporate raiders can be observed trying to pick clean the carcasses of such humbled companies as U.S. Steel, with the names submerged under generic labels such as USX. There is even less profit in owning the raw materials themselves; the world recovery of 1983-86 left raw material prices as low in relation to the manufactured goods that they can pay for as they were at the depths of the Depression.

At first this was puzzling. When the recovery began in 1983, the analysts at the Geneva headquarters of the General Agreement on Tariffs and Trade, where they know more about world trade than almost anyone else, were certain that it could not last. Their records showed that industry's demand for raw materials was much lower than in past recoveries, which to them implied that the recovery would soon run out of steam because no one would be able to afford manufactured goods for very long. This relationship between the prices of raw materials and manufactures is called a country's terms of trade. Suppose the terms were still at the level of 1973 (once again, that year). America, which traditionally owes its prosperity to knowledge plus raw materials (or brains plus brawn), would have had a much smaller trade deficit. Most of the brawny countries of Latin America, traditional suppliers of raw materials ranging from copper to coffee, probably would not be suffocating in debt. But we do not, and they are. Now we are getting closer to the reasons for the change. Since 1900, there has been a steady decline of about one and one-quarter percent a year in the amount of raw materials needed to produce a car, a locomotive, and manufactured goods in general. That means 60 percent less coal, oil, iron, wood, copper, or whatever. Cornering the copper market would not help General Pinochet keep his job in Chile any more than trying to cartelize the oil market helped Sheik Yamani keep his. Hardly anyone needs the stuff as badly as before.

The details of this change have been winkled out by Peter Drucker, who probably has the most original mind in America regularly analyzing the way the economy works. Not surprisingly, the process industries need the most raw stuff. Sixty percent of the cost of producing pots and pans goes for raw materials, 40 percent of an automobile, but only between 1 and 3 percent of a semiconductor microchip. Fifty to a hundred pounds of fiberglass cable transmit as many telephone messages as one ton of copper wire, and

producing the fiberglass takes 5 percent of the energy.
High-strength plastics cost half of what steel does,
including its energy input, and they therefore are increasingly replacing steel. The big industrial input is
not oil, not coal, not steel, but brains. Seventy percent
of the cost of making a microchip represents knowledge—research and testing—and only 15 percent is
labor. Half the cost of prescription drugs represents
knowledge, and 15 percent labor. The costs of the raw
materials are negligible, but the profits on the finished
goods are not.

   Two tiers of manufacturing industry are slowly de-
fining themselves: the process industries that powered
the economy through most of this century in the lower
tier, and the knowledge industries based on information technology, which is where the high rewards are.
We see it happening before our eyes: among states,
Massachusetts beats Texas; among valleys, Silicon beats
Mississippi River; among belts, Rust is trying to polish
itself while Sun is wilting. Industry does not even need
the invention of a new institutional model, and the
best one we have is undergoing some overdue downsiz-
ing: International Business Machines, the most successful high-technology company in the world. The
white-shirted men of Big Blue, like an army of Jesuits,
take risks because they have something few other corporations offer: training, technology, research support,
and, above all, a secure base from which to take on
competitors. Not one has ever been laid off in midcareer
for economic reasons since Thomas J. Watson Sr.
formed the corporate culture, company songs and all.
Already smaller companies are beginning to digest the
new technology in their own way. They are the ones
that will help us make things smarter, cheaper, and
better. The following, from an article by Gene Bylinsky
in the May 26, 1986, issue of *Fortune* magazine, is the
literary lineal descendant of that article about the Ford
assembly line in the 1915 *Factory* magazine.

   It is 7:30 A.M. on the eighth floor of an
   80-year-old Allen-Bradley Inc. building on Mil-
   waukee's South Side. Two-and-a-half hours

ago, an IBM mainframe computer at the company's nearby headquarters relayed yesterday's orders to a master scheduling computer. Now, at the scheduling computer's command, what may be the world's most advanced assembly line comes to life with pneumatic sighs and birdlike whistles. Lights flash. Without human intervention. plastic casings the size of pocket transistor radios start marching through 26 complex automated assembly stations.

Bar code labels, computer-printed on the spot and pasted on each plastic casing by a mechanical arm, tell each station which of nearly 200 different parts to install in what combination. As the casings move along a conveyor belt, tiny mechanical fingers insert springs, another mechanical arm places covers over the casings, and automatic screwdrivers tighten the screws. At the end of the line a laser printer zaps detailed product information onto the side of each finished plastic box. The boxes are then packaged, sorted into customer orders, and shunted into chutes ready for shipment—all automatically. The four technicians who stand by to unclog jams are rarely needed. Elapsed time per box from start to finish: 45 minutes.

The company makes industrial controls, which are ordered in constantly varying sizes and specifications. The line is the only one in the world that can execute a special order without stopping or slowing down. It can grind out six hundred electromechanical switches an hour, every one of them different if customers so request. The technical conundrum was unlocked by the simple application of supermarket bar codes to announce the different specifications of each item to the robots as it moved down the line. Other companies' automated lines can make different-sized tractors, or produce automobiles with different engines or radios, but not without slowing the line to readjust it by hand. Allen-Bradley's line cost $15 million to build, and it cut production costs by one-third. It does all its own quality control by laser gauges, can produce a special switch on one day's notice, and is irrelevant to direct on-line labor costs. Assembly-line workers previously represented less than one-tenth of the cost of a switch. At one point, the company looked into the possibility of shifting its manufacturing to Mexico, where workers earn a dollar an hour. But it calculated that with warehousing, transport, and other overhead—most of it eliminated by the automated line—its costs would really be about $13 an hour or only $3 less than the cost of its workers in Milwaukee. And those workers now are employed in the far more challenging task of making the robot lines that Allen-Bradley sells to other companies. They have moved into the knowledge industry. What they probably do not realize is that their products are what will help keep the country's living standards up and its foreign creditors at bay. The business of America is more than just business.

There is no magic solution to any problem of this magnitude, and that automated assembly line did not spring out of thin air. No one was even thinking of special tax breaks for investment or similar so-called supply-side carrots. On the contrary, the company acted under the threat of the heaviest of sticks: automate or die. The new line was created by a team of almost thirty people of different technical disciplines. Like people on Route 128 in Massachusetts, these Wisconsin workers live in a state with a history of radical solutions in politics, a tradition of cooperation in industrial relations, and an endowment of an excellent system of higher education. Teamwork and social consensus, education for social and individual improvement, and cultural traditions that enhance identity and pride: Yankee ingenuity in one place, German thoroughness in another. This is the opposite of the economic policies devised and followed by most American governments in the past generation. No country can suddenly pull ahead of its competitors by some quick financial fix, like cutting loose from gold or cutting income taxes, and then declare that it is back as Number One. The remedies, like those propelling all economic development, are social, cultural, and profound.

30

Instant Troubles

There is an old saying that, rather like a good luck charm, "God protects fools, children, and the United States of America." As seen from abroad, our country seems to regard itself as quite exempt from outside influences. As seen from the inside, it seems blithely unaware that they even exist. Until the middle of this century, that innocence and isolation had its own charm and hardly mattered anyway. Even after the United States assumed international leadership, it had such vast resources relative to the rest of the world that its inevitable stumbles could be made good in the way a visiting rich uncle leaves a present behind to help excuse any inconvenience. But since the mid-1960s, that margin of maneuver has narrowed without anyone much noticing it. With the exponential growth of foreign debt, it is narrower than ever. As the world becomes more interdependent, we are less the masters of our own fate than we would like to believe.

Every major shift in economic policy during the past fifteen years has had a foreign trigger. The underlying faults have been in ourselves and not in some distant star. But the timing or the direction of the adjustment has been forced on the United States from abroad. In all cases, we probably would have had to change course anyway, but perhaps not as sharply if we had moved with more prudence. Debts, deficits, dollars, and most things financial are like rubber bands. The farther they are stretched, the harder they snap back. In 1971, foreign treasuries were taking in dollars but feared that their value would be inflated away. The U.S. Treasury drew up plans for wage and price controls even though they were anathema to Richard Nixon. It urged the idea on the White House but got nowhere until, one week in August, the British government asked the United States to guarantee the value of the $3 billion in its reserves against any possible dollar devaluation. That was when the President and his entourage withdrew to his Camp David retreat and solved America's problems, or so they thought, by breaking up the postwar Bretton Woods System.

The abandonment of international financial discipline in 1971 helped produce the next huge economic shock: the first OPEC oil price rise two years later, which also originated abroad. In 1977, Jimmy Carter's expansionary plans were checked by a flight from the dollar, which his government had decided to let drift downward to help U.S. exports. In 1979, after floundering for half a decade between recession and inflation, the United States sharply shifted course again when inflation had become socially intolerable. The Federal Reserve had been working out new techniques to combat it, but its timing was heavily conditioned by fears for the dollar, and even by fears for the political stability of the United States, which were being expressed sotto voce at the annual September meeting of the International Monetary Fund in Belgrade that year. Paul Volcker left in the middle of the meeting and flew home to announce his program on a Saturday. Then, in the summer of 1982, came the next major shift, when the Fed loosened money after sending interest rates to 20 percent and more to stop inflation. Once again, the proximate cause for the sudden change of course lay abroad. Mexico and other foreign debtors were strangling on high interest rates and could take the international financial system and its major banks with them if they succumbed.

If this book has demonstrated anything, it is that the American economy is seriously askew, mainly because of our voracious appetite for credit in order to live beyond our means. Domestic budget deficits of $200 billion simply cannot continue "as far as the eye can see." The United States does not save enough to finance these deficits, which is another way of saying that there are not enough people willing to put aside money and defer their pleasures until later so that others can borrow their money and take their pleasures now. This domestic imbalance radically redirected the flows in the world's pool of capital early in the 1980s. It is the prime source of our foreign trade deficit, of the gyrations of the dollar, and, finally, of some of the most pressing problems of our industries. But the United States no longer enjoys the protection of being the world's rich uncle, its financial leader with special responsibilities and privileges. We let that role go by default under Richard Nixon when we closed the gold window, mistakenly believing we could continue to exempt ourselves from the rest of the world. Although our size, the efficiency of our capital markets, and the sense of confidence engendered by the character of Ronald Reagan gave us a period of grace, the size of our debt both domestic and foreign has created a situation that cannot last. Anything that cannot last, will, by definition, come to a stop. The question is how: slowly and manageably, or with a crash? No one knows that, only that we are vulnerable, and all the more so because of the internationalization of the financial system.

That system itself has changed beyond imagination in less than a decade. This permitted the United States to milk it for billions while refusing to allow it to influence national policies on the budget, interest rates, or jobs. But financial markets are unbearably swift, and they no longer are subject to the regulation of the world's leading power, as they were when London ruled until World War I and Wall Street ruled during our postwar *belle époque*. So much money is involved that even if the United States tried to regulate the markets, it could not do so alone. The financial world thus transmits economic shocks with a speed and force beyond the power of any single government to control. A concert of powers performing in the classical sense would be essential, but no such concert is playing nowadays. A century ago, a default by Argentina would take days to send its shock waves through the London markets, which gave the bankers time to retreat to the comfort of their clubs and devise a plan to protect the system against shocks. Even in the normal course of events, when one country wanted to expand its industry while another found itself overstretched, the financial imbalances equilibrated more slowly, although sometimes they overwhelmed the markets. "Today's troubles travel instantaneously," writes Professor Kindleberger in his charmingly titled study, *Manias, Panics, and Crashes.*

The technological revolution that has linked computers by satellite and then by telephone enables trading in stocks, bonds, and cash to operate across national borders for twenty-four hours a day. The market moves from Tokyo to London to New York, like Apollo on his chariot. The world's financial markets exchange about $150 billion *a day* in currencies alone. The money moves instantly, often in response to the vaguest of political rumors and speculations. Its movements are reflected in price quotations that can change by the minute on computer monitor screens and thus affect a country's economic destiny. Only about $15 to $20 billion of the money actually represents trade and investment. The rest represents banks balancing their books and hedging their clients' or their own financial bets by constantly shifting money from one pocket to another. Any financial or political shock could set off a rush for the exit in which the entire system tilts like a pinball machine. In a fright over a new prime minister, a new policy, or even just some new economic prognostication or statistic, everyone could decide to shift his money into his Tokyo or his Frankfurt pants pocket, so to speak, creating the same kind of imbalance, but more quickly, as when billions poured into the New York pants pocket in the early 1980s.

Thus the highly lubricated international financial mechanism that permitted the Wizard of Oz in Washington to help us borrow our way to prosperity can also be our undoing, by the speed at which it could unravel our credit abroad far more quickly than it was created. In more stable times, such quick unraveling would be tied up again quickly by a bold and powerful central bank that agreed to serve as what is called an international lender of last resort. In the nineteenth century, the Bank of England performed that function, and when the action shifted to Wall Street, it was the Federal Reserve. But the Fed alone no longer has the resources. When Mexico, followed by half of Latin America, threatened to go under in 1982, it had to seek help from Europeans through the Bank for International Settlements in Switzerland. If a panic ever developed involving the credit of the United States itself, we cannot be sure that conservative and insecure Japanese and West German financial officials, who do have the money, would move with speed and decisiveness to exert financial leadership.

For a government whose solvency depended on the foreign understanding and cooperation that is the foundation of credit, the Reagan administration maintained a surprisingly cavalier attitude toward its economic partners. Since 1981, the U.S. budget deficit has been the major focus of complaint by America's major allies at each of the annual economic summit meetings held by the world's seven largest industrial nations. The script has been tiresomely repetitive. Nevertheless, it is worth rehearsing one of the better performances. The one in June 1982 took place at a location that had an appropriately antediluvian resonance, Versailles. With the world heading straight into recession, President Reagan excused himself briefly from the discussion to make his regular Saturday-afternoon radio broadcast, which began, "Good day to you all in America, or perhaps I should say, *'Bonjour.'* I am speaking to you from the Palace of Versailles right outside Paris, France, and I am not over here on a vacation."

He explained that he was discussing economic cooperation at the summit with Allied leaders. In an effort to demonstrate the President's wise participation, the then Secretary of the Treasury, Donald Regan, later gave an exceedingly rare account of such a summit dicussion by reading directly from his notes. The level of discourse was not exactly elevating.

The June day was sultry, and the Salle du Sacre, hung with huge portraits of pivotal events in the life of Napoleon, was close and stuffy. The men had their jackets off; and even Mrs. Thatcher in her light summer dress showed a few beads of perspiration along her impeccable upper lip. The debate on economic and monetary affairs droned on. The President amused himself by doodling neat pen portraits of imaginary figures: a nondescript little man with a moustache, something that looked like a smiling Marlboro cowboy, and the head of a horse. The Secretary of the Treasury passed a note to the Secretary of State, saying, "We should be out swimming in that fountain." The Secretary of State scribbled back: "Yes, without all these clothes on." R.R. signed on: "I agree." Then, in full view of the heads of government of West Germany, France, Italy, Britain, Japan, and Canada, his eyelids drooped, and the President of the United States dozed off.

Given the predictability of the rhetorical contributions, including his own, Reagan's lapse of manners may be explained if not exactly excused. Pierre Trudeau of Canada had begun in hectoring style by asking whether inflation could be stopped without unacceptable levels of unemployment, and whether interest rates would come down. "And," he added pointedly, "if that depends on deficits coming down, how long can we wait?" Ruffles and flourishes followed: "We are moving from crisis to catastrophe." Trudeau asked Reagan what political support he and the others could offer that might help cut the U.S. budget deficit. Reagan then held forth for twenty minutes. He started by recalling that Franklin Roosevelt had run for re-election in 1936 on a promise to reduce unemployment by deficit spending, and that had not worked. "It

took World War II to cure that," said the President.
Then followed a survey of the postwar failings of
Keynesianism, followed by a primer on the virtues of
Reaganomics. He explained his program to cut spending, stimulate investment, and remove regulatory restraints from business. Unemployment, he hastened to
stress, had started rising before he was elected. It was
the fault of the Federal Reserve anyway for ratcheting
back the money supply. He agreed that the deficit was
too high, but "we're working on that," and Congress
would vote in the following week.

Mrs. Thatcher was loyal to a fault, pleading with her
ideological comrade to return to the old-time religion.
She said, "It is wrong to assume that deficit spending
works. Even Keynes didn't think so, and I know because I've been reading Keynes. There is not necessarily a tradeoff between inflation and unemployment."
The impenetrable Zenko Suzuki of Japan followed,
claiming that inflation in his country remained low
because of the consensus in Japanese society and its
cooperative character. Helmut Schmidt of West Germany, growing noticeably restless as this self-satisfied
(but not totally unjustified) Japanese morality tale
droned on, seized the chance to speak. He complained
that high interest rates were choking off new investment, and he pounded the table as he gave a fore-
shortened history of the previous fifteen years: "Inflation
began with the Vietnam War. It let us off from the
discipline of the Bretton Woods System. We printed
money to pay for oil—all of us."

The discussion then ran in circles around the problems of high interest rates, how long they would continue to prop up the dollar, whether anything could be
done about that, and whether it would make much
difference to the world economy when they came down.
Treasury Secretary Regan warned that falling rates
would be "no panacea." Ronald Reagan supported
him with a brief homily about there being "no quick
fixes" for the world's economic problems. Well, said
President François Mitterrand of France, summing up
the discussion he had just chaired, "Nobody can accuse Ronald Reagan of going back on his principles."

They were the principles of yesterday's world. One might wonder why such meetings are held at all. They were begun in 1975 to fill the vacuum created by the lack of international rules and structure, following the destruction of the Bretton Woods System. Under the influence of the publicity machine in the Reagan White House, they degenerated quickly into media spectaculars, producing little genuine interchange and even less original thought. It is a pity that their participants never bothered to read Keynes' *General Theory* right through to the end, where he wrote, "Practical men, who believe themselves to be quite exempt from any intellectual influences, are usually the slaves of some defunct economist."

31

Could It Happen Again?

Could it happen again? Depending on how old you are, "it" means different things. For people just starting their careers, not much seems to have happened in a sufficiently dramatic way to imprint itself on their formative consciousness in the 1970s and 1980s; it all snuck up on you. For those approaching middle age, "it" almost certainly means Vietnam, the first liberated encounters with sex and pot, and an unexplained economic equation that has made their lives and prospects uncomfortably different from their parents'. For my generation, "it" means only one thing: financial crash, economic depression, and the risk of war. When I was a small child in the 1930s, one worker out of every four could not find a job, and that doesn't just mean NO HELP WANTED this summer at McDonald's. It mainly meant fathers who could not feed their children. I can recall holding my mother tightly by the hand as a gaunt, unshaven man who seemed to have emerged from a narrow closet approached her at the corner of Atlantic Avenue and ll2th Street in South Queens and begged a nickel for a cup of coffee. She gave it to him, but I had no idea how much it meant to either of them. Years later, my father told me how close to the edge he had come. One day his business grossed the grand total of three dollars, not enough to pay the rent or even the light bill.

What we learned indelibly in those years is that the financial world affects the real one. When stocks collapse, when promissory notes cannot be paid, when debts go sour, the lives of men and women go sour, too. This is not just some big paper chase in which clever people try to hit it big by outwitting the system, and then the government borrows some more to keep the wheel spinning. Economists say they now know enough to contain such things. But the history of the past twenty years demonstrates that they really do not, or that if they do, their political masters will gag on the solutions they propose. Both the economists of the world and the economies they watch over are subject to surprises. Professor Kindleberger warns that modern economic analysis is so incomplete as to be misleading, "if it leaves out the instability of expectations, speculation, and credit."

The politicians and the economists left all that out in New York City, the brashest, cleverest, richest city in the world, which went broke like a third world country just over a decade ago. The country slickers then shrugged off the spendthrift New Yorkers and delighted in pulling them down a peg. Now we would do well to read the story again in the shadow of the present National Debt of the United States. In the 1960s, a municipal reform administration had more than doubled spending on welfare, hospitals, and higher education, which benefited its electoral clients and the city's employees. The lower-middle class householders in the outlying reaches of the city refused to underwrite these benefits with higher taxes. The City of New York therefore borrowed in short-term notes from the local banks, which made a handsome profit on the transactions. In the 1970s, inflation exploded the city's wage costs. Its interest bill almost quintupled like vigorish, to $2.3 billion by 1974, and its total short-term debt was twice that figure. If it had continued borrowing at the same rate in 1975, New York's short-term debt could have taken up one-third of all the municipal credit in the entire United States. That figure alone should have warned the city that its borrowing was unsustainable. The city fathers (Democrats) appealed to Washington (then run by Republicans headed by Gerald Ford) for financial help. Its refusal was reported in the memorable headline in the New York *Daily News:* FORD TO CITY: DROP DEAD.

When the bankers were shown the same numbers as Washington but realized the federal government would do nothing to help them, they panicked. Exhibiting their characteristic loyalty to their clients, they dumped the city's paper, thus quickly devaluing it. Likewise, with characteristic financial foresight, they realized that unless the city could reestablish its credit, they would never get their money back. They held so much of its paper that New York was Too Big to Fail. It was almost a dry run for what would happen to them later with Mexico, and perhaps late in the 1980s to . . . But we are getting ahead of the story. Working with the New York State government, the banks established their own sort of IMF to monitor the city's financial affairs. Bond buyers went on strike until the city cut its spending by firing or retiring one municipal worker out of five. That's how New York City went bankrupt. And not for the first time, either. The notorious Tweed Ring of municipal grafters overextended the city's credit by developing municipal services for its immigrant political clients until the bankers stopped borrowing in 1871 and insisted on the installation of a reform administration to keep their money under surveillance. New York now has a reform mayor of a different cast. With no major source of new revenue to service the city's debt except rising property taxes, City Hall has accommodated a thriving school of real estate sharks. The developers now have made New York City as plausible a place for an honorable middle-class family to live as Buenos Aires or Mexico City. That is one way to climb out of debt.

The classical alternative to retrenchment has been to blow away debt with inflation, which is as American as apple pie. The American Revolution was financed by the printing press, and the Continental Congress saw no harm in it. When Benjamin Franklin argued for loans in 1775, one Congressman said, "Do you think, gentlemen, that I will consent to load my constituents with taxes, when we can send to our printer and get a wagonload of money, one quire of which will pay for the whole?" The currency quickly depreciated. A barrel of flour cost $1,500, a pound of butter $12. These were notional prices; because the economy was overwhelmingly agricultural, it slipped back into barter. A commentator in the *Pennsylvania Packet* of January 20, 1780, justified the monetary scam on the ground that "every possessor of money has paid a tax in proportion to the time he has held it. Like a hackney coach, it must be paid for by the hour." Since the main holders of money were the merchants who had originally agitated for the Revolution, the episode is hardly remembered as one of crying injustice.

The inflation of the Revolution tells us that the virus is always in our blood. The inflation of the Weimar Republic tells us that it also is in our nightmares. The German hyperinflation of 1923 also grew out of the way Germany financed a war. At the start of World War I, its thrifty and obedient middle classes had given their gold to the government in exchange for bonds to finance war production. The bonds formed the basis for cheap credit to Germany's factories, whose owners made huge profits out of war matériel but were left with debts to the government and, through it, to the middle classes. The tax base of the new government was too small to service the debt, and the first democratic regime in Germany's short history as a nation dared not alienate its supporters by raising taxes. The circle still might not have been broken—indeed, total output kept rising until the terrible year of 1923—had it not been for the heavy reparations of one billion gold marks exacted by the victorious Allies.

That's when the Weimar government threw in the towel. It printed money to pay the debts to its middle class supporters and thus sold them out. The industrialists paid back the government at worthless pfennigs to the mark. The government skimmed the profit from the debasement to pay the reparations, and the middle class was left holding the bonds, which had face values of hundreds or even thousands of marks. Except that it now cost billions to buy a postage stamp. Norman

Angell, a celebrated English idealist of the interwar years, wrote about this hurricane of devaluation in *The Story of Money:* "It had inflicted rickets on a whole generation of undernourished babies, it had stopped schools, it had crippled the colleges and universities; it had transferred real wealth from weak hands to strong; those who had trusted it for a week, a day, an hour, fell with it, while those who juggled with it rose." He was writing in 1930, and no one could then imagine the unspeakable things that were yet to emerge from the rage of a nation so cheated.

You might think that would teach a lesson never to be unlearned, but not at all. Not to the governments of Argentina or Brazil in the 1980s, nor even to the government of Israel. But it can't happen here: not in America; never in America. Correct. America is different. Like Tolstoy's unhappy families, unhappy countries are unhappy in their own way. In America, it is very unlikely we could escape with a short, sharp inflation to leave our debts or even manage a slower, more climactic inflation like that of the 1970s. The world's financial markets would smell it immediately; and dollars would be pulled out before they could be devalued further. Listen to this presidential message to Congress on the State of the Union: "In the domestic field there is tranquillity and contentment and the highest record years of prosperity." Ronald Reagan in 1986? No. His favorite president, Calvin Coolidge, in 1928. Or this piece of Wall Street euphoria: "Nothing can arrest the upward movement of the market." Donald Regan, formerly of Merrill Lynch, late of the Treasury? No. Charles E. Mitchell, chairman of the National City Bank, predecessor of the irrepressible Citibank, in October 1929, only weeks before the Great Crash (and four years before he was tried for income-tax evasion). There are many, very many, curious but chilling parallels. Things are never exactly the same, of course, but that does not necessarily mean they are better.

The United States now is diverted by a war against motorboats bringing in cocaine instead of prohibited liquor. In Nicaragua, covert operatives of the Central

Intelligence Agency are active against a government regarded as fecklessly threatening, instead of Marines collecting debts in the Managua Customs House. The hot stocks in Wall Street are still high-tech, but instead of some company started by a high school dropout in his California garage, the company to watch then was called Radio; RCA had been put together by an immigrant telegrapher named David Sarnoff. Instead of mutual funds, futures, and other exotic financial instruments invented and peddled by twenty-five-year-olds from Brooklyn for whom a market collapse is something that only happened in the ancient agora, Yale men wearing Brooks Brothers suits and bearing impeccable pedigrees sold their rich friends and relations bonds guaranteed by reliable foreign governments and newly pyramided investment trusts that soon would be worth less than wallpaper. The entrepreneurs who flaunt their wealth in skyscraper erections now carry bridge-game names like Trump instead of solidly engineered ones like Chrysler. A class of new rich will buy anything bearing a label with only a polo player on it instead of Brooks Brothers, which, until conglomerated, proudly stood behind its own name. The Polo label's chief marketer of illusion, Ralph Lauren, has ended up on the cover of *Time* magazine, which compared the taste of his customers with that of Jay Gatsby. It forgot that the Great Gatsby was a rum-runner named Jay Gatz and that the green light of his illusion on Daisy Buchanan's dock went out at the end of the book. *Plus ça change. . .*

And then there was the rhetoric of the 1920s. Not just the constant false assurances that prosperity was just around the corner, but the use of euphemisms that continues to this day. It comes from the understandable human reluctance to face unpleasant facts. One expedient is to invent words to disguise the shifts in the business cycle that inevitably are part of capitalism. In the nineteenth century, the word *crisis* was used by economists and businessmen alike. Like old-fashioned doctors, they recognized the need for an occasional purgative to cleanse the system of high wages, profitable speculation by new money, and other undesirable elements. Andrew Mellon, Coolidge's millionaire Treasury Secretary, was an apostle of this school, holding that an occasional financial panic "will purge the rottenness out of the system. High costs of living and high living will come down. People will work harder, live a moral life. Values will be adjusted, and enterprising people will pick up the wrecks from less competent people." With Social Darwinists like that on the loose, the word *panic* had to be phased out quickly. The result was the appropriately abstract Latinate word *depression*. Alas, that was promptly discredited forever in its first canter around the course in the 1930s. The English, usually plain-spoken in such matters, use the word *slump*, while the French never had one because they devalued their currency. The Germans spent their way out of it by building autobahns but got something far worse, Hitler. After the war, the more neutral word *recession* came into use, but even that was too strong for the businessmen in the Eisenhower administration, and they tried to get away with *rolling readjustment*.

But the word *recession* stuck. The National Bureau of Economic Research served as the official arbiter of when a recession had occurred: there had to have been at least six months of falling real output. There were three such periods under Eisenhower. But if there was anything Nixon hated, it was that word with his name stuck in front of it so that it would come out (as it did in the papers) as "Nixon Recession." His economists insisted on the word *recedence*, and they got into furious fights with the National Bureau to avoid using the nasty word for the 1970 recession. But then we had the Great Inflation later in the decade, and Alfred Kahn, an exuberant Cornell University economist in the Carter White House, was given the unenviable task and title of fighting it. He was warned by presidential publicists to tread softly in the linguistic thickets, so when he felt the need to warn that a recession could remain the only curative for inflation if other measures were not taken quickly, he adopted a code word, saying that the country could be heading for a terrible "banana." While campaigning for the presidency, Ronald Reagan liked to tell the joke about a recession being when your friend loses his job and a depression when you lose yours, but "recovery is when Jimmy Carter loses his." Once in office and presiding over the worst recession since World War II, he stopped joking about the word and barely used it. When did you last hear him use one of the favorite scare words of his political initiation? I mean the term National Debt.

But there are less frivolous similarities with the 1920s. Two of the most striking and important are a long U.S. farm depression and a collapse in world commodity prices. Throughout the twenties, farm income slumped from its wartime levels and never recovered beyond two-thirds of its wartime highs. In the cities manufacturing wages kept climbing. Some parts of the nation and the world, but not all, thus benefited from price deflation. At the height of the boom, from 1926 to 1929, wholesale prices fell 5 percent and energy prices 17 percent. Of today's gluts, grain and oil are only the most widely advertised. Copper, tin, lead, and other raw materials produced both by America's heartland and the third world are also unlikely to recover in an economy where profits accrue to knowledge and not brute matter. Very few people know how to make money in collapsing markets, and when they do, they usually carry famous speculative names like Joseph Kennedy or Bernard Baruch. It is mostly ordinary people who get socked when prices fall too hard. Just as in the 1920s, the high leveraging in finance, the euphoric stock market, the banks that turned themselves into brokers on their own profitable account were attempting feverishly to catch up with a fundamental shift in the economy. Then the migration went from the farm to the factory. Today it is from the factory to the service industries.

Even after half a century, economists still are not certain of the causes of the era's most pervasive economic upheaval, the Great Crash and the Great Depression (another proof that they are not scientists; even historians have a better idea of what caused *both* world wars). Milton Friedman, as usual, has come up

with the easy answer by accusing the Fed of turning a
financial panic into an economic collapse by not supplying enough money to the economy. No doubt there
is some truth in his analysis; there is more than enough
blame to go around, but it is not sufficient to blame
the troubles of the real economy merely on the mis-
management of the money that symbolizes it. As Friedman himself concedes, "money is a veil" for the labors
of ordinary people. Nor is it sufficient to blame the
disaster on speculative mania, which seems to be the
residual popular myth. John Kenneth Galbraith culti-
vates it wonderfully by concentrating on the rich comedy of the financial mountebanks who have been
imprisoned forever in his classic, *The Great Crash*. But
much closer to his profoundly populist instincts than to
his elegant literary ones, I suspect, are the important
reasons he gives for describing the economy of the
1920s, in a modification of Herbert Hoover's famous
cliché, as "fundamentally unsound."

The causes of weakness that Galbraith describes are
nowhere near as extreme today, but there is more
than just a passing resemblance. Before the Crash,
there was maldistribution of income between rich and
poor, augmented by a flow of *rentier* income that was
twice as high a proportion of personal income as in the
postwar *belle époque*, when hard work paid better.
But the huge interest payments on our National Debt
now are shifting this proportion back in a more un-
equal direction. The middle class, which is the fount of
economic demand in our country, is shrinking in size
and spending power, and we are attenuating into a
two-tier society. During the 1920s, there was also a
shaky corporate structure of holding companies and
investment trusts that were, Galbraith remarks, "in
constant danger of devastation by reverse leverage."
In plain language, they were up to their eyeballs in
debt and could sink overnight if the income from their
component companies stopped. That historical parallel
with today's takeovers, mergers, leveraged buyouts,
and junk bonds speaks so plainly for itself that there is
nothing more to say about it. So does Galbraith's
reminder of the dubious banking structure, which then

was too fragmented and is now, if anything, too closely knit together by streams of paper whose strength has yet to be tested.

The financial vulnerabilities are among the most frightening echoes of the 1920s. In those times, banking was a freewheeling casino using other people's money as chips, but mainly within domestic boundaries. Now the riptides flow across frontiers, beyond the control of national authorities. The excesses disclosed by the Crash led to forty years of stringent U.S. banking regulation, a straitjacket that the bankers were just about to wriggle out of in 1982 when the revelation of their folly in the third world demonstrated they clearly were unready. Instead, they have concentrated their more daring, and therefore unregulated, activities in their foreign subsidiaries, but at a time that offers huge risks as well as opportunities. It happens also to be a time when the capitalist world's largest economy and most powerful government is totally dependent upon foreign borrowing to balance its accounts and to prevent its economy from tipping into recession.

There is one difference between this time and last time. Unlike the 1930s, we are not moving in the dark. Across the capitals of the world is a cohort of experts who know the way out; a number of them have been consulted over the years, and specifically for this book. Of course, the United States must lead the way by trimming its own appetites; for Americans it means an unfamiliar dose of austerity. Japan has the money to boost world production by spending on itself after two generations of unremitting toil. It also has enough to invest in the third world. Spending on housing and roads would be an appropriate national reward for Japan; sending funds to the third world would be one of Japan's tasks in its new role of global responsibility. Germany, Europe's most serious country but most reluctant leader, must assume its role as the continent's stabilizer, paradoxically by raising its national spending. Finally, an international financial safety net must be organized to decrease the risk of the world economy tipping over while it rebalances itself. Rebalancing would protect the world's largest debtor, the

United States, from financial collapse while it starts the slow, painful climb back to productive efficiency and solvency. It would also help the debtors of the third world. All must play their roles, and this means yielding national preference, changing national habit, indeed, sharing national sovereignty. With such political cooperation, Black Monday will have been only distant thunder, warning of what might have happened. Without it, we can easily glimpse the disaster that will certainly happen.

If the speculative bubble bursts into a real crash, we know well in advance this time what the cause will be. We simply do not know whether it will take place, and if so, when. During the 1920s, many sensible people knew that the stock market could not go up forever, and for their pains they were reviled as prophets of doom. Now, even a bookkeeper doing the National Accounts of the United States knows that foreign borrowing cannot go on forever, that we have put ourselves on a political and economic collision course by borrowing from others against the living standards of the future. The United States cannot continue piling up debt to countries that are free to decide at any time that they have had enough of it. Some day they will want the money back. Controlling a financial panic by definition means controlling mob psychology, and that demands huge resources to induce calm and firm measures to maintain control, whether by central police headquarters to deal with a riot or the central bank to avert a crash. On an international level, there is no central financial headquarters, no lender of last resort, that can move quickly enough, especially if the panic is touched off by the world's largest and richest debtor. We are indeed in uncharted territory.

Some of the little fables that appear toward the end of the first part of this book are designed to help explain how government finance can affect our lives. They are not predictions, only straightline extensions as they are, and what they might be if they continue unchanged. Of course, things always do change; the question is how. In explaining his book *1984*, George Orwell, the century's greatest fabulist, said that his nightmare of the future did not necessarily have to happen, and he tried to warn his readers: "Don't let it happen to you. It depends on you." These fables give some idea of how things might be handled without a crash. But that does not necessarily mean that they would be handled to our advantage. The story about Toyota and General Motors hints at how things might happen. It is just as likely that we could follow England's fate and simply muddle through. But there is a cost, no matter what. Already we see the social consequences of mistaken policies: families where husband and wife must work, often in insecure and repetitive jobs, just to approach the living standards of their parents; generations with different and declining expectations. We also see an America potholed: bridges, roads, schools in disrepair for lack of public investment. And, finally, we could see an America spending its energy satisfying its creditors instead of its own aims. The geopolitical consequences of that are yet to be addressed: Japan wealthy but adrift and a neutralist Europe inhospitable to leadership by a foreign debtor.

Books that try to unravel complex dilemmas like this are supposed to end by proclaiming to the government The Proper Course of Action and then warning the public, in large black letters, **WHAT TO DO ABOUT IT**. Editors demand it, critics insist on it, the public is pining for it. I doubt it. They already know, because the answers are obvious. As Ronald Reagan himself said upon being sworn in as Governor of California in 1967, "The truth is there are simple answers. There are just not easy ones." Twenty years may have been a long time a-learnin', and I hope he really has, but what he said is so.

First, there is no real protection for the ordinary citizen if the government deliberately sets out to welsh on its debts by debasing the currency they are written in. Some will win and some will lose, and it is literally a toss of the coin that will determine who they will be. Some may even get caught in a crossfire between the government and the markets. There is little a citizen can do short of opting out of society, which is what the survivalist movement is all about: a nasty retrogression to Hobbes' War of Each Against All that risks the imposition of peace by the hard hand of his Leviathan state. No investment can guarantee safety, and it is important to recognize that different investments represent different bets on the future. Gold bars and coins in fact represent a bet against your own government; they protect against the collapse of the currency but not the breakdown of society. They also do not necessarily pay off. Those who bought gold at the height of the scares over inflation and Afghanistan in 1980, and held on, have lost about half their investment and missed the biggest stock market boom in a generation. Neither the gold investors nor anyone else foresaw the determination of Paul Volcker to restore the worth of money and the value of corporate profits. They would have had to be nimble to get out at a profit.

Real estate bought on mortgage represents a bet that inflation will flare up again, but if the monetary authorities suddenly change course, as they did early in the 1980s, you could lose your bet. Collectibles are a faddish new inflation hedge promoted by art auction houses; unless you buy Old Masters, they are no protection against the fad going the other way and the bottom dropping out of the market. Then there are options, currencies, cocoa futures, and pork bellies. A lot of money can be made in the trading pits by those with nerve and skill. The only problem is that making it is a full-time job. Finally, there is considerably less certainty that the government could actually inflate its way out of debt, even if it wanted to, because of the sensitivity and awareness of the markets. They could well take fright and try to sell out all at once, forcing a panic and a price collapse. Real estate, collectibles, cocoa futures, even gold then goes up in smoke. Property bought on mortgage as a hedge against inflation could turn into a financial deadweight in a crash and deflation like that of the 1930s. The cynic who bets that the government will certainly steer out of debt by inflating the currency may learn that the government is unable to steer at all in the huge tidal waves of the international markets. There are better ways to secure a steady future, for everyone.

The most important element is to understand the problems we face. As Peter Drucker remarks, the first rule in finance is, "don't be clever, be simple and conscientious." Reducing the budget deficit is not an Augean a job awaiting some economic Hercules. On the contrary, the first attempts augur the need for a real-life political Pericles who can persuade the country to give up fair shares. It is both good politics and simple arithmetic to take small amounts from many people instead of large amounts from a few. This accents the sense of general sacrifice and community that has long been missing from our political life.

An oil tax of $5 a barrel would yield more than $20 billion and hardly be noticed when oil prices are falling. A cut of less than 10 per cent in defense spending would raise $25 billion. As long as inflation remains dormant, raises in social security payments could be slowed. Limiting cost-of-living adjustments to 2 per cent, for example, would cost each recipient about $160 in a year and yield about $10 billion in savings. A 5 per cent value-added tax along the lines proposed by Bruce Babbitt (with exemptions for food, housing, and medical care to lessen the impact on the poor) would yield $60 billion. Like an oil tax, it would leave us no worse off against our international competitors. It could also provide a broader base for social spending when our society regains its sense of solidarity and awakens to its responsibilities to the poor.

Negotiating savings like this demands a President willing to serve as a mediator among society's competing interests and not as some Olympian ideologue casting occasional thunderbolts on the warring armies below. He must pose hard questions about such unexamined subjects as the military and social security. How much are we willing to pay to defend our allies as well as ourselves? And what would we lose in power and influence if we decide to pay less? How much are the young willing to pay to support their parents? And how much do their parents need to live decently? Once this process of political clarification begins in earnest, the financial clouds will start to clear, because America will be seen confronting its problems instead of living on illusion.

Consensus on such fundamental issues enabled the government to function in the 1950s when the Democrats ran Congress and Dwight Eisenhower was a respected national leader of the opposite party. He reflected the country's values but also set its limits as well as its goals. For a while in the 1980s the country had, and then lost, the possibility of creating another era of good feelings under Ronald Reagan, one of the most popular presidents in a century. People enjoyed his cheerful personality, but they also want things sensibly run and well managed, and that did not turn out to be his strong suit. If the bizarre finances of the war in Nicaragua had not come to light, some other harebrained scheme of zealots would have surfaced, because as President he unwisely allowed the country to be run by the Snopses. Faulkner's ambitious and avaricious creatures despoiled the land and destroyed a settled society as naturally as they breathed. In Washington (as on Wall Street) they took root like kudzu and spread with equal ease on Capitol Hill.

Fiscal policy by gridlock has proven no more suitable than foreign policy conducted from the White House basement. The President was able to make both work for a while because he radiated the confidence of the true believer and had the country's gratitude for helping to pull it out of a psychological hole. But that did not keep the country out of a financial hole; in the long run, markets are unforgiving. Ronald Reagan's final years in public life did not have to mean the same tired finger-pointing, the same tired confrontations over vague ideologies that have never been worked out in terms of public finance.

Under Reagan, conservatives made an attempt, not altogether successful, to redefine what they stand for. But no one has successfully redefined the meaning of liberalism for half a century, and it is long past time for the Democrats to determine what they stand for. The nation needs to develop a new consensus about how much it wants to spend and for what. This means a debate on the role of the state in the economic and social life of the nation. Until both sides define their views of what people want from government—and what they want badly enough to pay for—then government will remain crippled and the Snopses will rule. That is not conservatism. It is anarchy.

We now must face the huge debt for the spending spree of the first part of the decade, and that means adjusting to a lower standard of living. This will be a new thing for America. Some specific priorities are obvious: better education to create a smarter work force, management trained to produce things that people want to buy instead of chasing bottom lines on paper, a more affordable housing stock for workers and their families. Personally, I would put a low ceiling on the amount of interest deductible for home mortgages and abolish it entirely for vacation homes, in order to favor renters and mobility and to stop obscene speculation in one's own home. Everyone has his pet ideas, and that is as it should be. But they are valuable to anyone else only in an open debate. We need to start one right away with the explicit goal of restoring national solvency. That is what makes good government instead of the borrowed illusion of it. From there on, the solutions are both simple and easy, because most people do know what to do. There probably is a new national consensus waiting to be formed around simple goals, if the right leader can articulate the aspirations of ordinary people instead of playing on their fears. Improve the schools. Learn to live with just a bit fewer creature comforts. Pay your taxes. Help the poor. Save your money. Leave the land of illusion, go back to Kansas, take Toto if you want, but forget about Dorothy's silver slippers and go to work. That hardscrabble program is a natural concomitant to Ronald Reagan's legacy of huge debt. His presidency has proved the certain truth of one of his original rallying cries, although not in the way he expected or intended, and now we will have to live by it: There is no free lunch.

Notes and Acknowledgments

Although this book makes no pretensions to formal scholarship, it is the product of years of research. The most concentrated work has taken place during 1986, as the problem of the National Debt clearly began to grow out of control. It consisted mainly of organizing the thoughts and experiences of reporting during a quarter-century in the United States and Europe, and clarifying them by reading and research. This is not meant to be a reporter's book; there are no hot scoops in it. In an earlier and more unbuttoned time in the history of the Republic, it probably would have been called a tract. That is what it is. The economics profession, upon which I draw freely after a journalistic career spent learning, and just as often unlearning, its many and varied hypotheses, may not look kindly on this invasion by a nonunion competitor. But many have kindly given their time and thought, and, in the special case of Alice Rivlin, director of economic studies at the Brookings Institution, and her predecessor, Joseph Pechman, the invaluable hospitality of their library. In particular, for many hours spent steering me through minefields, my thanks also go to Daniel Brill, former chief economist of the Federal Reserve System; Michael Emerson, director of macroeconomic forecasting at the European Community in Brussels; and Joseph White, visiting scholar at Brookings, who understands more about the politics of budgeting in

Washington than many people who spend their lives in it. More help came from three old friends who gave their time to read the manuscript: Murray Weidenbaum of Washington University in St. Louis, former chairman of the Council of Economic Advisers; Robert Hormats of Goldman, Sachs, former assistant secretary of state for economic affairs; and A. Gilbert Heebner, author, economist, and executive vice president of CoreStates Financial Corporation in Philadelphia. My dear friends Juan and Nora Cameron, and Stanley Cohen and Toby Molenaar provided sustenance and personal support when it was badly needed, and my wife, Edith, a thorough comprehension of the project from the beginning. These are no small things. But without Robert Cowley, not only my friend but an editor whose imagination and punctiliousness would be the dream of any writer, this project never would have been started or carried through.

Others also gave their time and generously shared their ideas, some of them government officials who prefer not to be cited. While I take full responsibility for everything in this book, I want simply to list in alphabetical order the names of those who helped me, as a way of thanking them.

Peter Bakstansky, David Beckwith, William Beeman, Wendell Belew, John M. Berry, Barry Bluestone, Barry Bosworth, Anthony Botterrill, Samuel Brittan, Ralph Bryant, Arthur Burns, James Capra, Guido Carli, Joseph Coyne, Archie K. Davis, Neil de Marchi, Sir Roy Denman, Joly Dixon, Edward Frydl, Herbert Giersch, Malcolm Gillis, Amy Hertz, Charles Kindleberger, Joseph Laitin, Robert Z. Lawrence, John Llewellyn, John Makin, Stephen Marris, Hans Mast, Sylvia Ostry, John Palmer, Art Pine, Carol Poirier, Myer Rashish, Christopher Redman, Daniel Rosen, Kathy Ruffing, Charles Schultze, Nicholas Sargen, Peter Skaperdas, Robert Solomon, Herbert Stein, Frederick Ungeheuer, Paul Volcker.

In footnoting (which I have always found a bore in general works like this), I have adopted a method specifically designed to help guide the general reader to the main sources for each section or chapter, mainly for further reading. Some information that may be questioned is sourced where possible for those who wish to verify it for themselves. Some of the odd facts come from *The New York Times,* the *Washington Post,* and the *Financial Times* of London, and I have cited them mainly when the information might be questioned. In general, the numbers come from reporting or massaging published figures—a technique I have learned from masters in the field of economics. The basic statistics are drawn from volumes that have served as my primary reference books: the *Budget of the United States Government,* the *Annual Report of the President's Council of Economic Advisers,* and the *Economic Outlook* of the Organization for Economic Cooperation and Development. In these areas, the general reader will fear to tread, and the specialist is already in familiar territory.

PART I

The Government's Debt—and Ours (Chapters 1-6)

The arrogant citation at the end of the first paragraph of chapter 1 comes from page 25 of Professor Harris' book *The National Debt and the New Economics* (McGraw-Hill, 1947). It is quoted by James M. Buchanan on the very first page of his attack on deficit finance, which he calls "the new orthodoxy," in *Public Principles of Public Debt* (Richard D. Irwin, Homewood, IL, 1957). Professor Buchanan, then very much outside the mainstream, has received vindication not only from events but from the central bank of Sweden, a country he would no doubt call socialist. It awarded him the Nobel Prize in Economics in 1986 for his work in applying economic methods to political theory.

For general information and some calculations on the disposition of government spending, I have drawn on several books here and in Part II. One of the most readable is Herbert Stein's *Presidential Economics: The Making of Economic Policy from Roosevelt to*

Reagan and Beyond (Simon and Schuster, 1984). Those who want to pursue the subject in greater depth should read Dr. Stein's *chef d'oeuvre, The Fiscal Revolution in America* (University of Chicago Press, 1969). In both books he attempts to prove, not entirely convincingly, that even in the Roosevelt era, Republicans really were in favor of deficits and government stabilization of the economy. No doubt some were, but in any case, there is no more scholarly or readable guide through this thicket than Dr. Stein.

The current debate is enhanced by *The Deficits: How Big? How Long? How Dangerous?* by Daniel Bell and Lester Thurow. These readable essays were given as the Joseph I. Lubin Memorial Lectures and published by New York University Press in 1985. Other sources include the *Report of the Congressional Joint Economic Committee* (March 11, 1986) and *Toward an Economy Without Deficits* (January 10, 1986), very trenchantly written by the Committee's Republican minority. On January 16 and 17, 1986, the JEC held a symposium, subsequently published as A *Symposium on the Fortieth Anniversary of the Joint Economic Committee*. The printed transcript, available through the Government Printing Oflice, is an excellent compendium of the best thinking on economic policy.

For a glimpse of the past (which probably never existed or at best was like the ephemera of a summer's day), see Walter Heller's Godkin Lectures at Harvard, published as *New Dimensions of Political Economy* by Harvard University Press in 1966. Another charming look into a simpler past is *Our Public Debt*, by Harvey E. Fisk (Bankers Trust Company, New York, 1919). Mr. Fisk wanted to sell bonds for his employer (there is a full calendar of available issues in the back), and in giving an excellent short financial history of the United States, he writes charmingly: "The people of the United States may well be proud of the debt paying record of their government." (Alas, a short time later, the government aggressively bid for funds with higher interest rates, thus driving down the prices of Liberty Bonds bought by patriotic citizens during World War I, including a retired artillery captain who never forgave or forgot, one Harry S. Truman. Unfortunately, this affected his attitude toward government finance and crippled the Fed's monetary weapons until the central bank was freed from Treasury control in 1951.)

I have also drawn on *The Origins of Hamilton's Fiscal Policies*, by Donald F. Swanson (University of Florida Monographs, No. 17, Winter 1963). For a good summary of the theoretical issues and history, see the August 1982 special issue of the *Review of the Federal Reserve Bank of Atlanta*, entitled "The Deficit Puzzle." E. Gerald Corrigan, president of the Federal Reserve Bank of New York, sketched out some of the worst-case debt scenarios in a speech to the American Bankers Association Chief Financial Officers Forum on September 16, 1985.

Two excellent and readable articles on deficits both domestic and international by distinguished economists are "Fiscal Fitness: Deficit Reduction and the Economy," by Barry Bosworth (*The Brookings Review*, Winter/Spring 1986) and "The Second Debt Crisis Is Coming," by C. Fred Bergsten (Challenge, May-June 1985).

The quotation from General H.M. Lord comes from the Brookings Institution's *Setting National Priorities: The 1973 Budget*, edited by Charles Schultze, who was Lyndon Johnson's budget director. In this publication, Mr. Schultze announced the discovery that there would be no Vietnam dividend, just in case Richard Nixon hadn't noticed it in his 1972 election year. As we shall see, he had; he printed money instead.

The statistics on ownership of government bonds are based on a survey of "The Financial Characteristics of High-Income Families," published in the March 1986 issue of the *Federal Reserve Bulletin*, and written by Robert B. Avery and Gregory E. Elliehausen of the Federal Reserve's Research and Statistics Division. It says many interesting things about the concentration of wealth, and Mr. Elliehausen was kind enough to do a special computer run to obtain information on the holdings of government (as distinct from corporate and municipal) bonds. He himself was impressed by the figures when his computer spat them out.

The famous passage about creating jobs by burying money appears on page 129 of John Maynard Keynes's *The General Theory of Employment, Interest, and Money* (Harcourt Brace, 1964). This is a hard book to read without a guide, but passages like this repay the effort. Here it is in full: "If the Treasury were to fill old bottles with banknotes, bury them at suitable depths in disused coal-mines which are then filled to the surface with town rubbish, and leave it to private enterprise on well-tried principles of *laissez-faire* to dig the notes up again (the right to do so being obtained, of course, by tendering for leases of the note-bearing territory), there need be no more unemployment and, with the help of the repercussions, the real income of the community, and its capital wealth also, would probably become a good deal greater than it actually is. It would, indeed, be more sensible to build houses and the like; but if there are political and practical difficulties in the way of this, the above would be better than nothing." In this passage, one also can discern an argument over the relative merits of military spending (i.e., throwing money down a coal mine) and wise domestic investment. *Pace* the Pentagon, note that even Keynes would insist on competitive bids. No wonder Paul Samuelson, Keynes's most famous American guide, once wrote that the book "abounds in mares' nests and confusions . . . When finally mastered, its analysis is found to be obvious and at the same time new. In short, it is a work of genius."

My sources for Robert Eisner are his book, *How Real Is the Federal Deficit?* (Free Press, New York, 1986), plus his articles expounding the same theme in *The Washington Post* and *Challenge,* and his testimony before the Joint Economic Committee of Congress. His thesis was challenged there by another fiscal specialist, John Makin of the American Enterprise Institute, and similar questions were raised more gently by Professor James Tobin of Yale, a Keynesian and a 1981 Nobel Prize winner, in his September 1986 article reviewing the subject in the *New York Review of Books.*

It is somewhat harder to find out what the RATs really believe, since they prefer to talk and write in algebra. The supposed impotence of deficits was originally mooted by Robert Barro in "Are Government Bonds Net Wealth?" in the *Journal of Political Economy*, November/December 1974, pages 1095-1117. Good luck to any noneconomist who can follow the argument there. The best place is an excellent book that flushes RATs out of their holes: *Conversations with Economists* by Arjo Klamer (Rowman & Allanheld, Totowa, N.J., 1984). Unfortunately, the most cogent description of what they believe and its implications is provided not by them but in the conversation Mr. Klamer held with a formidable critic, the 1985 Nobel laureate Franco Modigliani of MIT.

Debts: Business, Oil, Farm, Plastic, Junk (Chapters 7-8)

For research and guidance in this area, I am indebted as always to my *Time* colleague Frederick Ungeheuer. He even found a Debtors Anonymous and went to a meeting. One of his discoveries was a curious one: a young man who fell into debt almost as a disease because he didn't like his job. Surprisingly, he was working at the magazine *Psychology Today*. He changed jobs and lost his cravings.

The numerous dangers of commercial and personal debt, and what they can do, are catalogued in speeches and Congressional testimony by Paul Volcker and Gerald Corrigan of the Fed, and the respected calculations of James J. O'Leary of U.S. Trust Company in New York. Some of the most prudent—and clear—early warnings have been sounded in the newsletter of A. Gilbert Heebner of CoreStates Financial Group in Philadelphia. For general thoughts on the economy and its relationship to debt, I would direct readers to any of the regular articles by my professional colleague and friend for many years, John M. Berry of *The Washington Post*. His lucid and scholarly pieces there (as well as *The Financier*) are as solid as anything about the American economic outlook appearing in the daily press.

Books about insider trading and the Wall Street scandals are developing into a minor industry rivaling junk bonds; they will, I am told, soon be issued with about the same regularity. For the present, the daily and weekly business press has reported in satisfying depth. I have drawn in particular on *The New York Times,* November 16, 1986, Section 3, page 1, "Can Salomon Brothers Learn to Love Junk Bonds?"; November 21, page D1, "Drexel's Junk Bond' Wizard"; November 23, 1986, Section 3, page 1, "How Wall Street Bred an Ivan Boesky"; *Time,* December 1, 1986, page 51, which quotes Boesky's sister-in-law. For Ted Turner, see London *Financial Times,* March 17, 1986. International Capital Markets survey, page 8.

Some other factual sources:

Credit-card profits: *The Washington Post,* May 11, 1986, James L. Rowe, Jr., "Rates for Bank Credit Card Loans Stay High." Spencer Nilson, publisher of an industry newsletter, says that in 1985 the industry earned 5.37 percent on outstanding credit-card loans. This contrasts with an estimate of only 1 percent on all bank lending, according to a study by Representative Charles Schumer of New York.

Second mortgages: "Putting the Homestead Deeper in Hock," *New York Times,* November 24, 1985, Robert A. Bennett.

Third World Debt (Chapters 9-11)

The many books on Third World Debt and what to do about it now are an industry of their own. They should be, not only to assist in the bankers' repentance, but also because this is a fascinating story. For the general reader, I recommend *The Global Debt Crisis* by John Makin (Basic Books, 1984), which is written with great style and takes a broad, historical view. I drew on it in Part II to discuss the collapse of international financial order in 1971, when Dr. Makin was inside the U.S. Treasury as an official and I was outside reporting on it. Richard Lombardi, a banker with a conscience, was the first to bring home to me, while I was reporting on third world debt in 1982 for *Time* magazine, that banks had changed themselves into brokers. (He formerly was with First Chicago.) For his pains and his moral fiber in making his thoughts public, he was blackballed by some banks. His book *Debt Trap* (Praeger, 1985) is a profoundly moral examination by a profoundly moral man. Authoritative and specific is the book *Debt and Danger* by Harold Lever and Christopher Huhne (Atlantic Monthly Press, 1986). Lord Lever has been an invaluable guide to me and others on this subject over the years. Two studies done under the auspices of the Twentieth Century Fund are worth reading. They are *The Costs of Default,* by Anatole Kaletsky (1985), and *The Mexican Rescue,* by the late Joseph Kraft (1985), who tells the story with all the excitement usually accorded a Wild West rescue, which this was.

The most careful scholarly examination to remind us that nothing really is new was written by Albert Fishlow, and I have drawn heavily on it here. It is "Lessons From the Past: Capital Markets During the 19th Century and the Interwar Period" *(International Organization,* Number 39, Summer 1985). In addition, see "A Proposal: How to Resolve Latin America's Debt Crisis," by David Felix *(Challenge* magazine, November-December 1985) and "What Are We Doing in Kansas?" by Carlos F. Diaz-Alejandro (Brookings Papers on Economic Activity 2:1984), with comments and figures on capital flight by Jeffrey Sachs of Harvard. The quotation from Walter Wriston gracelessly accusing Paul Volcker of stopping the wheels of the world is in Dr. Makin's book, from *Euromoney,* October 1983, page 296 ("Champion of the CITI").

Calming noises about third world debt by bankers were frequent, but one that bears notice occurred in a speech by Hans H. Angermuller, vice president of Citicorp, to cheer up his dispirited troops at a company dinner in London on February 7, 1983. He began: "A recent issue of *Time* magazine featured on its cover a story entitled 'The Debt Bomb—The Worldwide Peril of Go-Go Lending.' The gist of it, and countless other cautionary tales in the media, is simple, and simplistic: International bankers, motivated by greed, have made huge, imprudent loans to a variety of countries; now those countries can't service their debt, and this poses a mortal threat to the international financial system unless the banks are 'bailed out' with taxpayers' money." This was an excellent précis of both the story and the situation, with one exception: the story nowhere recommended a bailout by taxpayers, however welcome it might have been in the boardroom of Citicorp. Quite the contrary, it urged bankers to continue to lend in order to keep their clients afloat until better times, as bankers traditionally do. This was not exactly Citicorp's favorite solution. According to Sir Derek Mitchell, formerly of the British Treasury and of late an adviser to indebted third world governments, the bank was among the most voracious in trying to get its money back.

America in Hock to the World (Chapters 12-15)

Much of this section is based on my own reporting. Professor Lamfalussy's remarks were made (June 1984) at the annual press conference of the Bank for International Settlements in response to my questions. I am particularly grateful for advice and thought in this speculative new area from Edward J. Frydl, assistant director of research for the Federal Reserve Bank of New York; James Capra of Shearson Lehman; Nicholas Sargen, who is Salomon Brothers' specialist in Japanese bond-buying habits. None of them are in any way responsible for either my conclusions or my way of putting things. Mr. Gyohten, who received me in Tokyo in the autumn of 1984, is not responsible for my speculations about the later policy considerations of his government. Neither are Messrs. Cross and Schlesinger, whose characters are known to me and anyone else who follows these things closely.

I am grateful to Stephen Marris, author of *Deficits and the Dollar: The World Economy at Risk* (Institute for International Economics, Washington, DC, 1985) and the most celebrated proponent of the hard-landing thesis, for thoughtful and provocative help over the years when he was chief economic adviser to the secretary-general of the OECD. He is also wise enough to know that the very act of forecasting the future may alter it by changing the perceptions of the actors—a sort of economic Uncertainty Principle—and he prefaces his book with an Arab proverb: "He who foretells the future lies, even when he speaks the truth."

The interesting parallel with Sweden has been drawn by Barry Bosworth and Robert Z. Lawrence of the Brookings Institution. Robert Solomon, former international adviser to the Fed, has done an interesting monograph under Brookings auspices, *The United States as a Debtor in the 19th Century,* which argues that we set the pattern for Brazil in the twentieth. The article by George Kennan, entitled "Morality and Foreign Policy," appeared in *Foreign Affairs,* Winter 1985-86. It is worth reading in full.

Although Mrs. Thatcher once boasted that she would never make a policy U-turn ("The lady's not for turning," she said of herself in 1982), she finally did. (London *Sunday Times,* November 9, 1986, and *Boston Globe,* November 10, 1986.)

For the ingenious idea of saving a government bond auction, I am indebted to Stanley Cohen, formerly a lawyer in Paris for such clients as the French and British Rothschilds, who are not known for unimaginative or unintelligent associates. Mr. Cohen now is a successful financier in New York. He has in fact discussed the idea, and not altogether in jest. At this stage such ideas must be entirely conjectural, and the role of any person mentioned in the more fanciful passages in this chapter is of course entirely fictional. As for Mr. Mulford, it is certain that his unquestioned loyalty to the U.S. government's banker, the Federal Reserve System, would preclude him from considering such a scheme on behalf of the Treasury. At least for the present.

Fiction rarely outruns fact in our time. There is indeed such a monastery as described, complete with

Texas-born monk and cordless phone. It is named Shogen-In, and its address is 350 Hazama, Ouda-cho, Uda-gun, Nara Prefecture 633-21. The monk is named Taler Sogaku, although he was born John Taler in Texas. His former sidekick, one Zuiken, had an even more incredible career. A former youth leader of the Japanese Communist Party, he spent four years trying to find God in Israel but seems mainly to have learned to speak English with a pronounced ghetto accent. He later was reported to have married, moved to Hawaii and started a monastery of his own. I have not forgotten Mr. Gyohten; he visits there on occasion. The night I visited Shogen-In his wife telephoned to arrange a stay at the monastery.

Finally, anyone who seriously questions the plausibility of this chapter—and I have had to revise it several times to keep a few steps ahead of events—would be well advised to ask himself whether he would have believed a thriller that had the Ayatollah Khomeini indirectly financing the Contras' war against Nicaragua. Where it all will end, knows God.

Further details on the prestidigitation of Third World Debt, which I investigated with the help of Christine Bogdanowicz-Bindert and Kenneth Hoffman of Shearson Lehman, may also be found in *The New York Times*. The sale of debts was uncovered by Nicholas D. Kristof in September 1985 (reprinted in the *International Herald Tribune*, September 19, 1985), and the swapping of debt for a piece of the country was revealed by Eric N. Berg one year later *(International Herald Tribune*, September 12, 1986). See also *Time* magazine, October 13, 1986 (International Edition).

Those who may be shocked to learn that the market capitalization of General Motors is smaller than that of Toyota—or at least it was in 1986—need only consult figures compiled by Morgan Stanley. IBM led the world with a stock market value of $85 billion, followed by Tokyo Electric, Exxon, Nomura Securities, General Electric (U.S.), Sumitomo Bank, Toyota, AT&T, Shell, General Motors. The figure for Toyota was $27.8 billion; for GM, $23 billion.

PART II

How We Got From There to Here (Chapters 16-20)

An amazing compendium of documents on industrialization, finance, and policy, with a useful introduction by the editor, is *American Economic Development Since 1860*, edited by William Greenleaf (Harper & Row, 1968). Other sources, in addition to the books by Drs. Makin and Stein cited in Part I, are as follows: *The Barbaric Counter-revolution: Cause and Cure,* by W.W. Rostow (University of Texas Press, 1983); *America's Competitive Edge,* by Richard Bolling and John Bowles (McGraw-Hill, 1982). Representative Bolling of Missouri develops the importance of the idea of consensus with great skill and passion. *The Seven Sisters,* by Anthony Sampson (Viking, 1975). This is the classic on Big Oil; it was he who uncovered the long-forgotten State Department policy statement on oil and the Middle East (page 290 in his book). *The Limits to Growth* (Universe Books, 1972). One of the most elegant charts is on page 127 of this book, opposite the cited passage; after that, the diagrams lose their aesthetic balance, I fear. *Before the Fall,* by William Safire, was published by Doubleday in 1975. An invaluable memoir and reference is *The International Monetary System 1945-81,* by Robert Solomon (Harper & Row, 1982). A full examination of the closing of the gold window appears in *The U.S. International Monetary System,* by John S. Odell (Princeton University Press, 1984). An excellent and readable source on the 1970s also is Leonard Silk's *Economics in the Real World* (Simon and Schuster, 1984).

Another source for those who want a good and brief summary of postwar economic management is *The President and the Council of Economic Advisers: Interviews With CEA Chairmen Edwin C. Hargrove and Samuel A. Morley* (Westview Press, 1984). The brief description of each chairman's problems is superb, but the interviews themselves are to be avoided on the advice of no less than Herb Stein himself (who steered me to this excellent volume). "They are so self-serving . . . ," said Nixon's former CEA chairman. He argues that nobody realized how strong the economy really was in 1971-73—when it was in fact being pumped up for the election.

For a review of the Great Inflation, I recommend *The Politics of Inflation and Economic Stagnation* (Brookings Institution, Washington, 1985). The symposium papers were edited by Leon N. Lindberg and Charles S. Maier. The utility of this book lies in the fact that most of the important contributions come from political scientists and not economists: Maier himself and, in particular, Robert O. Keohane on the subject of oil and money.

The quotation from Keynes is from *Essays in Persuasion* (W. W. Norton, 1963). Keynes is one of the great English stylists of the century, and his essays are still a joy to read for anyone interested in public affairs.

Charles Kindleberger's remark on responsibility appears in his study *The World in Depression, 1929–39* (University of California Press, 1986), page 239, wherein he defines the leadership roles in trade and finance. We will have occasion to look at this later in wondering whether it could happen again.

The cost of the Vietnam War is estimated by Bolling on page 60 of his book. Vietnam's first five years up to Nixon's election at the end of 1968 cost $47.2 billion. He matched it in the next five years at $59.7 billion for 1969 to 1973. (With inflation, the numbers come out about even.)

For those who were unaccustomed to frankness from Professor McCracken when he was in Washington (he regained it with an honorable vengeance when he returned to his professorial chair at the University of Michigan), consult *The Wall Street Journal,* May 23, 1986.

For the importance of the GI Bill, Social Security, and FHA mortgages, I am indebted to Professor Barry Bluestone of the University of Massachusetts—Boston.

Lest anyone doubt that an American secretary of the Treasury might use such a testiculate metaphor—

although no one who knew John Connally would ever have doubted it then, and anyone who later came across the expletives deleted from the Watergate tapes would ever again have doubted it about any member of the Nixon administration—the offensive phrase attributed to him in chapter 18 was in fact published in *Time* magazine in its issue of March 27, 1972. I am not naive enough to believe that any sensible person would take this alone as proof certain. However, less than twenty-four hours after it had appeared in print, I was stopped in a corridor of the Treasury building by Connally's chief of public relations and quickly ushered into the Secretary's huge office. I was confronted by his tall, imposing figure standing alongside his desk, peering at a copy of *Time* through his half glasses. "You write that?" he snarled, in an accent that nowadays might be called early Dallas. I hesitated. "You mean you *didn't* write that!" Drawing breath, I replied that I was fully responsible for reporting the offensive phrase, having heard of it from one of his own senior officials (who later went on to higher things), but that in addition, my colleague who reported from the White House had heard it independently. Furthermore, I added, both our informants were staunchly Republican.

Connally was taken aback, but only momentarily. He may have suspected what I could not have known at the time, that Nixon was going to deny him the vice-presidential nomination he badly wanted, and that this was part of a characteristic White House whispering campaign. He insisted he had never said any such thing. I replied that if he wished to deny it, he could write a letter to *Time*, which I assured him would be printed in the next issue. He then turned bashful. "I know I curse too much," he conceded, "but I would never say a thing like that. It's like saying 'shit' in front of a woman. Anyway, why didn't you call me about it?" Because, I told him, I knew he would deny it. I did not say that I would no more believe his denial before publication than afterward, but I did stress that his right to make such a denial would be honored. "That's right," he shouted. "I deny it now." This circular exchange continued for a few minutes, whereupon I was invited politely to sit down to a cup of coffee and was fed interesting news about something or other. Needless to say, no letter of denial ever was sent, although Connally had succeeded in leaving with me a scintilla of doubt, which of course was his intention. I pursued the matter several months later over dinner with Arthur Burns, seeking additional confirmation of the offensive phrase. Dr. Burns replied, "Not only does he say that, but he also says, 'Let's pull his pants down.' " Such is the elegance of Washington powertalk.

The figures on return on investment during the Great Inflation come from calculations by Salomon Brothers through June 1, 1982. The numbers were produced by a scion of that great bond house to argue on June 8, with great foresight and impeccable timing, that "Bonds May Still Be the Only Bargains Left." Fearful of a financial crash, the Fed loosened its reins that summer, and the prices of bonds and stocks went through the roof—as interest rates and inflation finally began to come down. The precise rates of return deserve to be recorded. The concept means that if on June 1, 1972, you had invested $100 in gold, real estate, oil, or whatever, you would have earned a specified percentage annually during the decade. The point of all this, of course, is that some of those investments were not worth holding at all. From 1972 to 1982, oil returned 29.9 percent; U.S. coins, 22.5 percent; U.S. stamps, 21.9 percent; Oriental rugs, 19.1 percent; gold, 18.6 percent; Chinese ceramics, 15.3 percent; farmland, 13.7 percent; silver, 13.6 percent; diamonds, 13.3 percent; housing, 9.9 percent; Old Master paintings, 9 percent; stocks, 3.9 percent; foreign currencies, 3.6 percent; and bonds, 3.6 percent. The consumer price index was 8.6 percent, so that anything that returned less represented a loss. These numbers also are worth considering in relation to wage earners, many of whom ended up even worse off than bondholders.

It should be obvious from the context that the source of much of my material on the Fed is my own reporting there and at other central banks and ministries of finance stretching back (as in chapters 2-4) to the 1960s. Some of this was published in "A Practical Politician at the Fed" in *Fortune* magazine, May 1971, but much has appeared in bits and pieces of weekly journalism. Paul Volcker's words (all of them) may be found (repeatedly) by reading the testimony that he has given semiannually under a law Congress passed in the 1970s that, characteristically, was designed to achieve simultaneously the mutually incompatible but politically attractive ideals of full employment and the steady growth of the supply of money.

Readers wishing to acquaint themselves with the work of Milton Friedman can consult any library for his essays and other brilliant polemics, all of which will demonstrate the effects of a mercurial temperament on an obsessive mind. No matter how his views are summarized, he is bound to disagree and insist that the subtleties of his scholarship have been misunderstood. No doubt, he will insist that they have been misunderstood here. Far more technically versed people than I have had to shrug off similar complaints. In any case, for a reader who really wants to immerse himself in a fascinating history of the U.S. economy from Professor Friedman's viewpoint, nothing can be more highly recommended than the magnum opus he completed with Anna Jacobson Schwartz, A *Monetary History of the United States 1867-1960*, available in a Princeton University Press paperback.

The comparison between monetarism and Mary Baker Eddy is not meant to cause offense, and is hardly as flippant as it sounds. Professor Kindleberger writes, "The monetarists are to the market what Christian Scientists are to the body. They think the market is never wrong; the Christian Scientists think the body is never sick."

Readers may wonder why the president of the Federal Reserve Bank of New York, who at last published report earned a respectable banker's salary of $170,800 a year, has been receiving roughly twice the salary of the Chairman of the Board of Governors of the Federal Reserve System, who, when Volcker occupied the post, was consistently rated in polls as the second most powerful man in America. (His subordinates lived in fear that he would one day emerge an egregious first.) This absurd situation derives from the creation of the system early in the century. It was supposed to provide "an elastic currency" as protection against financial panics by operating through a system of regional reserve banks. Populists insisted that only through this regional base would the Fed have a strong foundation, close to the concerns of the country. Like most populist idealism, this was quickly belied by events as financial markets centralized and government took on responsibility for the level of economic activity after World War II. But the regional banks, whose directors are leading members of the local business community, still retain a certain latitude in the salaries they can pay, and they tend to pay well in order to attract competent people. The governors in Washington, however, are presidential appointees and therefore tied by law to federal pay scales, which at the upper levels are mean and distinctly uncompetitive for people of the competence of Paul Volcker. Fortunately for the country, he is dedicated to public service. But the country is left with a situation not unlike that of the British Constitution as described in the nineteenth century by Walter Bagehot, where the distinction is made between the "efficient" part of the government (the prime minister) and the "dignified" (the monarch). The gap in pay and perks between Washington and New York is not as wide as that between Downing Street and Buckingham Palace, but the idea is the same.

Is Economics for Real? (Chapters 21-22)

The statistical information on economics as an industry comes from a lecture entitled "The Washington Economics Industry," delivered by Dr. Stein at the annual conference of the American Economic Association and reprinted in its *Journal*, May 1986. It is funnier than anything ever written by Dr. Laffer, despite his name, or by most other economists.

For further reading on the present state of economic

thought, consult *The Crisis in Economic Theory,* edited by Daniel Bell and Irving Kristol (Basic Books, 1981). This is a mite overwrought, since events have proven that straight Keynesianism in large doses can work wonders, even if that wasn't the original idea. But as historians of ideas, Professors Kristol and Bell have few peers.

For the comparison between biology and economics I am indebted to Friedrich A. Hayek, the eminent economist, whom I interviewed in the summer of 1984 at his vacation retreat in the Alps at Obergurgl, Austria. His views and those of the "Austrian school" are well known—Arthur Burns was one of their most distinguished American exemplars, although he introduced modifications of his own from a lifetime study of business cycles. But since Ronald Reagan has named Hayek as one of his favorite economists, it is worth noting what he seems to mean by that, and what Hayek does, too. The president and the professor met for the first and only time in 1982 at a No. 10 Downing Street reception (both are among Mrs. Thatcher's favorites). Reagan told him, with characteristic charm and modesty, "At an early stage, one of your books came to my hands, and I learned a good deal from it." Hayek assumed it was almost certainly *The Road to Serfdom,* and probably the *Reader's Digest* condensation of it. This book has long passed out of fashion, but it was an international sensation when it appeared in 1944. It warned that intellectuals would be the unwitting instruments of a new totalitarianism if they persisted in their belief that they could know enough to manage society for its own good. George Orwell, a democratic socialist to his death, gave the book a good review in the London *Observer* of April 9, 1944, and focused brilliantly on the dilemma posed by Hayek's strictures against intellectuals: "Professor Hayek is also probably right in saying that in this country the intellectuals are more totalitarian-minded than the common people. But he does not see, or will not admit, that a return to 'free' competition means for the great mass of people a tyranny probably worse, because more irresponsible, than that of the State. The trouble with competitions is that somebody wins them."

Hayek remained unperturbed by such criticism, because he assumes that society needs winners and losers. He asserts that, beyond providing a minimum living standard for people "who are literally unable to keep going," no government should have the power of judging any individual's wants or needs. When that happens, powerful interest groups, whether labor unions or big business, soon grab first-class seats on the government gravy train. Like Adam Smith, Hayek worries that the stronger the interest group, the more successful it will be in gaining government subsidy or protection, thus permitting it to escape the rigors of the marketplace by keeping prices higher than they would otherwise be. His explanation for the endemic inflation of the postwar world is that economists believed they could iron out the self-correcting mechanisms of the business cycle. He argues that they can never hope to obtain enough information about the marketplace to make Adam Smith's invisible hand visible enough for them to guide the economy themselves, even benevolently. This severe hands-off approach has certain intellectual attractions, but it does leave unexplained how one strong-willed and public-spirited individual, Paul Volcker, was able to learn enough to drain inflation out of the system without changing the basic balance of American society. Here was Hayek's judgment on Reaganomics: "The President had some very good advisers, but was misled by Laffer. What he recommended was inevitably naive. You can do it, but not on the scale he imagined, and now the debt is beginning to alarm me a little,"

Reaganomics Revisited (Chapters 23-24)

In reconstructing the early days of Reaganomics, I have drawn on several sources that the general reader should find hospitable. They naturally include David Stockman's misnamed book, *The Triumph of Politics: Why the Reagan Revolution Failed* (Harper & Row,

1986). *The Truth About Supply-side Economics*, by Michael K. Evans (Basic Books, 1981), gives a sympathetic economist's account of this viewpoint but avoids excessive claims for it. The best overall book, however, is *Gambling With History*, by Laurence I. Barrett (Doubleday, 1984; also published in a Penguin paperback). I recommend Mr. Barrett's book not because he is my valued colleague at *Time* (we have together reported somewhat hectically on five successive economic summit meetings) but because he was the first to preserve—in amber, so to speak—the events of the period before they subsequently took on the burnished patina of age when reappearing in memoirs such as Stockman's. His reporting and analysis have proven so durable that two of the more intelligent and dispassionate of those present at both the creation and the destruction of Reaganomics, Murray Weidenbaum and Richard Darman, who was the President's gatekeeper before becoming Undersecretary, of the Treasury, ask anyone who seeks to interview them on that period, to read Barrett's book first.

The effect of limiting bracket creep on the choice of national priorities was pointed out to me by John Palmer of the Urban Institute in Washington, which has done some of the most careful analysis of the social impact of the Reagan administration in its study *The Reagan Record*, published in 1984. Mr. Palmer made his point months before the 1986 tax reform bill seemed to have even a hope of passage, and events proved how right he was. What could not be foreseen was how the bill would combine with the Reagan priorities to affect the revenue positions of states and cities. The unexpected fiscal results of the Reagan Revolution in federal-state relations may thus be felt for years.

The bizarre discovery of where the investment money actually went was made by Barry Bosworth of the Brookings Institution (Brookings Papers on Economic Activity: I, 1985, page 34).

Society and Business (Chapters 25-29)

The work on changing incomes appears in a readable article entitled "An Economic Bust for the Baby Boom," by Frank S. Levy and Richard C. Michel *(Challenge* magazine, March-April 1986). It was also issued by the Joint Economic Committee of the U.S. Congress in December 1985.

Sometimes statistics do tell true stories; people are stuck in a rut, and the movies get it right about people down on the farm. For those who wish to verify the figures on average family incomes, they come from the 1986 *Annual Report of the Council of Economic Advisers,* page 286, Table B-29. Net farm income in constant dollars back through the Depression—I mean the first one—is on page 360, Table B-93, last column. For some reason, the 1986 report takes median family incomes only back to 1960, but the 1985 report (Table B-27, page 264) goes back to 1947. From 1950 to 1970, average family income (in constant dollars) almost doubled, from $13,736 to $25,317.

What happens to workers when they get laid off is drawn from an in-depth survey of 320 auto workers: "The Unemployment and Reemployment Experiences of Michigan Auto Workers," by Avery F. Gordon, Paul G. Schervish, Barry Bluestone of the Social Welfare Research Institute of Boston College (December 4, 1984; unpublished).

Further statistics on employment are from an in-progress discussion paper by Richard B. Freeman for the National Bureau of Economic Research, which is headed by Martin Feldstein of Harvard, former chairman of the Council of Economic Advisers. Just before Professor Feldstein left the Reagan administration (under a cloud for telling the truth about the deficit), he was asked whether he thought the rise in employment under the Reagan stimulus had fundamentally altered the structure of the U.S. economy. He said he would take a "side bet" that it had not, and then mused, "Have the workers gone from steel to McDonald's and high-tech? Probably not." He said that he would like to look into it before leaving the Council, but he seems to have left too precipitously. The National Bureau study shows that his instincts were right. It appears they went mostly to McDonald's. Further figures on hamburger jobs come from a first-class job of reporting by William Serrin in *The New York Times* of June 8, 1986, which his paper wisely put on the front page.

Further sources: "Wage Inequality Takes a Great U-Turn," by Bennett Harrison, Chris Tilly, Barry Bluestone *(Challenge* magazine, March-April, 1986). Housing figures are from the National Association of Homebuilders and the National Association of Realtors. Some material also has been provided by Philip Longman (see his articles in *The Atlantic Monthly,* June 1985, and *The Futurist,* January-February 1986). Mr. Longman is research director for a curious organization called Americans for Inter-Generational Equity, the political direction of which is obscure to most political observers known to me in Washington. It seems to contain the germ of the idea of organizing the entire Baby Boom generation into a political bloc. Its 75 million voters could cream all comers, including the elderly, in the event they could agree on anything, which, given the diversity of their interests, seems unlikely in the extreme.

The literature on declining productivity is positively liturgical in its repetitiveness. Everyone has the same laundry list of causes, and too many people have their own magic cure (for which read political hobbyhorse). I read *The Zero-Sum Solution* by Lester Thurow (Simon & Schuster, 1985), a snappy *tour d'horizon* for Democrats who don't know what to think; and *Can America Compete?* by Robert Z. Lawrence (Brookings Institution, 1984), which shows that all we need to do is tighten our belts and let the dollar dive. The standard scholarly examinations are *Trends in American Economic Growth 1929–1982* and *Accounting for Slower Economic Growth in the 1970s*, both by Edward F. Denison, both published by the Brookings Institution, and both of which take a great deal of numeracy to read. Many papers have been helpful, but mostly the work of Robert S. Gay and Stephen S.

Roach in Morgan Stanley newsletters, especially April 10, 1986; and, equally, a fascinating paper entitled "Productivity Growth, Convergence and Welfare: What the Long Run Data Show," by William J. Baumol, published in August 1985 by the C.V. Starr Center for Applied Economics of New York University. Both avoid announcing that the sky is falling and wisely approach this phenomenon from the view of history, which is sensible when dealing with something everybody can see but no one fully understands.

Any businessman who wishes to absorb W. Edwards Deming's ideas, before the race is lost irrevocably, may consult "Quality, Productivity, and Competitive Position" (MIT Center for Advanced Engineering Study, 1982). For the dark side, see "Quality on the Line," by David A. Garvin *(Harvard Business Review,* September-October 1983), which does not contain good news for manufacturers of American air conditioners.

On computers: "The New Technology Cycle," by Stephen S. Roach (Economic Perspectives, Morgan Stanley, September 11, 1985); "Productivity and the Electronics Revolution," by Martin Neil Baily, (Brookings Institution, mimeo, 1986); "The Productivity of Information Technology Capital," by Gary Loveman (MIT, mimeo, January 31, 1986).

Easy to read and essential is "The Changed World Economy," by Peter Drucker *(Foreign Affairs,* Spring 1986).

The World Intrudes (Chapters 30-31)

The information and views in the chapter on the international dimension stem entirely from my own reporting over seven years as European Correspondent for *Time.* One person not cited previously but whose views I have borrowed shamelessly is Sylvia Ostry, former Chief of the Economics and Statistics Division of the OECD in Paris. She has now returned to her post as a senior civil servant in Canada, where she is her country's Ambassador for multilateral trade negotiations and her Prime Minister's personal representative for arranging the Economic Summit meetings. (These officials are informally known as "sherpas.") Two good books on summitry are *Hanging Together: The Seven-Power Summits* by Richard Putnam and Nicholas Bayne (Harvard University Press, 1984), and *International Economic Policy Coordination* by Michael Artis and Sylvia Ostry for the Royal Institute of International Affairs (Routledge & Kegan Paul, London and New York, 1986).

The story of New York's bankruptcy is drawn from "New York City's Fiscal Crisis: The Politics of Inflation and Retrenchment" by Martin Shefter in *The Public Interest*, Summer 1977.

The statement by George Orwell was part of a lengthy explanation of *1984* dictated by the author, literally on his deathbed, to his publisher, Frederic Warburg. (See "Halfway to 1984," *Horizon* magazine, Spring 1970, page 38.)

This is not a book of investment advice; there are plenty on sale. But it would do the frenetic New York art world good to consult the May 1986 *American Economic Review*, page 10, for a paper presented by Professor William J. Baumol at the American Economic Association's annual convention. The title alone tells it all: "Unnatural Value: Or Art As a Floating Crap Game." He calculates the rate of return on an average painting held for three centuries would have been only one-third that of a government bond. But more fun to own.

There is a morbid fascination with reading about the Crash and the Depression, especially for anyone who has lived through even some of it. It would be salutary especially for those who know about it only as ancient history. I have drawn on several books that are accessible, none more so than John Kenneth Galbraith's *The Great Crash*, available in a Penguin edition. Professor Galbraith also fears a replay, as he explains in an article in the January 1987 issue of *The Atlantic Monthly*, "The 1929 Parallel," which he was kind enough to show me in advance. Charles P. Kindleberger is a student of this subject on an international level, and his book *The World in Depression, 1929-39* (he was gracious enough to give me the revised edition in exchange when I showed up at his house with the 1973 edition) is essential reading and easy to follow. So is his book *Manias, Panics, and Crashes* (Basic Books, 1978), a fine study of human financial folly through the centuries. Like Professor Galbraith, he also has an uncomfortable feeling in his fingertips. Finally, if all this about the Depression still seems like some impossibly bad dream, go read about the Okies on the move in John Steinbeck's *The Grapes of Wrath*. It was real, and it was dreadful.

Index

There's an epidemic with 27 million victims. And no visible symptoms.

It's an epidemic of people who can't read.

Believe it or not, 27 million Americans are functionally illiterate, about one adult in five.

The solution to this problem is you... when you join the fight against illiteracy. So call the Coalition for Literacy at toll-free **1-800-228-8813** and volunteer.

Volunteer Against Illiteracy. The only degree you need is a degree of caring.